Tragic Conditions in Shakespeare

RETHINKING THEORY

Stephen G. Nichols and Victor E. Taylor, *Series Editors*

Tragic Conditions in Shakespeare

Disinheriting the Globe

PAUL A. KOTTMAN

The Johns Hopkins University Press

Baltimore

© 2009 The Johns Hopkins University Press
All rights reserved. Published 2009
Printed in the United States of America on acid-free paper
9 8 7 6 5 4 3 2 1

The Johns Hopkins University Press
2715 North Charles Street
Baltimore, Maryland 21218-4363
www.press.jhu.edu

Library of Congress Cataloging-in-Publication Data
Kottman, Paul A., 1970–
     Tragic conditions in Shakespeare : disinheriting the Globe / Paul Kottman.
        p. cm. — (Rethinking theory)
     Includes bibliographical references and index.
     ISBN-13: 978-0-8018-9371-1 (hardcover : alk. paper)
     ISBN-10: 0-8018-9371-2 (hardcover : alk. paper)
        1. Shakespeare, William, 1564–1616—Criticism and interpretation.   2. Shakespeare,
William, 1564–1616—Tragedies.   3. English drama (Tragedy)—History and criticism.
I. Title.
     PR2983.K67 2009
     822.3′3—dc22   2009002890

A catalog record for this book is available from the British Library.

*Special discounts are available for bulk purchases of this book. For more information,
please contact Special Sales at 410-516-6936 or specialsales@press.jhu.edu.*

The Johns Hopkins University Press uses environmentally friendly book materials,
including recycled text paper that is composed of at least 30 percent post-consumer waste,
whenever possible. All of our book papers are acid-free, and our jackets and covers are
printed on paper with recycled content.

For Sophia and Helena

CONTENTS

ACKNOWLEDGMENTS

Because I have been fortunate to talk about Shakespeare with so many lively and engaged students over the past few years in my seminars at Eugene Lang College and the New School for Social Research, my attempt to sharpen my understanding of Shakespeare has never felt like a lonely pursuit.

Conversations and exchanges with two friends, Agnes Heller and Julia Reinhard Lupton, kept me mindful of what Shakespeare demands. I am grateful to them for their encouragement and camaraderie.

Jay Bernstein deserves a special acknowledgment here. This book simply would not be what it is were it not for the education that he has given me over the past several years. Numerous thoughts he has shared or provoked have found their way into these pages. His singularly helpful set of comments on a late draft helped make this a better book and therefore is something for which readers of it will have reason to be thankful. But, as far as I am concerned, his response to the book, on its own, makes me happy to have written it.

A sabbatical leave granted to me by the New School, for which I am grateful, allowed me to write these pages. An earlier version of chapter 2 appeared in *Revue Internationale de Philosophie* 63, no. 247 (2009).

My father, Karl Kottman, read drafts of each chapter with indispensable scrutiny and acumen.

Sakura, Sophia, and Helena make me thankful for more than I can acknowledge.

Tragic Conditions in Shakespeare

Disinheriting the Globe

THE WORLD, such as it is left to us, seems more unwieldy, troublesome, and broken than the world left to our forebearers.

As we know, our forebearers suffered much. So, it cannot be said that our experiences are somehow more wrenching than those of our ancestors. If the social world we inherit—our institutions, possessions, ritual practices, kinship ties, and political prerogatives—now seems less desirable, less manageable, or less comprehensible, it does not necessarily mean that we suffer more than those who bequeathed this world to us. Instead, it may be that the shared social horizons through which such sufferings can seem meaningful, or yield insight, appear less determinable. We have perhaps lost something of our collective capacity to make sense of what we undergo. "The oldest hath borne most," Edgar reflects at the close of *King Lear*. "[W]e that are young / Shall never see so much, nor live so long" (5.3.325–26).[1]

And yet it is not that we suffer any less than our forebearers. After all, we still have our experiences—we undergo transformative periods, we suffer losses, we endure what befalls us. "Those ills" we bear, and of which Hamlet speaks so memorably—"[t]he heart-ache and the thousand natural shocks / That the flesh is heir to" (3.1.62–63)—are not unfamiliar to us. His words still speak to us. But it may be that the drama of such suffering and endurance—our experiences and their attendant affects—corresponds less and less to inherited ways of making sense of what we actually do and say with one another.

Shakespeare's *Hamlet* still moves us, perhaps, but can we articulate why, or how? If, as Aristotle teaches, our affective responses to tragedies are expressions of the social stakes of the events tragedies portray, then can Shakespeare's play be said to yield insights into the significance of our own actions?

In the wake of his father's murder, Hamlet stands to lose a world of authoritative norms and principles that lie beyond his own desires, thoughts, and improvised actions. Or, rather, insofar as the normative or dutiful activities still open to him—vengeance or displays of courtly obedience—appear to him as less and less worthwhile, his life's experience, his suffering and grief, come to seem increasingly divorced from the activities he is called on, socially, to perform. ("I have of late, but wherefore I know not, lost all my mirth, forgone all custom of exercises" [2.2.295–97].) He therefore finds himself unable to make sense of his experience—the suffering he feels, the pain he registers—in a way that might meaningfully correspond to what he himself is doing: reading books, practicing his swordsmanship, disposing of dead bodies, or avenging his father's murder. Indeed, it is only insofar as Hamlet does not do these things—refuses to do them or delays doing them—that he is able to make sense of his experience at all.

There seems to be a gap between what we feel ourselves go through—both the events themselves and our affective response to them—and our inherited social activities; whatever we routinely, or on special occasions, do and say with one another. The meaning and worth of our activities—those rituals and "custom[s] of exercise" we undertake that bind ourselves to one another, living and dead—thus appear opaque and questionable. "The uses of this world," as Hamlet says, come to seem "weary, stale, flat, and unprofitable" (1.2.134, 133). What we do and say together—at work, at home, in public, among friends—no longer determines, establishes, or clarifies the meaning of what we experience; and, therefore, our experiences themselves seem weirdly divorced from what we spend our time saying and doing. Our own activities end up leaving us without the transmissible insight that our very "experience" should provide. "That it should come to this!" concludes Hamlet (1.2.137).

Perhaps this sense of having lost shareable insights into the meaning of our activities might itself become the basis for our shared experiences. Our drama might unfold, henceforth, as a procession of the suffering, who no longer know what to say to or do with one another in order to make new sense of that suffering or in order to offer some insight into the experience itself. Rather than "learn" from our mistakes and missteps, therefore, we proceed by trying to come to grips with our inability to see ourselves more clearly in the wake of what we have gone through.

And because it even starts to seem inappropriate to use words like "insight," "recognition," or "wisdom" to name the fruits of such "coming to grips," the statements of philosophers and charlatans, wise men and fools, the experienced and the inexperienced become harder and harder to distinguish from one another. "This cold night will turn us all to fools and madmen" (*King Lear*, 3.4.78–79). Like Edgar and Gloucester, we grasp one another's hands on foggy terrain that we cannot even see; we speak much less of understanding our position than of enduring it. "Men must endure / Their going hence, even as their coming hither," says the son to his father, refusing to let the latter "rot" alone beneath "the shadow of [a] tree" while the kingdom falls: "Come on" (5.2.9–11, 1, 11).

Processions like these unfold not only because of the errors and missteps of our forebearers—missteps whose impressions and shapes may become clearer to us with time because they have been trodden again and again—but also because the terrain, indifferent to their suffering, remains to be covered once more by us and by whoever may follow. Edgar will have to walk this same ground once Gloucester has gone. Indeed, we must cover it at an ever-quicker pace, at a younger age, if we are finally to arrive at an individual or collective fate that we might call our own. For, "we that are young / Shall never see so much, nor live so long" (5.3.325–26).

We have perhaps now reached a point at which we find ourselves saddled with the errors and sufferings of our ancestors even before they themselves have been fully crushed by the weight of their own misdeeds. So that we have the additional burden of witnessing the fall at close range, as if having to bear up under the aftershock of the collapse were not already enough.

Such is our predicament. This is what the world stage, Shakespeare's Globe, looks like upon our arrival. Hercules, child of the gods, straining under the weight of what his forebearers have wrought.

~

In the following chapters, I offer readings of four of Shakespeare's mature dramatic works, *As You Like It* (c.1599), *Hamlet* (c.1601), *King Lear* (c.1605), and *The Tempest* (c.1611), that examine how Shakespeare increasingly dramatized the fate of protagonists whose lives are conditioned by authoritative social bonds—kinship ties, civic relations, economic dependencies, political allegiances—that end up unraveling irreparably and who therefore find that they can neither inherit nor bequeath a livable or desirable form of sociality. In *As You Like It,* Orlando and Rosalind inherit "nothing . . . but growth" (1.1.13–14) before becoming refugees in the Forest of Arden; Hamlet is disinherited not only by Claudius's election and the insufficiency of natural-matrilineal ties but by the sheer vacuity of the social activities that remain open to him, such as revenge or life as a courtier; Lear's disinheritance of Cordelia bequeaths a series of events that finally leave the social sphere itself forsaken of heirs and forebearers alike. I approach the plays as offering different dramatic retrospectives of such predicaments of social disinheritance in order to determine the extent to which these dramas might still offer us insights into the inheritable conditions of our lives together.

Shakespeare's dramas, I argue, compel us to regard the social bonds on which we depend for the meaning and worth of our lives together as being, in spite of that total dependence, fully dissolvable. The plays therefore throw into question the very inheritability, or transmissibility, of human sociality.

Indeed, such crises come to form the dramatic horizons against which Shakespeare increasingly challenges his audience, as if to see whether they will be, or can be, moved by what they see. If we consider that theories of tragic representation from Aristotle to Hegel (and beyond) teach us to regard dramatic representations as portrayals of a series of actions that expose the strengths and limitations of various forms of social life, portrayals offered to an audience whose affective response to the drama is by the same token inseparable from a critical reflection on the social stakes of the actions that they represent to themselves, then the radical nature of Shakespeare's dramatic strategy becomes apparent. For Shakespeare not only challenges his audience to consider the fates of protagonists whose lives depend on political, familial, or economic bonds that are then put into crisis; his plays also dare us, I argue, to respond to predicaments in which the transmission of any inheritable sociality is radically imperiled.

Shakespeare's dramas therefore ask to be understood as staging the limits of tragic representation itself, even in the context of plays not traditionally regarded as tragedies. The "tragic" in Shakespeare can, in this sense, perhaps be usefully approached as the exposing of tragedy itself to a tragic downfall. Whether this downfall provides some measure of satisfaction or enjoyment (and is therefore perceived as "comedy") or is experienced as something that frustrates our desire (and is therefore perceived as "tragedy"), the outlook—a perspective revealing the undoing of social inheritability through concrete, individual strife and struggles—does not fundamentally change.

At the same time, the ritual practices that had sustained and performatively bestowed the authority of inherited social bonds in the plays—funerary rites, the performance of "noble" or "honorable" deeds, military service, conventional uses of language, rituals ways of bequeathing the material world, formal modes of punishment or retribution—appear in these plays as increasingly perverse, inadequate, or insufficient. As a result, the protagonists of these plays are routinely vexed by deep crises in their own agency. The question is not simply "*Can* the protagonists act?" but "Will their actions, once done, be perceived as being socially meaningful or consequential?" And if so, how? By improvising their courtship and wedding, Rosalind and Orlando can "begin . . . rites" (5.4.196), but what inheritable form of sociality do these rites augur? What are the ethical stakes of Hamlet's actions, his slaughter of Polonius, say, or his refusal to treat his dead body with care? What do we make of Cornwall's torture of Gloucester? How are we to grasp Prospero's "art" and "project"? Do Shakespeare's protagonists undergo transformations or experiences from which, or through which, *we* might learn about our lives together?

Because Shakespeare's plays challenge us to take seriously the irrevocable fragmentation of the very sociality that forms their and our own dramatic horizon—their "internal" context (the breakdown of Lear's kingdom, for example) as well as the "external" relation to an audience (as manifested, for instance, in the uncanny immediacy of Rosalind's and Prospero's epilogues)—these plays test both the conditions of their own possibility to move us dramatically *and* our own capacity to be moved by them.

I would like therefore at the outset to frame the chapters that follow with a simple question that has been missing from recent critical writings on Shakespeare: are we still moved by the fates of Shakespeare's protagonists, and, if so, can we articulate not only how but also why?

⁓

In posing the question this way, I would like first to advance our understanding of the ways in which Shakespeare's drama pushes us to move beyond the classical (Aristotelian) question of *how* we respond affectively to the representation of significant human actions, to mimetic reenactments of what human beings might potentially do to one another. For, the question of how we are moved supposes *that* we are moved and therefore presumes a detectable relationship between the social or ethical stakes of the drama and the sociality of our response to it.

When Aristotle defined tragedy in the *Poetics,* he not only offered an account of the internal structure of tragic dramas—an account that stressed, above all, the notion that plot or *mythos* is the "soul" of tragedy—but he also linked this account to a normative understanding of their impact on the audience. In this way, the plots of tragedies—their staging of the vicissitudes of human actions—make a partial claim about the nature and conditions of those actions that cannot be separated from the way in which these actions move us; that is, the feelings induced in us are constitutive of the social bonds that connect us to our fellow audience members (*katharsis*). If the tragic story moves us, in other words, it does so in a way that lays bare our communal bonds—which must be strengthened, broken, or altered through these fearful and pitiful events, just as the protagonists' social bonds (as Aristotle points out) ought not go unchanged by these events.[2] At stake is not just the community "internal" to the play—the family or civic drama itself (whether in Thebes or Elsinore)—but the community that stages the drama and finds itself moved by it. The way in which we are moved is—as Aristotle sensed—the arbiter of the social bonds our responses effect.[3]

Taking affective responses for granted, however, not only presumes that by representing communal principles (like matrilineal descent) and their correspondent ritual activities (such as burying the dead) in crisis or dissolution, our dramas "know"—or furnish some understanding of—how we are bound socially to one another. Additionally, supposing *that* we are moved by what we see presumes that something *about* the actions we witness is learned, grasped, and transmissible. "Because we suffer, we acknowledge we have erred," writes Hegel, translating Sophocles' *Antigone.*[4]

Speculating on the "central feeling" aroused by Shakespearean tragedy, A. C. Bradley suggests that the downfalls suffered by Shakespeare's protagonists leave us with "the impression of waste" and this impression "makes us realize so vividly the worth of that which is wasted that we cannot possibly seek comfort in the reflection that all is vanity."[5] Bradley's lectures, which are well known for their focus on Shakespeare's characters, are in fact of perhaps greater distinction for the fact that Bradley tries to account for the affective response elicited by Shakespearean tragedy without relying on more familiar terms such as grief, fear, or pity—indeed, without relying on any positive moral categories. Departing from the Aristotelian inheritance, Bradley notes that Shakespeare's protagonists are not compelling because of their moral righteousness— far from it. Hamlet, Macbeth, Othello, and Lear perform all manner of cruel and violent acts. Because they are not morally righteous, Bradley goes on, our "moral" judgment of the protagonists' actions ends up being detached, or detachable, from our affective response to the plays. Our feelings about Hamlet or Lear or Othello cannot be understood solely as expressions of a judgment of them or their deeds, which means, again, that our sense of meaningfulness or loss in relation to Shakespeare's protagonists is not function of a moral disposition. The "impression of waste" we are left with means simply that we feel that these lives matter—independently, as it were, of the rightness or wrongness of the deeds they perform or the sufferings they endure. Moreover—and this may be Bradley's larger point—if we affectively sense meaning and "worth" in these lives (and perhaps, by extension, in our own lives) through "the impression of waste" elicited by the dramas, then in Shakespeare ethicality appears in a "negative" form, as it were, through the experience of its resounding lack or defeat.

Our philosophical categories for understanding affective responses to tragedy—whether Bradley's "waste," Plato's "grief" (*achos*), or Aristotelian *katharsis*—are not first and foremost theories about our emotions; nor are they primarily terms we invent to characterize our experience of dramatic representation. Rather, these terms are above all how we understand our investment in what we do and say with one another and how we measure the transmissibility of that investment beyond our immediate horizon. They are nothing less than categories around which coalesce the ambitions of any philosophy that tries to speculatively account for human sociality or ethical life or that aims to grasp how our activities become inheritable and meaningful from one generation to the next.

That we can be moved—that we experience grief or fear and pity in response to correspondent sufferings and actions—is simply the classical philosophical way of plumbing the depth of our investment in our lives together, of gauging the aptness of our shared self-understanding and testing its transmissibility. *How* we are moved, therefore, becomes an essential measure of the extent to which any given sociality—any "we"—can learn from and about itself and devolve from past to future. Our affective response is a manifestation that we care, individually and collectively, about our bonds to one another, living and dead, just as our categorical terms for such affects—fear, grief, waste—are a sign that we can achieve a level of insight into these bonds.

~

However, Shakespeare's plays increasingly trouble this association of affective response and comprehending insight into our social bonds, first of all by upending the plot structure on which tragedies and tragic experience have been understood to depend. According to Aristotle, it is one of Sophocles' great merits to have distilled the essential actions of the story of *Oedipus the King* into the plot of the tragedy that is so familiar to us. Picture, by way of contrast, the awkwardness that even the Shakespeare scholar feels when, upon sitting down with her friend at the playhouse to catch the latest production of *Hamlet* or *The Tempest,* she hears her companion's request for a quick recap of the story.

It is worth remembering that our typical understanding of tragedy, derived from Aristotle and advanced by Hegel and his followers, arises from the thought that tragic plots are the most refined form of narrative, mythic, or historical expression.[6] Like history or epic, tragedies portray a sequence of human actions; but unlike history or epic, tragedies condense that sequence in such a way as to most fully contain, and therefore intensify and reveal, the significance and consequentiality of what human beings might do to and with one another.[7] In this way, tragic plots furnish insights into human actions and their conditions that are not to be gained outside of tragedy. Similarly, for Hegel, the way in which philosophical insight follows on "experience" (*Erfahrung*) corresponds to the consequential, yet utterly contingent, structure of classical tragic plots. Tragedies are set in motion by specific deeds and transgressions—Oedipus's slaying of his father, Antigone's burial of her brother—whose power, as Hegel says, "breaks forth only after the deed is done."[8] This temporal interval between the deed and the "recognition" that follows is central to tragic structures, whether "dialectical" or as "plots" in which "events occur contrary to expectation yet on account of one another."[9] What Aristotle and Hegel are developing, in short, is the thought that it is only through a retrospective view or "recognition" of this unexpected consequentiality that we learn something about the social, ethical, political, or personal stakes of the transgressions themselves. Tragedies teach us that whatever we can learn about what we do with and say to one another is available only through "experience"—the consequential separation of deed from recognition that Aristotle calls "plot" and that Hegel has in mind when he writes, "Reality . . . stems from the action itself and results from it."[10]

But do Shakespeare's dramas furnish insights in the same manner? In the chapters that follow, I endeavor to articulate how the tragic conditions Shakespeare represents confound the consequential separation of deed from recognition on which philosophical and ethical accounts of tragic action have traditionally rested, pushing us to read Shakespeare in ways that go beyond the Aristotelian, the Hegelian, and the Bradley models.[11]

Consider, as one example, that it is unclear what insight, if any, is afforded to Hamlet—or to us—consequent to Hamlet's actions, much less what "new reality" breaks forth as a consequence of his deeds. Indeed, Hamlet's predicament is characterized by the failure of his words and deeds—his murder of Polonius, his betrayal of Rosencrantz and Guildenstern, his production of "The Mousetrap," his very speeches ("words, words, words")—to bring into being any new social consequence or ethical insight within the context of the drama. If classical tragedies spring consequentially from the crime, misdeed, or transgression of their "hero," *Hamlet* offers a protagonist for whom the very possibility of transgression appears foreclosed.

This preemption of new realities—and the consequent foreclosure of ethical insight—is even more ferocious in *King Lear,* which stages for us a tragic predicament or plot structure in which there is no "consequential" delay between Lear's disinheritance of Cordelia and the recognition of the blindness his action manifests. As a result, there is no further turnaround, no further experiential insight—only a coming to terms with what it means to have been blinded. The tragic blindness of Lear is not subsequently revealed by means of a mythic or historical "reality" that "stems from the action itself and results from it"[12] Rather his deed *im-*

mediately expresses his blindness—as well as the meaning of that blindness—for all to see. (Hence Kent's quick response: "See better, Lear" [1.1.158].)

Consequently, the ethical stakes of Shakespeare's drama cannot be grasped by means of our inherited poetic-philosophical categories, such as plot structure, reversal, recognition, experience, or pity and fear. For Shakespeare increasingly confounds the unexpected, yet irreversible, consequentiality of our deeds that, according to the philosophical tradition, tragic plots reveal. In *The Tempest,* as we shall see, Prospero's activities serve to deny the irreversibility of human actions by vexing any historical or narrative orientation for what happens on the island. Indeed, Prospero's torment of the others on the island is characterized by a negation of its claim to be a substantial deed at all.

If Shakespeare's mature drama, and the ethical predicaments they offer, are not structured as "plots"—inasmuch as they do not offer insights pursuant to the unexpected consequentiality of our actions—then Shakespeare's drama compels us to revise not only our inherited poetics and philosophy of tragedy but also, correspondingly, our understanding of our very activities as human beings.

If we are denied tragic insight into what we see ourselves to be doing within a graspable social horizon, then how are we to understand our activities at all? How are we to understand our experience of what we see ourselves say and do, if the meaning of our actions is not revealed in their consequences—whether intended or unintended?

Is what we "learn" from Shakespeare what it means to "live on" without, however, being able to regard self-induced transformations in our lives together as directing us toward any more advantaged position for self-understanding?

❧

Shakespeare's disregard for classical poetic principles has, of course, long been noted in critical responses to his work. A common neoclassical complaint about Shakespeare's work was that his plays do not obey the Aristotelian principle of unity of time and place, essential to the poetics of classical tragedy (as well as to the subsequent philosophy of the tragic).[13] Taking issue with this neoclassical response to Shakespeare, Johann Gottfried Herder usefully observes that formal rules and inherited categories are of no help at all for understanding a body of drama that has to solve for itself, again and again with each new play and performance, what it means to be dramatic—and therefore what drama might now become.[14] What Herder is driving at is nothing less than the thought that we simply do not know, after Shakespeare, what "drama" is—for we cannot claim to know what Shakespearean drama represents, what insights it offers into our experiences, or what understandings of our activities it stages. Suggesting that Shakespeare's work has not yet found, as it were, its correspondent Aristotle, Herder argues further that the distinction between genres—comedy, tragedy, pastoral, romance, historical drama—is confounded in Shakespearean drama not simply because Shakespeare is an unruly artist with little regard for classical principles of dramatic representation but because the historical world itself, in which and of which Shakespeare writes, knows no "unity of time, place, action."[15] Shakespeare does not give us, as Aristotle's Sophocles did, poetic genres mimetically suited to the relatively closed social world in which he composed them; rather, says Herder, Shakespeare gives us "history in the widest sense" in all of its complexity and disunity.[16]

With this, Herder usefully points toward the source, and the significant stakes, of neoclassical anxiety about Shakespeare's drama. It is not only Shakespeare's "poetics"—his unraveling of "plot" as a contained sequence of actions, for example—that provoke critical anxiety. The problem is not confined to "aesthetics" (or poetics) as a discourse, because it cannot be contained *by* that discourse. Indeed, new critical discourses on aesthetic experience that arose in the late baroque period in tension and debate with neoclassical principles—and in which German philosophy (and contemporary critical theory) takes root—is itself propelled by the need to account for the crisis in self-understanding and self-representation that Shakespeare's work exhibits.[17] What neoclassical aesthetics finds disquieting in Shakespeare, at bottom, is the way in which Shakespeare's drama throws into crisis our inherited understandings of human actions and their consequences in general.

Because the very conditions for human activity—social, historical, political, economic—have themselves been transformed and must therefore be seen as transformable still, our representative understandings of those activities must also be seen as transforming and transformable. This radical mutability no doubt characterizes the way that Shakespeare's drama

—as historical artifact, literary text, and theatrical practice—looks, to Herder as well as to us; hence, the singular variety and sheer quantity of critical responses occasioned by Shakespeare's drama in universities, playhouses, and popular culture since the late eighteenth century.

Taking this mutability seriously means that there can be no "poetics" of Shakespearean tragedy in the classical philosophical sense, because our very understanding of *what drama is,* and of *what is "dramatic,"* is itself subject to radical revisions in the social conditions of our shared activities. Any understanding of Shakespeare to which we can aspire must therefore start by tracking such revisions, and their consequences, in Shakespeare's work itself and in subsequent emergent human activities and their changing conditions.

This endeavor of understanding can, of course, be undertaken in any number of ways. Without presuming to prescribe a critical orthodoxy or methodology, I nevertheless wish to offer the following chapters as one attempt toward such an understanding.

⁊

My initial, guiding contention in this endeavor is that Shakespeare's mature drama enacts the failure of inherited forms of social organization—such as matrilineal descent, denaturalized patrimonial inheritance, state-sanctioned property rights, and military services—to govern, prescribe, and determine the meaning of the activities that might establish and sustain familial, political, economic, or civic relationships from generation to generation.[18] In this way, Shakespeare's "plots" do not reveal the consequentiality of a set of actions *within* a closed world of determinable, inherited social principles—the way that, for example, the consequences of an individual action in Sophoclean drama could be said to represent concerns proper to the Attic world. Instead, Shakespeare's "plots" unravel the "closed-world" conditions under which plot structures can reveal the social significance of our actions. Protagonists of Shakespeare's dramas—Orlando, Hamlet, Edmund, or Prospero—increasingly find themselves in situations in which the authoritative social ties that bind them to others are undone or shown to be wholly undoable and nonbinding.[19] They move from a closed world to a newly infinite "desert" (as Orlando calls the Forest of Arden), which means that Shakespeare's "plots" track and demonstrate the disappearance of the conditions under which "plot structure" can anchor tragic significance or under which the consequences of our actions might come to reveal their meaning.

Often, this demonstration unfolds in the wake of an act of betrayal or as the consequence of some interpersonal breach or infidelity—such as Edmund's treachery, Claudius's murder of his brother, Oliver's attempt on Orlando's life, or Antonio's usurpation of Prospero's dukedom. It is practically a critical truism, with good reason, to note that throughout his career Shakespeare stages forms of betrayal, infidelity, usurpations, and perfidy of all sorts. In fact, this truism may serve to illustrate the manner in which Shakespeare reveals inherited forms of social life not only in crisis but also in radical dissolution. For, like all tragic deeds, acts of betrayal—whether of individuals or of collectives—lay bare, and threaten to devalue, the worth of the social bonds and attachments that they tear asunder.

Like crimes and misdeeds that break a prior law or bond—such as Antigone's burial of her brother, Oedipus's murder of Laius, or Romeo's slaying of Tybalt—acts of infidelity or betrayal are typically thought to bring down, or necessitate, some active ethical response.[20] If the misdeed triggers no further deed as its social or ethical consequence, it risks not appearing as a misdeed at all. Indeed, our inherited ways of responding to such transgressions—inasmuch as our responses to misdoings imply an understanding of how the deed constitutes a *mis*deed—form the poetics of our ethical life and thought: revenge, punishment, or forgiveness. We might say that when our actions appear to others as acts of betrayal, criminality, or infidelity, their meaning—their ethical stakes, so to speak —are in great part illuminated by the reaction or reactions they set in motion. "Because we suffer, we know we have erred." Moreover, our inherited ways of responding to misdeeds—taking revenge, inflicting punishment, or offering forgiveness—constitute ways of understanding, reinstituting, or reelaborating the social bonds that were broken by the transgression.

In the following pages, however, I try to show how Shakespeare's dramas increasingly explore the breaking point of our inherited reactions to misdeeds—vengeance, punishment, or forgiveness—reopening, in this way, the question of how we are to think about the shared significance of our words and actions. If Shakespeare routinely represents acts of infidelity or perfidy—brother betraying brother, lover killing lover—he also goes out of his way to reveal the inadequacies and failures of our ethical "responses" that seek to make sense of such acts. In *As You Like It,* no one is punished or forgiven for past crimes; indeed, no accounting of past deeds is offered in the play's concluding acts. *Hamlet* portrays the deepening insufficiency of "revenge" as an ethical practice that would bind generations, the living and dead. In *King Lear,* crimes are neither avenged nor punished—as if the horizon of ethical response itself were radically narrowed, threatening our capacity to make sense of what we do with and say to one another at all. So, too, in *The Tempest*, through Prospero's acts and speeches, we confront a set of dramatic, ethical responses that cannot be grasped as the taking of revenge or the inflicting of punishment. And although Prospero offers forgiveness, his deeds are disquietingly proximate to torture.

In this way, I argue that Shakespeare increasingly challenges us to consider acts of betrayal not simply in light of the social values and normative ethics they might bring to light. Rather, betrayal and misdeeds in these dramas compel reflection on the inadequacy of our inherited ways of making sense of our shared words and deeds and of responding meaningfully to transgression.

The revelation of that inadequacy seems to imply, furthermore, that what betrayal affords is not an opportunity to heal the diremption but rather an occasion to learn, through the endurance of suffering, just what it means to live with the breach, with an irreparable split.

ᴥ

At times, acts of betrayals appear in Shakespeare's plays as wrenchingly personal—that is, almost irreducible to any inheritable form of social life whose value they might illuminate. In his 1909 lecture "Shakespeare and Modern Drama," Georg Lukács usefully notes that we misread Shakespeare if we understand the interpersonal rifts and betrayals as reducible to historically necessary conflicts between competing forms of social organization. Chiding Hegel for reading *Macbeth* as a "dispute between different systems of hereditary rights," Lukács suggests that we fail to perceive Shakespeare if we hear the plays as depicting an historically fateful conflict of principles or abstract universals; instead, he observes that "for Shakespeare, the dialectics of drama resides in the character." He also puts it thus: "Tragedy is a necessity, but how it takes place is not a necessity."[21] *How* tragedy unfolds in Shakespeare, to round off Lukács's thought, needs to be understood through the individual relationships whose personal conflicts, crises, and failures bear the full weight of the drama's meaning.

Think, to give a prominent instance, of Falstaff's banishment and humiliation toward the end of 2 *Henry IV* (c. 1597), at the coronation of Prince Hal as Henry V. Here the betrayal appears to be performed for the sake of *upholding* an abiding form of social life (like monarchical rule, or the House of Lancaster) that demands the cessation of any attachments and actions that might be seen as incommensurate with the sustenance and transmission of that sociality—or incompatible with the worldly inheritance in question.[22] And yet in cases like this, where Shakespeare stages the sacrifice of an individual, or of a uniquely personal attachment, for the sake of a collective sociality or a kingdom's endurance, our dramatic investment in the betrayal might nonetheless be said to depend on the strength of our attachment to, or sympathy with, the betrayed individual—rather than to the social principle for which he is betrayed. We are moved and provoked—according to predominant critical orthodoxy as well as audience responses since the reign of Elizabeth I—not by Prince Hal, future national hero, but by Falstaff.

Thus, even where Shakespeare does not elicit our dramatic interest through any anxiety about the survival of the social world in question because he is demonstrating, as in the *Henriad,* the historical survival and relative duration of social institutions and principles of generational devolution—the fortitude or resiliency of monarchy, patrimonial inheritance, or military service, he still shows us the interpersonal *cost* of that world's survival, the irreversible personal rifts and estrangements, the concrete struggles that become the condition of the social realm's durability.

This may in fact help us to make sense of a traditional perplexity regarding *1* and *2 Henry IV,* plays in which Shakespeare takes us on long detours through Eastcheap in order to represent the ascension of Henry V and the consequent succession of the English throne through the House of Lancaster. In those plays, Shakespeare seems to suggest that our understanding of Henry V's venerated position in the generational devolution of English monarchy as a social-historical form of life, or as a retrospectively grasped history, is aided by tarrying with Hal's singular attachment to, and betrayal of, none other than Falstaff, a drunk, aging solider. Indeed, the dramatic tension of those plays lies not only in the representation of competing social collectives or values (such as the House of Lancaster's transmission of the throne through the male lineage or passing of the throne through females by the House of Lancaster) but also in the considerable dramatic energy Shakespeare invests in Hal's relation to the fat, old, inebriated Falstaff. In this way, Shakespeare tests the extent to which Prince Hal can come into the matchless inheritance of land, title, property, and power to which his birth entitles him while at the same time actively sustain abiding relationships to others that might offer the chance for Hal to be loved and recognized for who he uniquely is, without the mediation of those inheritable rights and entitlements.

Can Hal be lovingly recognized by those who know—as Falstaff does —that he is also the crown prince, namely, someone whose entitlements will one day give him the power to bestow favors and worldly entitlements in turn? Can the crown prince, for his part, recognize or even acknowledge other people, especially those he loves, in ways other than by offering them worldly entitlements, privileges, or rights?

The prince's sojourns in Eastcheap are designed, I think, to at least let us imagine an affirmative answer to these questions. For Eastcheap is not merely a disreputable quarter of London; it names a set of conditions invented by Shakespeare—and given legitimacy as a invention, perhaps, by our own verisimilar experience of such conditions—under which social attachments are formed or improvised in relative independence of the inheritance and bequeathal of worldly rights and entitlements or as a parody of authoritative norms. Indeed, Eastcheap offers one of Shakespeare's first portrayals of those whose activities and interactions are not conditioned by any principle of generational devolution or prescribed by any ethical or worldly duty. As with the Forest of Arden, Lear's heath, the cliffs of Dover, or Prospero's island, no paternal authority, no matrilineal blood ties, no state-sanctioned property rights prescribe what is said and done in the Boar's Head tavern. Binding social duties or ethical obligations lose their weightiness and return to earth as nothing more than the play between these individual men. There, the drunkard Falstaff can take up the role of king; and the prince can play the fool. Rights and entitlements are as empty as the principles of duty and honor to which they correspond. "What is honour? A word," declares Falstaff. "What is that word 'honour'? What is in that honour? Air" (1 Henry IV, 5.1.133–34).

Falstaff's critique of honor stems from his sense that the inheritance and bequeathal of worldly rights and entitlements cannot replace, furnish, or provide authentic gestures of loving recognition.[23] From Falstaff's perspective, it is only by actively loving and being loved—without being able to prescribe or regulate the "form" that loving should take—that one can come to seem entitled to anything whatsoever in the world. ("sweet Jack Falstaff, kind Jack Falstaff . . . banish not him thy Harry's company. Banish plump Jack and banish all the world" [1 Henry IV, 2.4.462–67].) Accordingly, he imagines that Hal, once crowned, will welcome him to the court and bestow entitlements upon him because of the free, unconstrained dutyless words and deeds of loving friendship they shared together in Eastcheap.

This is the belief that Hal betrays upon his ascension, as he rejects Falstaff himself. It is, for most students and audiences (at least in my experience), almost unbearable to watch. The prince's inheritance of the kingdom—with all the rights and entitlements this inheritance brings—impedes him from recognizing the man who bends before him. "I know thee not, old man," he says:

Presume not that I am the thing I was;
For God doth know, so shall the world perceive,
That I have turn'd away my former self;
So will I those that kept me company. (2 Henry IV, 5.5.56–59)

Shakespeare shows worldly rights and entitlements, and the social worth they express—the normative prerogatives and values that we require to reproduce a sustainable form of social life—to be precisely that which invariably blinds us to the recognition of others. Recall that in Aristotle's account, tragic ignorance (hamartia) signals our blindness to the ways in which, even without knowing it, we are bound in socially inheritable ways to other human beings—by blood or civic ties. In Shakespeare, by contrast, such "universal" principles threaten to blind us to the recognition of those human beings to whom we might wish to be bound irrespective of inheritable forms of social life.

❧

Conversely, in Shakespeare, to be bound meaningfully to another—to love or to fail to love—will entail not an individual renunciation of worldly rights or institutions but the very failure and collapse of the worlds that sustain them, along with those worlds' gods and values. It is not simply that universal values collapse, leaving only particular individuals, naked in their imperfections and limitations; rather, it is that these limited and imperfect human beings appear as the bearers of these collapsed values. How *they* bear up under the weight *completes* the collapse. "Let Rome in Tiber melt and the wide arch, / Of the rang'd empire fall!" cries Antony, as he embraces Cleopatra (1.1.35–36).

In Hegel's *Phenomenology of Spirit* it is comedy—symptomatically, the comedy of Aristophanes, as it supersedes Sophoclean tragedy—that completes the speculative passage of the abstract universal to the concrete universal. Comedy, it should be understood, does not just augur a shift from the perspective of universal values to that of limited and imperfect individuals in their concrete materiality, as if it were a turn *away* from universal values. Rather, for Hegel, comedy lays bare the limitations and imperfections of the abstract universal itself—and thus brings to light the manifold concrete, dramatic perils to which our deepest values are exposed in the extraordinary and surprising lives of individual human beings. In other words, comedy demonstrates that these values—our grand social principles—turn out to be no more and no less grand than their appearance on the world stage, in our lives and loves, our ups and downs.[24]

Furthermore, inasmuch as these values, these gods, are no longer separate from these individuals, they are no longer "represented" by them (as was the case in Attic tragedy). This is why, for Hegel, comedy is not simply mimetic or representational. The actors on stage, along with the characters they play, no longer "represent" any external meaning or truth—some "value" that is beyond them, or greater than themselves (blood ties, civic status), by sole virtue of which we see their fates as meaningful or socially significant. Instead, the actors and characters stage *themselves* so to speak (which, again, means that we are no longer dealing with mimetic representation); they appear as human beings on the world stage, meaningful or valuable for who they are and not only for what they also happen to be (prince, actor, whore, courtier, servant, poet, merchant, and so on).

Thinking for a moment in terms of Hegel's comments on comedy, we can challenge a deeply entrenched truism about Shakespearean drama—one that is no doubt bound up with limitations that still adhere in our theatrical practices and institutions. The truism is that there are "roles" in

Shakespeare (Hamlet, Othello, Lear, Lady Macbeth) that actors "play" within a representational domain, the "theater," designed to keep separate our recognition of the role from our social recognition of the actor who plays it.[25] It is presumed for instance that we watch *Laurence Olivier*'s Hamlet or *Paul Scofield*'s Lear—that is, Olivier and Scofield take on the "role" of Shakespeare's characters for some period of time, garnering our accolades as themselves after the performance has finished. I would challenge this truism on two scores. First, there are numerous occasions where this neat separation of our recognition of the actor from our recognition of the role is clamorously thrown into crisis by the very movement of Shakespearean drama—for instance, in Prospero's epilogue. Second, if Olivier is truly successful at acting Hamlet—meaning, here, if he succeeds in revealing to *us* something of why this individual called "Hamlet" might matter to us (as distinct from whatever we might take "Hamlet" to represent or stand for)—then Olivier himself will also be recognized by *us* as Hamlet, independently of Olivier's own desire or intention in this regard and in spite of the artificial or mimetic limits of the "theater." Put starkly, if Olivier's performance succeeds (and is not such "success" the aim here?), then this success will mean that Hamlet ceases to be a mere "role" that is detachable from the actual life of Olivier, like a mask that he might put down at will.[26] This is the risk that the actor invariably takes when playing a "Shakespearean" role (in acting without a mask); namely, that his success will mean a certain, perhaps uncomfortable, coincidence between himself and the role by virtue of *our* recognition of this coincidence.

Of course, that this happens to actors quite often—and not only in the performance of works by Shakespeare—means that what is at issue here is not something Shakespeare or others accomplish through sheer poetic invention or skill; rather, we are dealing with a dissolution of representational thinking and mimetic distance in our own dramatic self-conception—a breakdown that in fact makes new recognitions of one another possible.

With this in mind, it should become clearer that it is precisely such new recognitions that might be occasioned by the drama. Therefore I propose that our task in understanding Shakespeare is not—as we too often imagine—to figure out what Hamlet's fate "represents" (for society, for modernity, for humanity), as if that meaning could be determined independently of the fact that it is *Hamlet's* fate. Rather, our task is to figure out why (or if) Hamlet or Lear or Rosalind matter to *us*—which is to say that we need to determine the conditions under which individual lives can be recognized as meaningful, without relying on any external, transcendental values that could claim to anchor that meaning.

Can we matter to one another not only in virtue of what we might "represent" but also with nothing to offer but ourselves—our foibles, passions, strengths, weaknesses, or peculiarities? Can we recognize one another, in our very ordinariness, as of extraordinary worth?

There is a strong humanist dimension to the movement Hegel ascribes to comedy. He makes this clear when he notes that in comedy human beings drop the "mask"—which in (Attic) tragedy had separated "the person in the play and the actual self"—in order to let "the self [appear] in its significance as something actual . . . stand[ing] forth in its own nakedness and ordinariness."[27] Something of this humanism, I am suggesting, might be recognizable to us on the Shakespearean stage as well. One might wish to hear a faint echo of this same humanism, minus its (necessarily) attendant atheism, in Harold Bloom's claims regarding Shakespeare's "invention of the human."[28] But Bloom, of course, celebrates this humanism by promptly reinstalling a new god, a new "universal"— none other than Shakespeare himself.[29] "Shakespeare," writes Bloom, "is my model and my mortal god."[30] We might be tempted to regard such a notion—Shakespeare as "mortal god"—precisely as comedic were it not for the fact that Bloom's notion here betrays hidden stakes. Shakespeare's mortality, for Bloom, is that he was after all only a mere man from Stratford, whereas his divinity lies in his powers of representation, his poetic invention of us—his "invention of the human." But it is exactly this separation of representational form from individual human being, of poetic artifice from actual self, that is undone in the movement Hegel attributes to comedy—where what is meaningful makes it appearance on the world stage *as* human beings, which also means that human beings are not "merely" human beings. Indeed, in his discussion of Aristophanes, Hegel appears to be inadvertently offering a far more appropriate description of Shakespeare than does Bloom when he writes that "the actual self of the actor coincides with what he impersonates, just as the spectator is completely at home in the drama performed before him and sees himself playing in it."[31]

Why, then, do I persist in using the term "tragic" to describe conditions in Shakespeare if these conditions resemble, at least in this regard, the upshot of a movement that might appear in the guise of comedy or humanism?[32] What are the "tragic" conditions here, beyond the (Attic, "representational" tragedy) "tragedy" whose overcoming comedy was supposed to signal?

~

Tragedies have always compelled us to reflect on what makes our lives together livable, desirable, or worthwhile. This is why tragic representation becomes central to civic discourse in moments at which the city seeks to question its own value or sustainability, as in fifth-century BCE Athens. Tragedies like *Oedipus* or *Antigone* ask us to consider how we can best and most desirably sustain and transmit the conditions of living with one another. They challenge us to regard our lives not only in terms of the minimum requirements for biological life or in light of the claims of nature but also in terms that make sense of how we are socially or culturally bound to one another, living and dead, from generation to generation—such that our lives together might seem meaningful and worthwhile. Indeed, it may be that we come to measure the significance or value of our bodily lives together in terms of its worldly inheritability—the relative transmissibility of rights, entitlements, possessions, institutions, and prerogatives that we might wish to bestow on those we love.

Similarly, the dramatic horizon of tragic conditions in Shakespeare can be understood as a struggle over how particular human beings aim to properly suture the claims of nature and the demands of culture. However, in Shakespeare—precisely because this suturing responds to what must, in modernity, be faced as an ongoing diremption—this struggle unfolds without being able to understand nature as a precultural condition of cultural life or culture as a process of denaturalization. Breaking the Sophoclean mold, Shakespeare understands this work of suturing not as a precondition for the emergence of any inheritable form of cultural life but, on the contrary, as the ongoing horizon and limitation of any transmissible or inheritable sociality—and therefore as a perhaps insuperable potential for dramatic tension and strife between individual lives.

Stretching well beyond the Greek horizon, Shakespeare's dramas balance, weigh, and reveal the stakes of social transmissibility by staging—

through the concrete and passionate conflicts of individuals—a persistent diremption of sociality from nature. In this way, moreover, Shakespeare's dramas show that the fate of the transmissibility of social life cannot be separated from the manifold and concrete-particular dramatic vicissitudes of this diremption. Indeed, these individual dramas *are* that fate.

By offering such contests as the very horizon for his drama, I maintain, Shakespeare—like the Greeks—represents the inheritability of cultural life, of human sociality, as propelled by shifting nonnatural accounts of nature's claims on us. And yet—unlike the Greeks—Shakespeare's dramas also depict the transmission, worth, and desirability of any sociality as hemmed in by what we now know to be the inherited failures of such accounts to once and for all satisfactorily or desirably bind us to one another. And this depiction is inseparable from—*it is nothing other than*—uniquely dramatic breakdowns in the affairs of particular human beings.

Which means, we can now see, that the "abstract" stakes that form the dramas' horizon—the diremption of sociality from nature—are no more and no less significant, moving, ridiculous, or gripping than are the lives, loves, words, and deeds of these unique human beings.

Their successes and failures, triumphs and miseries, *are* the materiality of the diremption; or rather, they are its dramatic movement, the fullest proof that it really matters.

Finally, therefore, to return to my opening sentiment, Shakespeare will compel us to consider our forms of worldly inheritance, on which we have depended in order to live together meaningfully at all, as insufficient, fragmented, weakened, or damaged. The activities that upheld and affirmed prior modes of social organization—burying the dead, military service, or courtly speech—will give way, as we proceed, to activities that break and destroy bonds on which we, in our lives together as individuals, rely, culminating with acts of torture—to which we will finally turn as we read *King Lear* and *The Tempest*.

All the same, failures of social transmissibility—viewed retrospectively by Shakespeare as dramatic failures that are borne by individuals like us—may still turn out to furnish concrete conditions, and unforeseen occasions, for further reflection on the worth and meaning of what we can do and say to one another, even when new realities appear foreclosed.

CHAPTER ONE

On *As You Like It*

Why, whither shall we go? (1.3.102)

WE FIND OURSELVES AMONG persons in exile in a makeshift refugee camp.

Trudging through Arden forest, the banished Duke Senior is exposed to nature's "icy fang, / And churlish chiding of the winter's wind," which "bites and blows" upon him until "[he] shrink[s] with cold" (2.1.6–9). "This is no flattery," he declares. "[T]hese are counsellors / That feelingly persuade me what I am." (2.1.10–11).

"What" he is, of course, is a human being—bereft of property, home, rights and entitlements, political allegiances, kinship ties, and material comforts of all kinds. He has been dispossessed of all wealth, domesticated resources, and established routines as well as their correspondent prerogatives. He has been divested of the worldly inheritance into which he was born, of all that he might have bequeathed—and of any abiding bonds to those to whom he might have bequeathed anything.

"Sweet are the uses of adversity," he remarks to his companion. "[T]his our life, exempt from public haunt, / Finds tongues in trees, books in the running brooks, / Sermons in stones, and good in everything" (2.1.12, 15–17). The harsh environment and freezing temperatures, we might surmise from this, have made the duke delirious. He seems determined to see a public sphere or human world in the natural surroundings, as if the organic material of the earth could serve as interlocutor. Or, perhaps—by imagining that the speech of flattering courtiers may be favorably substituted by the wind—Duke Senior aims to challenge any meaningful distinction that would privilege an inherited and inheritable world over the frigid forest in which he finds himself. What is clear, however, is that he has not yet managed to reconcile the awareness of himself as a natural creature—the self-consciousness attained through the "churlish

chiding of the winter wind" that "feelingly persuade[s] him what" he is—
with the natural world as such in its indifference to him.

⤴

According to tradition, *As You Like It* is a pastoral comedy.[1] On closer
inspection, however, it becomes clear that the play is not the latest itera-
tion of an untroubled pastoral-poetic tradition, in which the renewal or
rejuvenation of the human world is enabled by means of a sojourn in a
natural world free from history or culture. The duke, after all, does not
here address himself to the wind or the trees. His remarks do not constitute a poetic apostrophe, or animistic address, to a natural world to
which he might be reconciled or from which he might be expelled. The
duke inaugurates the scene by convoking his "co-mates and brothers in
exile" (2.1.1) to consider the surroundings as both hostile (and therefore
as affording no reconciliation) and inescapable. ("I would not change it,"
says Amiens [2.1.18].) Shakespeare, writes Jan Kott, "takes us into the
Forest of Arden in order to show that one must try to escape, although
there is no escape."[2] And faced later with Orlando's violent entrance to
his camp, the duke finally, observes W. H. Auden, "drops his pro-pastoral
humbug and admits that . . . exile to the forest of Arden is a suffering."[3]

We perceive that there are historical reasons—acts of banishment and
exile—for which Duke Senior finds himself in the Forest of Arden. Therefore we know that the forest is not an original state of nature but a condition or predicament consequent to a sequence of events for which, however, no narrative explanation is provided in the play—and into which no
insight, as a result, is forthcoming. We therefore meet the banished duke
and his companions in the act of hunting and gathering *as if* this were a
historical situation but without having been offered any dramatic retrospective for this state of affairs.

If accounts of dramatic representation from Aristotle to the German
romantics turn on the notion that the protagonist "picks the fruit of his
own deeds," to use Hegel's turn of phrase, then Shakespeare's mature
dramatic work offers us something decidedly different.[4] For we do not
learn what, if anything, Duke Senior has done; nor is it clear that he has
suffered a simple misfortune or survived a bizarre twist of fate. We are
thus incapable of determining whether his fate is sheer accident, as in the
fates that make up *A Comedy of Errors* (c. 1589–94), or if it is instead

something that he brought down on himself, as Romeo had done when he declared himself to be "fortune's fool." Duke Senior is someone in relation to whom we can offer no judgment, through whom we can gain no insight into past experiences; and, therefore, he is someone for whom our affective sympathies and dramatic investments remain undetermined.

At the same time, the refugees in the Forest of Arden remain unreconciled to the claims of nature by which they are now wholly seized. By this I do not mean to deny the obvious, any more than they do; we take seriously, with them, the "churlish chiding of the winter's wind," which "bites and blows." We can take for granted that they *feel* deprivation, cold, hunger, the stench of death; the immediacy of these feelings compels the hunting and gathering. That they are mortal and find themselves confronted as never before with the demands of bodily life is not in question. The issue, rather, is that they no longer know (if they ever did) how to make convincing social or cultural sense of the claims of nature or of the tug of mortality on their bodily lives. Thus Duke Senior, for instance, cannot decide if he has been freed from "the penalty of Adam" (2.1.5) or if he is, along with his companions, "not all alone unhappy" (2.7.136).[5]

At the start, therefore, they orient themselves by tending to immediate, quotidian necessities by hunting deer or gathering fruit. "Come," says Shakespeare's banished duke, as if challenging his audience to reflect on their own dramatic involvement in the proposed activity, "shall we go and kill us venison?" (2.1.21).

Like the protagonists we encounter in subsequent chapters, Rosalind, Orlando, Duke Senior, Jaques, and the others in *As You Like It* are not simply born into conditions of destitution, abjection, or cultural vacuity. Instead, they discover that the social norms, human fabrications, and institutions that not only might have given their lives meaning and orientation but in fact made them sustainable from day to day have been taken from them as they live, destroyed before their eyes.

If "statelessness" is "the most symptomatic condition of contemporary politics"—in the words of Hannah Arendt, writing in the wake of genocide and world war—then it might seem anachronous to apply the term "stateless" to the members of the dissimilar circle that accompanies the banished duke in Shakespeare's Forest of Arden, who are bereft of both asylum and the possibility of repatriation.[6] First staged at the earliest horizon of the modern nation-state—when the medieval adage of "Quid est in territorio est de territorio" no longer held full sway—Shakespeare's drama nonetheless poses questions that cannot be approached if we regard the play merely as a pastoral ode.[7]

Can we be reconciled to the disenchantment of nature? What does it mean to live not just without an inherited or bequeathable world but also *bereft* of such a world, of social and kinship ties, of institutions and principled duties? What does it mean to survive under conditions of exile, to survive, that is, not the nonexistence of the world but rather the divestment of a human world, familial ties, and authoritative communal bonds? What does it mean particularly when this disinheritance makes one a survivor of something that one cannot survive without at the same time undoing one's own sense of what it means to live on or not?

{2}

... and there begins my sadness. (1.1.4)

Orlando's eldest brother, Oliver, has prevented him from gaining the inheritance that he had been charged to provide.[8] The kinship ties that should have furnished Orlando with inherited worldly means and properties are instead responsible for denying him this inheritance. Worse, Orlando has been denied the education that his birthright should have guaranteed and which has been provided to his other brother. ("My brother Jaques he keeps at school, and report speaks goldenly of his profit: for my part, he keeps me rustically at home, or, to speak more properly stays me here at home unkept" [1.1.5–8].) Orlando's predicament is therefore not destitution but rather disinheritance—which here means the failure of fraternal and kinship ties to accomplish the inheritance of a shared world. Orlando's "condition of blood" (1.1.44–45) still determines the worldly conditions under which he toils as, in effect, his brother's slave; but these blood ties do not bring with them rights and entitlements that would make of them something more than base natural bonds. ("He lets me feed with his hinds, bars me the place of a brother" [1.1.18–19].)

Orlando's labor as a slave constitutes a shared investment in a common world, an investment he makes for the sake of a community—his brother's orchard—to which he ostensibly belongs, albeit as a bondsman. In this sense, Orlando is the laboring body whose toil furnishes the material conditions for his brother's—his master's—existence. Like Caliban, he does not even have the provisional freedom that comes from producing material goods; he simply labors to supply the daily needs for life. At the same time, he perceives his brother's community to be characterized, in turn, by a marked divestment of any future concern for his own well-being: "Besides this nothing that he so plentifully gives me, the something that nature gave me his countenance seems to take from me" (1.1.16–18). His own disinheritance appears, in this way, to be a condition of the community's prospering and continuance.

As a result, Orlando cannot find a way to distinguish his life from that of the animals he feeds and with which he sleeps. If anything, because he is himself "unkept," the conditions of his livelihood appear more debased than the livestock he maintains.

> . . . call you that keeping for a gentleman of my birth, that differs not from the stalling of an ox? His horses are bred better; for besides that they are fair with their feeding, they are taught their manage, and to that end riders dearly hired: but I, his brother, gain nothing under him but growth, for the which his animals on his dunghills are as much bound to him as I. (1.1.8–15)

If Orlando is "bound" to Oliver as are "his animals on his dunghills"—and indeed, *less* bound, insofar as his horses are at least "taught their manage"—then in what sense is he to understand his own form of life as human, as inheritable, at all? "Shall I keep your hogs and eat husks with them?" (1.1.37).

The sense of injury and injustice Orlando expresses in the play's opening lines arises, we might assume, from the self-perception of his own upright and "natural" humanity—he "think[s]" that the "spirit of [his] father" is "within" him (1.1.21–22). And he challenges Oliver on these grounds—"I have as much of my father in me as you" (1.1.49). But the problem here is not the perception of natural humanity—the sharing of inherited traits or anatomical features. The question, rather, is what recognition or entitlement might correspond to this perception?

Orlando's predicament, we might say, is that he is forced to appeal to his own bodily nature—his shared blood ties to a common father—in order to protest the reduction of his life to mere natural "growth" and animality. "The courtesy of nations allows you my better," he tells Oliver, "in that you are the first-born, but the same tradition takes not away my blood, were there twenty brothers betwixt us" (1.1.45–49).

Yet Orlando cannot easily protest his current condition, because the very grounds on which he would appeal his treatment—namely, an acknowledgment of the fraternal blood ties or common "natural" humanity—only beg the question of the conditions under which nonnatural rights and entitlements to property or education might arise.[9] Orlando's demand to be treated differently from oxen or hogs would have to include a claim to be recognizable as something more than the offspring of a shared litter, of "twenty brothers" sired by the same father; but this claim remains groundless, a mere gripe. Orlando thus fails to discover within the form of social life he has inherited any terms through which to transform his bondage.

> The spirit of my father . . . begins to mutiny against this servitude. I will no longer endure it, though yet I know no wise remedy how to avoid it. (1.1.21–25)

Rights and entitlements—to property, or education, or even to humane treatment—do not appear here as natural givens but rather as modes of recognition that follow on a certain social or ethical account of what it means to be a person, of what it means to be a bearer of such nonnatural rights. The "right" to inherit, own, or alienate property can therefore only be recognized, or bestowed, in a context in which natural life has been accounted for in a nonnatural way; for example, in a legal system that understands persons as capable of ownership and that thereby recognizes the "right" of owners to own. The transmission of worldly rights and entitlements follows from understandings of how we are bound to one another culturally, of how we account for our lives together in nonnatural terms. As such, worldly rights and entitlements cannot on their own be regarded as something "given" to everyone at birth—for their transmission and bestowal depend on a social understanding of the (nonnatural) significance of the rights one would bear.[10]

By the same token, it is only insofar as one is recognized in a certain way that rights and entitlements might follow as a way of binding their bearer and giver pursuant to the form that recognition takes. Hence, Orlando and Oliver's initial encounter in the play unfolds as a struggle for such recognition:

> *Oliver:* Know you where you are sir?
> *Orlando:* O sir, very well: here in your orchard.
> *Oliver:* Know you before whom sir?
> *Orlando:* Ay, better than him I am before knows me. (1.1.40–43)

Because Orlando, again, can only appeal to shared natural origins—"I have as much of my father in me as you" (1.1.49)—as grounds for this recognition, there is not yet any social compulsion for his brother to grant it. "What," comes Oliver's rejection, delivered with a physical blow and the verbal denigration, "boy!" (1.1.51).

And, because Orlando has no answer—that is, no nonnatural way to account socially for his bonds to the man before him and therefore no articulate basis for the entitlement he is demanding—he is reduced to trying to compel recognition through violent force, by demonstrating his physical mastery over the one whose bondsman he is.[11] ("Wilt thou lay hands on me villain?" Oliver asks [1.1.55].) Because Orlando is, in fact, stronger, he easily gains acknowledgment of his physical mastery over Oliver—just as he will shortly be seen as victorious over Charles the wrestler in competition at Duke Frederick's court. But being "recognized" for his superior physical strength or natural physique only brings with it the reaffirmation that his social life is reducible to such displays of brute force—at best, to mere contests of athletic prowess. He can therefore only aspire to the forms of social recognition open to such displays—villainy, slavery, or naked athleticism.

In this way, Orlando's struggles for social recognition of his natural condition and his enslavement to his brother only serve to further affirm the insuperability of those struggles. If "[I am] killed," concludes Orlando, "I shall do my friends no wrong, for I have none to lament me; the world no injury, for in it I have nothing; only in the world I fill up a place which may be better supplied when I have made it empty" (1.2.177–82).

Orlando's athletic triumph over Charles, another slave, cannot appear as a "deed" worthy of recognition in its own right insofar as Orlando's natural geniture—the "nature" on which he himself insisted in the opening scene—remains determinant for any social recognition to which he would aspire. Upon thrashing Charles to the point where the latter "cannot speak," (1.2.208) Orlando identifies himself to Duke Frederick as "the youngest son of Sir Rowland de Boys" (1.2.211–12) in the hope of finally achieving some measure of public acknowledgment. But he finds that athletic distinction (bordering on martial), like the fateful bloodlines with which, as the occasion itself demands, he must identify himself, fails to offer him any future. "I would thou hadst told me of another father" (1.2.219), Duke Frederick informs him, upon hearing his surname. "Thou should'st have better pleas'd me with this deed, hadst thou descended from another house" (1.2.216–18).

Orlando's athletic distinction betrays him in other ways. "Your virtues," Adam informs him, "are sanctified and holy traitors to you" (2.3.12–13) because they bring down the jealous rage of Oliver and Duke Frederick. ("O what a world is this, when what is comely, / Envenoms him that bears it" [2.3.14–15].) Orlando discovers the failure of kinship ties to make his life livable in even the minimum biological sense when Adam tells him that Oliver plans to murder him while he sleeps:

O unhappy youth,
Come not within these doors . . .

. . . .

Your brother, no, no brother, yet the son—
Yet not the son, I will not call him son—
Of him I was about to call his father,
. . . means
To burn the lodging where you use to lie,
And you within it. . . .

. . . .

this house is but a butchery.
Abhor it, fear it, do not enter it. (2.3.16–28)

The "natural" kinship ties, the intractability of which have enslaved him to his brother, are undone, inadvertently, by Orlando's display of athletic prowess. But, rather than being freed to pursue a more livable life, Orlando instead finds himself exiled, now bereft even of shelter and food. "Why whither Adam would'st thou have me go?" he cries in response. "[W]ould'st thou have me go and beg my food / Or with a base and boist'rous sword enforce / A thievish living on the common road?" (2.3.29–33).

Orlando's predicament, finally, is that the terms of his self-understanding—as his father's youngest son or as a highly capable athlete (the "something that nature gave me" [1.1.17])—do not suffice to furnish for him a desirable social existence, a way of binding himself to others (living and dead) as anything *other* than his father's son or a strong, young "boy." If Orlando had had the fortune, say, to live under conditions in which those terms carried with them the rights and entitlements to which he aspires, then his fate would no doubt have been a happier one. In this sense, it could be said, his "sadness" and fate is a social-historical misfortune. Orlando is not himself "responsible" for his undoing; nor can he, on his own, transform the social-historical circumstances into which he was born. He is not even called to do so.

{3}

Shall we be sunder'd? Shall we part, . . . ? (1.3.94)

Although not restoratively pastoral, we may say that *As You Like It* can still be enjoyed as comedy so long as what we mean by "comedy" is not that the protagonists somehow transform the awful things that happen to them into something positive, something to be laughed at and thereby learned from, ameliorated, or overcome. We miss something crucial if we only see here what we call a "feel-good comedy" or the power of positive thinking. An imperative happiness is no happiness at all.

As You Like It rather asks us from the very start to accept Orlando's "sadness" without passing judgment on him for being sad (1.1.4), just as Celia is asked to accept Rosalind's lack of mirth.

Celia: I pray thee Rosalind, sweet my coz, be merry.
Rosalind: Dear Celia, I show more mirth than I am mistress of, and would you yet I were merrier? (1.2.1–3)

The point is not, of course, that "feelings" of happiness or mirth are not desirable or important; rather, the point is that the action in *As You Like It* is not identical to how the protagonists *feel* about their fates at any given moment. Truth be told, it is not always clear that they themselves know how they feel. If anything, the dramatic action—which we may or may not enjoy as comedic—reveals an uneasy split between the protagonists' feelings and their activities. A satisfying way of tarrying with *that* split is just about the highest enjoyment to which they can aspire. ("From henceforth I will [be merry], coz, and devise sports. Let me see, what think you of falling in love?" [1.2.23–24].)

It is in this spirit of good sportsmanship that Celia, daughter of the usurping Duke Frederick, pledges to Rosalind her own inheritance:

> You know my father hath no child but I, nor none is like to have; and truly when he dies, thou shalt be his heir; for what he hath taken away from thy father perforce, I will render thee again in affection.
> (1.2.16–19)

Celia offers this pledge, as she says, in mockery of "the good hussif Fortune . . . that her gifts may henceforth be bestowed equally" (1.2.30–31). "Fortune," replies Rosalind, "reigns in the gifts of the world, not in the lineaments of Nature" (1.2.40–41), as if, in light of their current predicament, to affirm the desirability of separating worldly inheritance from natural lineage.

However, in presuming to insert Rosalind as her father's heir, and thereby effectively undermining her father's patrimonial authority by reducing her father to a natural creature whose death she eagerly awaits (1.2.17–18), Celia inadvertently makes her mirth-depleted cousin an intolerable presence at court. By offering "in affection" what Duke Frederick would render by paternal authority, Celia aims to bind herself to Rosalind independently of preexistent kinship or political ties—and, thus, her affection is perceived as a threat to the durability and viability of those other ties. This, at least, is the logic Duke Frederick offers for his sudden banishment of Rosalind.[12]

This act of banishment is, however, perceived by Celia as an occasion—a sporting chance, as it were—for divesting herself of all preexisting social ties, as well as the entitlements they would bring, and binding herself instead to Rosalind on her own terms.

> . . . thou and I am one.
> Shall we be sunder'd? Shall we part, sweet girl?

No, let my father seek another heir.
Therefore devise with me how we may fly,
Whither to go and what to bear with us,
And do not seek to take your change upon you,
To bear your griefs yourself and leave me out.
For by this heaven, now at our sorrows pale,
Say thou what thou canst, I'll go along with thee. (1.3.93–101)

I understand both the circumstances and the questions posed by Celia
—"Shall we be sunder'd? Shall we part, sweet girl?"—as that which pro-
pels all of Shakespeare's so-called romantic comedies as well as the dramatic stakes of modern romantic comedies more generally. How might
Rosalind be bound to Celia, once the intergenerational sociality that
brought them together—and the conditions for an inheritable life it provided—is sundered? The only way to find out, as lovers teach us, is to try
to deny those intergenerational ties. "Deny thy father, and refuse thy
name," is Juliet's challenge to Romeo; so, too Celia provokes Rosalind:
"Wilt thou change fathers? I will give thee mine" (1.3.87).

What forms of human attachment might survive the disappearance of
all preexisting social, familiar, or political bonds? Can any form of human
attachment or "affection" uphold itself—provide for itself a future—
fully independent of the preexisting social, or familial, or cultural dimensions that might sustain and facilitate such an attachment?

Do the conditions of refugees, exiles, the homeless, and the stateless
turn out to be conditions under which self-determining modes of loving
attachments are most neatly unveiled?

{4}

Art thou thus bolden'd man by thy distress? (2.7.92)

Early Christian articulations of *caritas* might be understood as indicating one form that "love," as a potential social principle or bond, might
take whenever our investments in worldly fabrications, entitlements, and
rights are most threatened.

When preexistent familial ties or other modes of civic or political sociality no longer hold people together, charity and criminality can appear

to be the only remaining social principles. The homeless—goes the thinking here—either steal or receive alms, since no other abiding form of human interaction is available to them. We might understand charity and criminality as zero-degree social principles, in that they afford the only social or ethical bonds possible under conditions of homelessness, although they are not themselves principles that might sustain a desirably inheritable social form of life.[13]

Orlando heads for the Forest of Arden, where circumstances soon lead him to "enforce / A thievish living" (2.3.32–33). Facing the near prospect of Adam's starvation (2.6.1), Orlando resorts to attempted robbery, threatening Jaques and the duke: "He dies that touches any of this fruit / Till I and my affairs are answered" (2.7.99–100).

But his criminality is almost immediately converted, as if through a self-sufficient dialectic into the principle of charity. "What would you have?" comes the duke's elegant response. "Your gentleness shall force, / More than your force move us to gentleness" (2.7.102–3). Duke Senior's response is often read and performed as an eloquent appeal to Orlando's better nature, a nicely phrased request for better manners. The rhetorical grace of the response is undeniable; for it succinctly collapses the two seemingly opposed principles between which Orlando had found himself trapped—criminality, on the one hand, and charity, on the other. But the force of the duke's response is dramatic, as well as rhetorical; it performatively undoes Orlando's ethical quandary—"beg or steal"—by effectively dissolving the opposition between charity and criminality, "gentleness" and "force."[14]

The difference between charity and criminality thus loses its moral bearing, so to speak, as if charity were already understood to name the bond between criminals.[15] Although neither charitable societies nor bands of criminals are capable of instituting a new world, the ties that bind these entities are capable of sufficing, as Hannah Arendt puts it, to "carry an essentially worldless group of people through the world."[16] It is surely the idea that such ties suffice to form a worldless society that Shakespeare means to invoke when he compares the banished duke to "the old Robin Hood of England" (1.1.116) and his band to "many merry men" (1.1.115).

The catch, as Arendt notes, is that where charitable or criminal bonds become the prevailing mode of community, worldlessness itself becomes, perversely, a "political phenomenon," a way that politics is reduced to the zero degree. "Worldlessness as a political phenomenon is possible only on the assumption that the world will not last."[17]

The Forest of Arden itself can become a place of self-fulfilling prophecies—a situation in which the survival of communal bonds is rooted in the presumption of the world's nondurability rather than in its inheritance or bequeathal.[18] And, for that reason, the banished duke expresses a loss of interest in any future investment. ("The Duke hath put on a religious life [5.4.180].) Correspondingly, his role in the action that follows is restricted, although he does prompt Jaques's well-known ruminations, from which the promise of futurity is rigorously excised: "Last scene of all, / That ends this strange eventful history, / Is second childishness and mere oblivion, / Sans teeth, sans eyes, sans taste, sans everything" (2.7.163–66).

{ 5 }

[He] . . . was converted
Both from his enterprise and from the world. (5.4.160–61)

Whatever Shakespeare's suppositions about his audience as he wrote *As You Like It,* one thing is certain. He did not imagine that we would care much, finally, about whether those exiled in the Forest of Arden manage to regain what they have lost, take revenge on (or offer forgiveness to) those who took it from them, or undertake a renewal of the forsaken courtly world.

In a sense, courtly activities continue, without seeming terribly remarkable in the forest. By hunting deer, the banished duke usurps more "than . . . your brother that hath banish'd you" (2.1.27–28).[19] For her part Rosalind, without much fuss, pays gold for food and shelter, making the forest into a landed estate:

Assuredly the thing is to be sold:

. . . .

The soil, the profit, this kind of life,
I will your very faithful feeder be,
And buy it with your gold right suddenly. (2.4.94–98)

The Forest of Arden does not, we can now admit, represent a critical vantage from which the "cultured" or "civilized" social world might acquire new meaning or be transformed for future generations. If anything, it marks a loss of collective investment in the generational devolution of sociality as such—the emptying or divestment of shared, worldly interests. This is why no one—not even Duke Frederick or Oliver—can, finally, bring himself to fight for the court's survival by, say, opposing the increasing flight of its inhabitants to the Forest of Arden. On the contrary:

> Duke Frederick hearing how that every day
> Men of great worth resorted to this forest,
> Address'd a mighty power, which were on foot
> In his own conduct, purposely to take
> His brother here, and put him to the sword.
> And to the skirts of this wild wood he came,
> Where, meeting with an old religious man,
> After some question with him, was converted
> Both from his enterprise and from the world,
> His crown bequeathing to his banish'd brother,
> And all their lands restor'd to them again
> That were with him exil'd. . . . (5.4.153–64)

That "exile," banishment, and disinheritance are now *willfully* undertaken—"every day / Men of great worth resorted to this forest"—is not a sign that "exile" and the daily suffering it brings (pains and labors more than once underscored by our protagonists here) are desirable fates in and of themselves. Rather, it indicates an increasing inability to recognize any self-evident or compelling distinction between exile and inherited forms of worldly belonging, between landed estates and "desert[s] inaccessible," between the "rustic revelry" of the forest and the ritual activities that had characterized courtly life.

Duke Frederick's conversion at "the skirts of this wild wood" is routinely taken as a mere artificial device employed by Shakespeare to bring about restoration or a happy ending. But this conversion "both from his enterprise and from the world" does not amount to a reconciliation between the brothers; it signals merely the duke's loss of investment in the worth of the "potent dukedom" (5.4.168) that he had, previously, been willing to kill for.

Moreover, the banished duke and his companions receive this news of "lands restored" as little more than a timely offering to the strange wedding ("to begin . . . rites" [5.4.196]) now under way in the forest (5.4.166). No one moves a muscle to hurry back to their lost homes—any more than they refuse return or repatriation.

It is as if the drama here does not regard the contest as being between exile (or the state of nature) and the worldly form of life. Rather, Shakespeare's dramatic challenge is to find something for us to do—something that might matter for us—in the wake of the disappearance of any persuasive difference between the conditions of exile and those that furnish the inheritable conditions of a livable life. We arrive on the scene after the diremption of culture from nature. Thus, our investment in our activities may have to be generated through the "doing" itself, irrespective of any external justification.

"First, in this forest, let us do those ends / That were well begun and well begot" (5.4.169–70), suggests the banished duke. "Meantime forget this new-fall'n dignity / And fall into our rustic revelry" (5.4.175–76). His aim, after all, has not been to achieve restoration. The form of sociality to which the duke and his companions once belonged, of which they were disinherited, is no longer capable of claiming their allegiance. The challenge is merely to discover activities that temporarily might bind them to one another, without past or future. To be sure, we might well ask ourselves, with Jaques, if there is a livable future in "rustic revelry" and conclude that there is nothing left to see and that it is preferable to retreat from the scene altogether.

"To see no pastime I. What you would have / I'll stay to know at your abandoned cave" (5.4.194–95).

{6}

There is sure another flood toward, and these couples are coming to
    the ark. (5.4.35–36)

Nevertheless—Shakespeare dares his audience—our dramatic investment may light on the relationships that emerge, or are transformed, in the worldlessness of the forest, regardless of whether those couples form a sociality that might be bequeathed to future generations.

In the *Politics,* Aristotle begins by proposing the aggregation of pairs —man and woman, ruler and ruled—as the archetypal, natural forms of human community (*koinonia*), from which community in its other various forms springs and develops. In *As You Like It* such pairings appear not as the origin of community but as an end toward which the drama bends in the absence any detectable natural teleology. To my eyes, one of the most striking features of the second half of *As You Like It* is that the world stage suddenly seems barely capable of supporting more than two individuals at a time. No ménage à trois is permissible in the saturnalia that unfolds. The preponderance of the action comprises one-on-one encounters, "couples . . . coming to the ark," as Jaques puts it.

Parallel to this is a loss of dramatic investment in the protagonists' *story*—the exile that we have been tracking thus far. The faint plot structure—of exile, loss, and sadness—transforms itself in the play's second half into scenes of wooing. In contrast to his earlier plays—think of *Twelfth Night* or *A Midsummer Night's Dream*—Shakespeare does not choose here to hold his audience until the end by means of a "plot structure" that sees Malvolio undone or Puck's magic go awry. The usual stuff of comedies—wooing, confused identities, gender trouble, or weddings —is no longer the organizing principle of the drama.[20] We know, or sense, perfectly well that Rosalind and Orlando will end up together, as we know that Silvius will have Phebe and Touchstone Audrey. Oliver and Celia's ultimate matching proves my point in a different way—it is so unforeseen by the previous action in the play as to be almost free of any narrative valence whatsoever.

The pairing off that dominates roughly the later half of *As You Like It,* therefore, might be best understood not as the unfolding of a plot that holds our attention in the manner of Lysander and Helena's misadventures in *A Midsummer Night's Dream.* In contrast to stories of love potions or mistaken identities, in *As You Like It* B does not follow A *consequentially.* It is true that Orlando and Rosalind do finally marry after their wooing, as do Touchstone and Audrey, but Orlando's wooing does not—through any unexpected consequence—*lead to* his marriage to Rosalind, any more than does Touchstone's wooing of Audrey.

Pairs simply meet each other in the woods, here and there, now and then, and speak with one another. Some encounters give rise to a desire between the pair to see one another again; some just the opposite (as in the case of Jaques and Rosalind). In this way, one scene leads into the next without, however, doing so in a manner that obeys a larger mythic or narrative purpose. It is as if Aristotle's teleological principle of aggregation—pairs, followed by households, villages, cities—were stripped of its developmental trajectory; or, rather, as if pairs now constituted the only community capable of bearing any ethical or dramatic weight.

One good way to better see this lack of narrative coherence might be to consider an element in the play that traditionally bewilders students and audiences alike for its apparent lack of narrative logic: the sudden appearance of the goddess Hymen at the close of the play to marry the couples. This is routinely seen as a deus ex machina device designed to fulfill Rosalind's promise (5.2.58–60) to marry the various couples. However, if we consider that there is not really any plot confusion to resolve at this point, then the deus ex machina interpretation begins to make less sense. Rather than resolve complications in the plot, Hymen simply enters in order to join the couples.

Nothing seems terribly peculiar about this, if we do not interrogate the truism according to which comedies end in weddings. And yet, on closer inspection, a few intriguing features of the episode emerge. Rather obviously, the marriages do not legitimate, establish, or reinstitute any enduring or inherited social order—as, for example, in the manner that some readers perceive marriage does in *A Midsummer Night's Dream*.[21] It is true that the wedding furnishes an occasion for Duke Senior and Rosalind to be reunited as father and daughter, but that reunion passes without any remarkable transformation in their relationship. Indeed, because the marriages take place before we learn of Duke Frederick's abdication, the matrimonies imply no inheritance or dowry, no worldly good to bequeath or bestow upon the couples. No preexistent, anticipated, social, or worldly fate hinges on the ceremony performed by the otherworldly Hymen. As the marriage pronunciation itself implies—with its simple cadence of "you and you" (5.4.130–32)—only the future pairings, all but nameless, are at issue here.[22]

Another way of putting the problem here is to simply note the obvious: namely, that there is no external "obstacle" to the relationship between Orlando and Rosalind—no necessary confusion of identities (due to magic potions, say, or a shipwreck). This does not just mean that nothing now keeps them apart or stands in their way but more significantly that nothing stands *between* them; nothing facilitates or necessitates a face-to-face encounter. Lacking obstacles—namely, a "third" force (society or fate)—their challenge is at once simple and daunting: how can they (really) meet one another, hook up, or make a date? How can they come together with nothing "in the way" but one another?

~

Where no "real" obstacle exists, of course, one can always be cooked up. The make-believe playfulness that sets in motion the "wooing" between Rosalind and Orlando—the disguise, the pretense—is, of course, not "necessary" in any strong social or fateful sense. Rosalind can (and, finally, does) drop "Ganymede" without having to wait (like Viola in *Twelfth Night*) for the occasion to arise. That the make-believe is so utterly unnecessary, however, should give us a clue to its meaning—it is an indication of the sheer force of their desire. The point is not that their desire for one another is so great that it stands ready to "challenge"—by force of opposition—an existent social or historical "reality." Rather, their make-believe games reveal that the "reality" of their desire has, as it were, a life of its own—over and beyond whatever the supposedly really real circumstances are.

This does not mean that, by wooing, Rosalind and Orlando are denying the reality they face. They know they are not out of the woods; they know that their make-believe marriage vows (which they repeat more than once) are not "really" binding; just as they know that they are playing a game. What it means, rather, is that if reality furnishes no means, no obstacles, no "third" party to come between them (and, thereby, to bring them face-to-face), then their desire for one another is perfectly capable of outstripping reality itself, of "making" its own reality.

Nothing is terribly unusual or surprising about this. Our desires routinely refuse to accept or conform to reality as given, whether by casting a suspicious eye on the givenness of "reality" or by making a new one up. It is tempting to regard *As You Like It* as an allegory of desire in this sense, or a comedy about the power of human desire to outstrip, or even make for itself, "real" conditions that might otherwise appear denied or foreclosed. Indeed, the protagonists in the play—particularly in the scenes following Rosalind and Celia's arrival in the forest—appear driven to and from one another by nothing more than appetite and satiation, desire and repulsion. Jaques and Rosalind are turned off by one another; Touchstone and Audrey are turned on.

So, why not stop here, with "desire"? Why doesn't the play stop there?

{7}

Now by the faith of my love, I will. (3.2.416)

The discovery or acknowledgment of the force of desire, its "real" power, is no doubt a part of what Orlando and Rosalind undergo in their initial scenes together: to deny this would require denying the obvious, palpable attraction they feel for one another. (How else can we regard Rosalind's heavy breathing at 3.2.215–20 or Orlando's obsession with Rosalind's name but as indicators of sexual desire?) And yet, Shakespeare refuses to allow the satisfaction or frustration of their desire to be the motivating principle in what follows (even though, of course, that motivation never cedes). If anything, Rosalind proposes a test of Orlando's will, not of his desire (which she never really doubts)—and she does so precisely to remedy the "ordinary" "lunacy" of desire that belongs to everyone (3.2.388– 93). To bind *her self* to *him* requires an individuation—of one another and of their life as a "couple"—that the recognition of desire alone cannot furnish.

Thus, while Rosalind seeks to bind Orlando to her without ready-to-hand ethical ties or social knots (chastity, say, or any other fixed duty), she *also* prescribes activities for him that obscure or evade the fervor of their sexual desire for one another. Without prescribing what wooing ought to entail beyond the act of wooing itself, she requires him to woo.

Manifestly, it is not Orlando's *desire* for her (or hers for Orlando) that carries them forward: on the contrary, it is precisely the urgent "reality" of their desire that she seeks to obfuscate with her theatrics. Again, I see this in her famous sermon about "curing" Orlando of his mere desire. ("Love is merely a madness. . . . Yet I profess curing it by counsel" [3.2.388–93].) If he is to (really) love her, the active form that such loving takes should exceed the prescriptions of inherited social principles, on the one hand, and the vicissitudes of sexual desire, on the other. Her "demand," therefore, derives its force from a reciprocal detection and measuring of the other's (individual) *will,* as a force over and beyond *both* the "real" inconstancy of desire and the "real" conditions of any inheritable sociality.

Hence, as she tells him, wooing means grappling with the "changeable, longing and liking, proud, fantastical, apish, shallow, inconstant, full of tears, full of smiles, for every passion something and for no passion truly anything" (3.3.398–402). She would, she goes on, "now like him, now loathe him; then entertain him, then forswear him; now weep for him, then spit at him" (3.3.403–5). Loving bonds are thus not to be found in any ritual display or duty, she wants to teach him, *nor* in libidinous drives. What is required of lovers—if "love" is to provide an adequate sociality of its own—is willful fidelity to a shared futurity, a vow to "woo" tomorrow without knowing in advance what that could possibly necessitate.

Demanding and exacting as she is in her interactions with Orlando, Rosalind (or Ganymede) requires nothing more of him than that he keep his promise to meet with her and woo her. ("[C]ome every date to my cote and woo me" [3.3.415].) There shall be no *content* to this promise, nothing specific that Orlando is required or bound to *do*—no ritual to be learned, no formula to pronounce, no task to perform. Making and keeping the promise—wooing—is both end and means and therefore an end in itself; it makes the *will* implicit in the act of promising into the "social" principle for the sake of which promises are made.

What therefore follows are promises kept and broken, appointments made and missed. Rosalind, of course, remains disguised as Ganymede pretending to be Rosalind, which in Shakespeare's theater meant that the boy playing Rosalind played Ganymede playing Rosalind. Commentaries abound with regard to the complex mimeses at work.[23] My own sense of these "disguises," however, is that they cast each interaction between Rosalind and Orlando as a freedom or "play" irreducible to (though, of course, still bound up with) the immediacy of overt sexual desire and therefore as a test of the other's willpower. Each rendezvous shall have no other *proper* purpose or end, after all, than performing the promise to meet again, to promise again—to affirm, thereby, the willful self-determination of their rapprochement.

Of course, we might ask: is a pairing that aims to exceed both its grounds in sexual desire and its role in foundational social principles (property, family life, childbearing, and the like) still a couple? That is, can it be regarded as socially significant or recognizable if its "purpose" is to test the relationship's capacity for free self-determination through a discovery of the other's will?

Orlando comes to have his doubts; or, rather, he fears that his will-power has its limits. "I can no longer live by thinking," he says (5.2.50).

But there is no other future for *them*—as a couple—in the Forest of Arden, aside from the willful performance of them as a couple. There is nothing more "sober" (5.2.69) or more substantial that Rosalind can promise Orlando at this point aside from the further promise to meet to-morrow. To sustain his interest (and not just his desire), to provoke his "belief," she can only up the ante by promising that she "can do strange things" (5.2.59–60). She promises that they "will be married tomorrow" —"*if [he] will*" (5.2.73–74, my emphasis)—but without, of course, ex-plaining what that marriage will mean, who will perform it, how it is to be done, or what his role will be. She simply vows that further vows will be taken, without promising anything in particular.

What she is asking, obviously, is not for Orlando's hand in somber matrimony, any more than she is presenting herself, or baring her body, as sheer seductive force. If we (and Orlando) continue to find Rosalind desirable then, I wager, this is not solely because of the boundlessness of our desire but also because we detect the strength of her will as an invi-tation to test our own. We are asked to gauge, for ourselves and with oth-ers, the capacity of individual wills to enact social bonds that matter.

"Dost thou believe, Orlando," asks the banished duke in a question that may as well be addressed to us, "that [Ganymede] / Can do all this that he hath promised?"

"I sometimes do believe," replies Orlando, "and sometimes do not, / As those that fear they hope, and know they fear" (5.4.1–4).

CHAPTER TWO

On *Hamlet*

—their writers do them wrong to make them exclaim
against their own succession. (2.2.348–49)

I WOULD LIKE TO FRAME THIS chapter with a straightforward question
about *Hamlet,* a version of which arises every time I approach the play
with students but that seems to me not to have been explicitly posed in
recent scholarly discussion of *Hamlet.*

Why do we care about Hamlet and his fate, if in fact we do? Does the
play *move* us; and if so, *why* and *how?* What is the relation, if any, between Hamlet's fate and our collective self-conception?

On the one hand, in stating matters this way, I am taking for granted
that gauging our affective response to the play implies thinking about the
collective, social stakes that the play dramatizes. That is, I am assuming
that Aristotle was onto something that still matters for us when he sought
to grasp the way in which the representation of a particular protagonist's
tragic fate can move us collectively. What I want to steal from Aristotle,
in other words, is the elegantly simple thought that tragedy affects us by
compelling us to reflect on, or be made affectively aware of, our actions
and activities in relation to inheritable social bonds—those being whatever we require in order to maintain the conditions for living together
from one generation to the next. The sociality of the affective response is,
indeed, the fullest manifestation of the social stakes of the tragic events
themselves.

On the other hand, the particular answer that Aristotle provides—by
proposing an intricate bond between a fearful and pitiful series of events
and the *katharsis* such a plot elicits—will not help us answer the question
of how, or if, *Hamlet* moves us. As I argued in the introduction, Shakespeare's "plots" do not reveal the consequentiality of human actions
within a closed world of determinable, inherited social principles; rather,

Shakespeare stages the disappearance of the social conditions under which "plot structure" can anchor tragic significance or under which the consequences of our actions might eventually reveal their meaning. Moreover, to again recall A. C. Bradley's discussion, *Hamlet* compels us to detach our "moral" judgment of Hamlet from our affective response to the drama; our "feelings" about Hamlet are not identical to a judgment of his virtuousness. Thus, I am also assuming that modern readers of *Hamlet*—Hegel first among them—were onto something in underscoring Hamlet's self-alienation as an individual subject.

Yet Hamlet's own fate is not solely, as A. C. Bradley puts it, "the expression of [his] character" or, as Hegel suggests, "the formal inevitability of his personality."[1] Rather, this fate calls to be read against the disinheritance of the social world—the disjointed time—into which he is born.[2] Indeed, if this is the tragic story of an individual whose relation to the social form of life into which he is born is not clear—or, at least, is undesirable and perhaps unlivable—then it is likewise not clear why the fearful and pitiful fate of this one individual should matter for *us*. In other words, the sociality of the affective response is rendered opaque by the opacity of the social world in the tragedy itself.[3]

In this sense, a reading of *Hamlet*—like Hegel's—that understands Shakespeare's protagonist as deprived of the "ethical pathos" that animated Sophoclean tragedy cannot but fail to account for why or how the play moves us.[4] It will therefore be necessary to revise Hegel's approach to Shakespeare by seeking to move toward an understanding of the relation between individual and community in *Hamlet* that keeps alive—as it must, if this relation is to make itself manifest—the question of our affective response to the drama.

{2}

A little more than kin, and less than kind. (1.2.65)

I propose to do this by considering Hamlet's fate in light of two competing, overarching principles of social organization that prevent Hamlet from taking up his life in the world as *his*. Yet, at the same time, I argue that these principles exert an insuperable and continual force on the conditions of what social life remains to Hamlet. They are, I suggest, his natural blood ties to Gertrude, or what we might call "matrilineal descent," and the election of Claudius, or what we might call the assertion of state-sanctioned "property rights" irrespective of natural geniture. I try to clarify the relation between these principles, and their role in the play, before returning to the question of our affective response to the play.

On the one hand, Hamlet is not permitted to sever the filial ties that chain him to Elsinore and oblige him to forebearers—above all to his mother ("Let not thy mother lose her prayers, Hamlet / I pray thee stay with us, go not to Wittenberg" [1.2.118–19]) and consequently to Claudius (who repeatedly calls him "son") and the incestuous bed, or "nasty sty," whose image he cannot get out of his head.[5] Insofar as this incestuous bond keeps Hamlet restlessly in his place at Elsinore—where he can be called to his mother's chamber at a moment's notice—it is clear that bonds of blood are still determinant for the devolution of one generation to the next. An enduring sense of matrilineal inheritance is invoked as that which ties Hamlet to Elsinore.[6]

This is, of course, not to say that the elective monarchy of Shakespeare's fictional Denmark conceives of its generational devolution in matrilineal terms. However we should remember that it is central to the play's dramatic claims that Claudius's acquisition of the kingship appear adjoined throughout the play to his sexual conquest of Gertrude.[7] Of course, Hamlet's sexual disgust at this "incestuous" union has received plenty of critical attention, and, though I do not mean to suggest that we discount sexual disgust at this point (it remains motivational in what follows), nevertheless, it is likely, as some recent commentaries suggest, that the intensity of Hamlet's disgust is in fact linked to the very real possibility of an utter alienation from his inheritance, were Claudius and Gertrude to have a child.[8] Indeed—in a total inversion of the Oedipal model—it is precisely because Hamlet did *not* have a child with his mother, and thereby insert himself between her and any further offspring, that he stands to lose everything.

Thus, a relative proximity to Gertrude's womb, to the matrix of power imbued by the flow of her blood, remains an essential social bond between one generation and the next.[9] Even the ghost instructs Hamlet to "[l]eave her to heaven": "Taint not thy mind nor let thy soul contrive / Against thy mother aught" (1.5.86, 85–86). Of course, the ghost's injunction only makes explicit something Hamlet well knows. He cannot harm Gertrude without destroying himself; he can speak daggers to her "but use none" (3.2.387).[10] In the wake of his father's death and Claudius's accession, Hamlet is thus "too much in the sonne" (1.2.67).[11] He is allowed to live, breathe, eat, command servants, speak publicly, stage plays, welcome guests, and wield a sword only inasmuch as he is conceived, by all those around him, to be of royal blood—meaning, now, that he is unquestionably Gertrude's child, fruit of her womb (newly adopted as "son" by Claudius).

As such, the very conditions of his worldly existence appear indistinguishable from *nature;* that is, from the sheer factuality of the conjugal blood of which he is, uniquely, both living proof and vessel. For Hamlet, to live in Denmark at all is to be thus bound. ("Denmark's a prison" [2.2.243].) He thus repeatedly doubts that he is anything more than a natural being. Already in his first appearance in the play, having just pledged allegiance to his mother—"I shall in all my best obey you, madam"—Hamlet's very next words, moments later, express the wish for a speedy decay of his natural life: "O that this too too sullied flesh would melt / Thaw and resolve itself into a dew" (1.2.120, 129–30). And insofar as this thought holds sway until the end, he inhabits the world in a suspended state of childhood, an interminable adolescence—living as a kind of mere offspring, unable to make of himself anything more than that.

Naturally, this thought only serves to further fuel his mounting disgust with that world and its inhabitants, as well as with the natural facts of organic life—above all wherever they make of themselves communal principles. ("[T]o me, what is this quintessence of dust? Man delights me not" [2.2.308–9].) For, if there is no way to account for nature in a nonnatural (say, "human") fashion, then the "natural" ties that bind—sex, embodiment, decomposition, blood—provoke only disgust.

Seen in this light, the questions that haunt and anguish Hamlet are no idle preoccupation. In their very adolescence, they are the founding questions for human culture.

Am I anything more than a natural creature? More than mere nature, worm food, a concoction of blood and soil? What am I—am I at all—without my family?

Now, if family life—common blood ties to this woman's womb—amounted to nothing more than an occasion for the continual posing of these questions, a continual provocation for disgust at natural, maternal origins from which one can never fully escape, then *Hamlet* would be about nothing else. But, of course, there turns out to be more to the drama than this. And so, we begin to suspect that perhaps the inheritance of these natural bonds—blood, family, kinship—brings with it something more than disgust.

~

But what else is a family for, if not the provocation of disgust?

Love? Economic security? The upbringing of children?

In the *Phenomenology of Spirit,* Hegel poses the same question, rejecting each of these possibilities.[12] The task of the family—he offers in a startling hypothesis that comprehends an entire field of subsequent anthropological inquiry—is to care for the dead, for one's *own* dead. It is by means of this care that the "natural" family makes of itself something capable of distinguishing itself *from* nature: "Blood-relationship," writes Hegel, "supplements the natural process by . . . interrupting the work of Nature and rescuing the blood-relation from destruction; or better, because destruction is necessary, the passage of the blood-relation into mere being, it takes on itself the *act* of destruction."[13]

Of course, the fact that care for his *own* dead presents Hamlet with a unique challenge will be apparent to all who know Shakespeare's play. But this challenge cannot be properly understood without bearing in mind the broader challenge to Hamlet's self-conception that his familial blood ties already pose, from the start. For the challenge that caring for the dead poses *is* precisely what the sheer fact of being born from this womb, bound by nature and blood to these others, carries with it. Namely: can I / we understand ourselves—as *human* life—as anything other than natural beings, as something more than "mere" nature, if upon dying we reveal ourselves to be nothing more than pieces of nature, destined to melt into the elements?

Is my life nothing more than a "natural" interlude *in* nature, nature itself being nothing more than the total sum of the dead and the dying? Is human life intelligible *as human* if it cannot furnish for itself an ongoing, nonnatural (cultural or simply "human") excess from within the active course of its natural life, between womb and grave? Sustaining this excess is the challenge of making of the "natural" conditions of one's existence

—above all, our individual uterine origins, and the irrevocable natural-familial bonds entailed by those origins, along with our eventual return to the ground as corpse—something more than sum total of those givens.

Confronting this challenge, of course, means recognizing the trajectory from womb to corpse as "natural." It is this very "nature"—"whose common theme is death of fathers" (1.2.103–4)—that Claudius invokes when berating Hamlet for "persever[ing] / In obstinate condolement" (1.2.92–93). Indeed, Claudius faults Hamlet precisely for failing to recognize his father's death as a purely natural event—as the *exemplary* natural event—and he therefore regards Hamlet's "unmanly grief" as a "fault against the dead, a fault to nature" (1.2.94, 102).

But what Claudius fails to acknowledge here is that this recognition of death as natural—of "death of fathers" as nature's "common theme"—in turn evokes a series of questions that, once posed, do not go away quietly.

What happens to someone once they are dead? Do they retreat immediately *back* into natural life? Do they then reveal themselves—no matter their actions in life—to have amounted to nothing more than a crumb of nature? "To what base uses we may return, Horatio!" remarks Hamlet later to his only friend. "May not the imagination trace the noble dust of Alexander till a find it stopping a bung hole?" (5.1.196–98). And when Horatio gently tries to change the subject, Hamlet will have none of it.

Imperious Caesar, dead and turn'd to clay,
Might stop a hole to keep the wind away.
O that that earth which kept the world in awe
Should patch a wall t'expel the winter's flaw. (5.1.206–9)

If being dead is a natural state, then all death is nothing more than a natural fact. But this thought must be intolerable to Hamlet, for it would mean that the death of his father has no *human* meaning and therefore no "particular" meaning for him. There would be no way to distinguish his father *as an individual* from Caesar, Alexander, Yorick, and the other crumbs of dead nature littering the earth. Indeed, no way to distinguish him from the earth itself. But we remember the lengths to which Hamlet, seeking to establish his father's death as particular, goes in the play to assert—and to push others to assert—his father's irreducible uniqueness.

This is why Gertrude's initial query to Hamlet is so galling! "All that lives must die," she chides, "passing through nature to eternity." "Why," she asks, "seems it so particular with thee?" (1.2.72, 75). Hamlet's immediate response, as we know, is to assert that it does not "seem" particular with him; it "*is*" particular with him. ("Seems, madam? Nay, it is. I know not 'seems'" [1.2.76].) This particularity is, to Hamlet, a matter of the utmost seriousness. For, without holding to this particularity *as serious,* there is no difference between seeming and being. All of which amounts to saying that Hamlet stakes his very being—stakes Being itself—on the seriousness of the particularity of his father's death for him and on what this death asks of him.

So, Hamlet's question must then be: *how do I make the death of my father—his sheer, natural death—particular? How do I assert the particularity of this death* for others *when it seems as though it is only particular for me? How do I make of* this *death, of my loss, a matter worthy of our note?*

And how, in so doing, *do I mark nature itself as something human?* For, it is not enough to oppose the human to the natural—for that would only make nature, as the "limit" of human culture, fully determinant of that culture by limiting its horizon of possibility. Rather, Hamlet's challenge with respect to his dead father—and, by extension, with respect to his family ties tout court—is to make the limits of culture belong to culture, as it were, rather than to nature. Claudius *must* have it wrong, from Hamlet's perspective at the play's opening. For if "obsequious" care for the dead appears to be "an offence to nature," then this is *precisely because* the accomplishment of that care cannot itself be a natural process.

Human hands, not the wind, must inter the corpse.

What, then, are we to make of the sequence of failed, botched, perverted, and aborted burials in *Hamlet?*

{3}

I have sent to seek him and to find the body. (4.3.1)

According to Hegel, burial of the dead one serves to make of her a *continuing* member of the community, thereby transforming her "return to the earth" from natural *fact* to human *deed.* ("in order that the individual's ultimate being, too, shall not belong solely to Nature . . . but shall be something *done*").[14] This ritual therefore constitutes a twofold transition: on the one hand, the interment of this individual is what binds him or her—more than anything in life could have done—to the organization of people to whom she now belongs irrevocably. *Only* burial can bind the individual to the community in such a lasting way. By the same token, it is through the ritual act of burying the dead that those still living demonstrate that they belong to these dead ones as well as to one another. On the other hand, burial brings about the fullness of this recuperation of the individual by the community because it converts the sheer fact of death—our inevitable bodily dissolution into earth—into *a deed,* something of human and not merely natural significance.

"Hamlet," thunders Claudius upon learning what he has done with Polonius's corpse, "this *deed* . . . // must send thee hence" (4.3.40–42, my emphasis). Tellingly, the "deed" to which Claudius refers that perforce demands Hamlet's immediate exile from the community of Denmark is not Hamlet's killing of Polonius but the perversity of his "secret" disposal of Polonius's body. "Where the dead body is bestow'd, my lord, / We cannot get from him," complains Rosencrantz to the king (4.3.12–13).

Of course, there are many ways in which one might interpret Hamlet's "deed"—one might read the way he literally "lug[s] the guts into the neighbor room" (3.4.214) and then dumps Polonius's body, leaving the corpse to reveal itself as mere stench, as "something rotten" within the house of Denmark, as a sign of his implicit refusal to return the body to the earth. "If indeed you find him not within this / month, you shall nose him as you go up the stairs into the lobby" (4.3.36–37).

In performances of the play with which I am familiar, the exchange between Hamlet and Claudius is frequently acted in a manner that emphasizes the dark humor of Hamlet's remark to the men sent to recover the body: "A will stay till you come" (4.3.39). However, I would propose that we attend instead to what I take to be Claudius's genuine horror at Hamlet's actions here. Indeed, Claudius seems at a loss even to name the "deed"—he refers instead to "*that which* thou hast done," after asking Hamlet in genuine bewilderment "what does thou mean by *this?*" (4.3. 42, 29, emphasis mine). After all, there is something horrific—unnamable—in Hamlet's deed, as well as in the callousness of his account of it: "Now, Hamlet, where's *Polonius?*" demands Claudius (he repeats the question twice, both times asking "where's Polonius?" rather than "where's the *body?*" [4.3.16, 32, emphasis mine]). "At supper" (4.3.17), comes Hamlet's retort. "Not where he eats, but where a is eaten" (4.3.19). Hamlet's extemporization on maggots, worms, and fish, which concludes with the thought that "a king may go a progress through the guts of a beggar," is doubtless yet another rhetorical deflation of Claudius-the-king. But we should not forget that Hamlet's observation that kings may go on journeys through a beggar's stomach is also a claim that is directed toward Polonius's corpse and that concerns Polonius as an individual within the community of Denmark. The depravity with which Hamlet chooses to speak of the body of someone he himself slew and dumped challenges the capacity of the onlookers to respond and indeed hastens Hamlet's departure from Denmark. With this "deed," he has become intolerable in the community.

Perhaps we might understand Hamlet here to be miming, all too literally, Claudius's and Gertrude's own earlier arguments to Hamlet regarding the "commonness" or the naturalness of death. Indeed, he seems in this later scene to be cruelly echoing Gertrude's careless truism: "Thou know'st tis common: all that lives must die, / Passing through nature" (1.2.72–73). "Ay, madam, it is common," sneered Hamlet in response in act 1, scene 2; and we hear that same sneer here again, as if his summary killing and disposal of Polonius under the stairs, along with his discourse on worms and guts, were a demonstration of that very commonness.

"You say the passage from life to death is mere nature? That I should not seek my noble father in the dust?" we might imagine Hamlet to be insinuating here.

Fine, I'll leave your courtier's body under your stairs.

You speak of the commonness of death as a return to nature?

Then surely you won't mind if I remind your very noses of that commonness by leaving the crumb of nature in your own walls.

Hamlet's eulogizing Polonius by speaking of worms, fish, fat kings, beggars, and guts might of course be heard as his dehumanization of Polonius. Or, perhaps, by showing Claudius and Gertrude just what the significance of burial should be, Hamlet challenges them to see if they can rehumanize Polonius as an individual, bring him back into the community. That is, Hamlet reopens the *question* of the individual dignity of the human body precisely by violating it—by testing the noses of his cohort.

But the deed might also be seen as Hamlet's dehumanization of himself and, thus, as Shakespeare's challenge to *us*.

I killed a man, and dumped the body, and I regard the act as nothing more than offering worms their dinner.

I have no remorse.

Will you, like Denmark, now send me 'hence with fiery quickness?' Am I still one of you?

Are we moved by Hamlet's fate? If so, how?

{4}

The pious giants who settled in the mountains must have noticed
the stench which arose from the corpses of the dead as they rotted
on the ground nearby, and must have begun to bury their dead.

GIAMBATTISTA VICO, *THE NEW SCIENCE*

Thus begins the passage of *The New Science* (1744) in which Vico connects the primitive origins of family or tribal life to the burial of the dead.[15] Vico's mythologeme locates the foundational claim of culture for itself in a repulsion for the stench that natural death brings.[16] Only if and where noses are offended by the natural decay of human remains does a not fully natural form of social life get a foothold. This form of life can therefore only sustain itself where such offense continues to be taken. (As Hamlet himself is disgusted by the smell of Yorick's skull—"And smelt so? Pah!" [5.1.194].)

What both Vico and Hegel imply, in their divergent ways, is thus that the care of one's *own* dead is not in the first place a moral obligation, still less some sort of natural law. Rather, it is a contingent, spontaneous practice that emerges from human beings' taking olfactory offense at the human piece of nature and that generates a principle of generational devolution by giving familial ties a proper purpose—thereby making of kinship something (slightly) more than the sheer fact of shared uterine origins, something more than being a member of an animal litter related by maternal blood alone.[17] The practice of caring for the dead thus becomes the condition of possibility for inheriting one's *own* life as human at all. It is how one reckons through one's own *deeds* the *fact* of having been born of this particular woman. Caring for one's *own* dead is the only way to actively take on oneself the fact of having been born *to this family,* as one of them.

More than half a century before Hegel wrote the *Phenomenology,* Vico moreover suggests, in one of his typically fanciful etymologies, that the Greek noun *phyle*—"tribe," or "clan"—derives from *phylax,* meaning "grave marker," or "guardian."[18] A lifelong student of Roman law and society, Vico goes on to associate the ritual care of the dead with genealogical devolution. The very notion of ancestry, Vico suggests, implies not only the burial of the dead but also a certain vigilance over the site of interment—such that being able to identify oneself as belonging to a family (the precondition of nobility and by extension of social life generally) means being tethered to, or not abandoning, the site in which one's dead is buried. As *Hamlet*'s Goodman Delver puts it: "There is no ancient gentlemen but gardeners, ditchers and grave-makers. They hold up Adam's profession" (5.1.29–31).

Funerary practices are, however, merely the minimum requirement for the transformation of natural fact into human deed. In order for this deed of burying the dead to be *sustained* as an ongoing, relative excess of culture within nature, the grave must be cared for, tended to, watched over. Care for one's *own* dead, therefore, implies a certain guardianship or vigilance with respect to the terrain or space occupied by the "natural" remains.

To be clear, this practice of vigilance does not yet entail ownership of territory or a notion of property and, therefore, of rights and entitlements. It is thus not *yet* a matter of guarding the site against others who might seek to appropriate it for themselves. Rather, such vigilance originally amounted merely to the sustenance of a certain testimonial proximity to the "deed" of burial. Caring for the grave or the urn is, at bottom, a ritual practice through which, again, culture reaffirms itself by performing itself into something more than the "fact" of its natural being.

However, a novel problem is not far behind. For, property rights—an extrapolation of ownership of land—emerges as a related, albeit subsequent, moment of this affirmation. Indeed, it is only against this earlier horizon of caring for the dead that the question of property as the orga-

nizing principle of an ulterior not fully natural conception of social life
emerges.

That property ownership emerges as the foundational principle of social life out of the care of the dead will be important for our understanding here, because it means that a society organized around the principle
of property rights continues, to some degree, to be conditioned by the ar-
chaic challenge to which caring for the dead is the response—namely, the
problem of our natural origins, of our relation to nature.

We will return to this momentarily, in our consideration of act 5, scene
1—which of course unfolds around, and in, a gravesite.

{5}

... that I ...

. . . . .

May sweep to my revenge. (1.5.29–31)

Before turning to the question of property, however, let us tend to some
unfinished business. I have been suggesting, for reasons cursorily sketched
thus far, that the insuperability of natural blood ties to his mother entails,
for Hamlet, the obligation to care for his dead father. And true enough, a
funeral was apparently conducted for old Hamlet—although, significantly, it is staged in no scene that Shakespeare offers in *Hamlet*. So, the
problem in the play is not that these ritual practices were not carried out.
Rather, as it turns out, the *problem* now is the clamorous inadequacy of
these practices as a means of making sense of communal bonds, of the relations between the living and the dead.

The burial of old Hamlet turns out to have been inadequate for a number of reasons; let me name only two for the sake of brevity. In the first
place, the burial was not sufficiently separated—in its very ritual doing—
from the marriage of Claudius and Gertrude. ("Thrift, thrift, Horatio,
the funeral bak'd meats / Did coldly furnish forth the marriage tables"
[1.2.180–81].) Indeed, what Hamlet finds vexing in the "most wicked
speed" with which his "mother's wedding" followed his "father's funeral" (1.2.156, 176, 178) is not only the implicit substitutability of his
father but moreover the enacted confusion of the rituals of burial and

marriage. In other words, Hamlet's complaint is that, by blending funereal rites into a wedding, the bonds that the care of the dead was meant to ratify get obscured, erased, by *another* practice, namely, marriage, that seeks to generate new, *nonnatural* family ties.

Secondly, and more significantly as far as the drama is concerned, the inadequacy of the burial is signaled by old Hamlet's return as the ghost. Of course, the ghost in *Hamlet* offers one of the richest exegetical opportunities in Shakespeare, and, given the fruitfulness of recent writings on the ghost, what I want to suggest here will perhaps seem retrograde or elementary to some.[19] But, as a way to underscore what is at stake in the *failure* of Hamlet (and of others in the play, like Laertes) to care for their *own* dead, I want to approach the ghost here in terms of its call for Hamlet to take revenge.

Let me quickly add that I am not suggesting that Shakespeare's *Hamlet* is reducible to the revenge tragedies on which it is ostensibly modeled. But I do think that we overlook something crucial if we move more quickly beyond the problem of revenge than the play itself does; after all, Hamlet *does* kill Claudius in the end—which means that revenge animates the drama until the end.[20] And he also articulates his revengeful duty throughout. ("O, from this time forth / My thoughts be bloody or be nothing worth" [4.4.64–65].) So we ask: if *Hamlet* is not a revenge tragedy "pure and simple," then what is the call to revenge doing in the play at all? What problem is revenge called on to solve?

If revenge were simply a matter of "evening the score"—for example, of making sure that Claudius, too, is "[o]f life, of crown, of queen at once dispatch'd" (1.5.75)—then anyone capable of doing the murder could do the deed. The ghost could have employed Horatio for the task, for example, in the play's first scene.[21] But at stake in Hamlet's duty to take revenge is not simply the principle of an eye-for-an-eye, a tooth-for-a-tooth. Nor is revenge to be understood here merely as a natural reflex to an injury suffered. Still less is Hamlet's revenge a matter of "justice," political or moral.

At stake, rather, is our very problem here—namely, generational devolution, care for the dead, and the possibility of inheriting one's own life as human at all. For, old Hamlet's ghost enjoins Hamlet *his son* to do the deed because what matters is not simply the accomplishment of the deed—namely, the assassination of Claudius—but also the generational bond thereby instituted between the deed, the one who does it, and the one for whom it is done.

In calling his son to take revenge (refusing in fact to speak to anyone else), the ghost is in effect calling Hamlet to do what the funeral itself did not accomplish. That is, he asks Hamlet to perform in fidelity to his *own* dead, thereby in effect asking Hamlet to *act* like a son—as though there would be no filial relation between them were Hamlet to fail to do this deed. "If ever didst thy dear father love," then "revenge," demands the ghost, "his foul and most unnatural murder" (1.5.23, 25). As far as old Hamlet's ghost is concerned, taking revenge is a family matter because it is how the family will reconstitute itself around him, old Hamlet, that is, around the avenged one.

But because it is a *ghost* who makes the appeal, we can conclude that revenge in fidelity to the dead is called for whenever the ritual ways in which the dead are buried no longer bind the living and the dead in a way that frees up the future for the living. Ghosts and revenge go hand in hand for this reason. That is, the appearance of the ghost signals some eruption between past and future, the insistent return of what should be over and done. Thus, the demand for revenge, like the return of the past, unfolds as radical denial of a new beginning, a new life. By demanding that his son take revenge in order to prove his love—that is, in order to take on himself a filial relation to the dead father who makes the demand—the ghost effectively denies that Hamlet might have something else to do with his life, that he could be otherwise meaningfully occupied in the present.

So, a revenge tragedy is symptomatic of its performers' failure to generate social bonds through the care of the dead; indeed, the tragedy itself signals that these bonds have remained sundered by *this* death. And this is why the task of revenge must fall to the one who—if he is to inherit *his* own life within the community—is called to recuperate the particularity of *this* death for the community.[22] To exact revenge, therefore, far from being the severing of communal or familial bonds, is rather to attempt to reestablish them there where they are in crisis. Hamlet must avenge his father in order to adequately bury him, in order to inherit his own life as humanly livable. The play is, in this sense, Hamlet's effort at burying the dead. But this effort is, the play seems to conclude, doomed to failure. For, it opens onto no future to which Hamlet himself might belong.[23]

But at least, it might be said, Hamlet has a potential duty, a social role to play, a cultural task to perform. The question, therefore, is: why is this duty not enough for Hamlet? Or, to put the question in its traditional form: why does Hamlet delay, when his course of action is so clear?

The delay itself must signal a shortcoming in the duty, an insufficiency of the very significance of the duty. It is as if doing this duty were not enough for Hamlet, in spite of its urgency, which he recognizes, or as if by delaying, Hamlet could show by sheer force of procrastination that his life is not reducible to the doing of this duty. After all, his delay shows, if nothing else, his relative individuality with respect to the performance of the filial task to which he has been reduced; or it at least demonstrates the *possibility* of his distancing himself as agent from the accomplishment of his father's demand and from the demands of family life in general.

The delay—and the play, therefore—tests our patience by seeking to make a drama out of letting one's family duty "sleep" (4.4.59), and without replacing this duty, indeed without replacing family life itself, with anything more meaningful to be accomplished. But when all is said and done, Hamlet's self-individuation as something more than filial duty doer threatens to amount to nothing more than this delay: "It will be short. The interim is mine / And a man's life no more than to say 'one'" (5.2.73– 74).

Whether or not we are moved by Hamlet must therefore depend on our patience with this delay, with this attempt at self-individuation. How badly do *we* want to recognize Hamlet as something more than the Dane he is "naturally" born to be—his mother's son, his father's avenger?

{6}

. . . with no less nobility of love
Than that which dearest father bears his son
Do I impart toward you. . . . (1.2.110–12)

Considered from another angle, however, Hamlet's social "duty" is much less transparent. Indeed, as far as his life at Elsinore is concerned, it is far from clear just what he is meant to do with himself, other than be proximate to Gertrude and Claudius—"Here in the cheer and comfort of our eye, / Our chiefest courtier, cousin, and our son" (1.2.116–17). In being passed over for the kingship—that is, by not inheriting the position and title that had been held by his father—it could in fact be fairly said that Hamlet, rather than delaying, is himself deferred. He is, at least according to Claudius's public declaration, "most immediate to our throne" (1.2.109). But what being "most immediate" means, or bodes, is far from clear. Just what, exactly, is someone in Hamlet's position meant to do? Practice his swordsmanship? Read books? Visit with friends?

Perhaps we might put the matter this way. Hamlet is, in essence, asked to obey without being given a particular duty other than the chore of this very same vacuous obedience. His very presence at the court, in fact, signals both his obedience and the emptiness of any content or principle for this obedience. Of course, courts of the period had names for such people: courtiers, noblemen, liege. I will return to this question shortly.

More generally, Claudius's accession to the throne shows that the principle of matrilineal descent—of "nature," let us say—has been emptied of its primary authority. Denmark, in Shakespeare's play, is an elective monarchy where the right of primogeniture does not hold sway.[24] Hence, although it is true that being born of Gertrude is essential to the social life that Hamlet lives, it is nevertheless not clear that Hamlet stands to inherit anything as a result of this fact. It is Claudius, not Hamlet, who wears the crown and wields power. Indeed, as elected king, it is now Claudius alone who can offer Hamlet at least the promise of a future. ("[T]hink of us / As of a father; for let the world take note / You are the most immediate to our throne" [1.2.107–9].)

Again, what makes this significant for our purposes is not the particular form of government that an elective monarchy might imply but rather the form of generational devolution, or worldly inheritance, that it reveals. If bloodline inheritance seeks to make of a "natural" fact—the fact of being *this* woman's child, for example—the founding principle of worldly inheritance and cultural life, then an elective monarchy such as Shakespeare's Denmark denaturalizes Hamlet's relation to those by whom he is preceded and followed.

In the most elementary terms, what an elective monarchy suggests is that the "natural" devolution of generations—the bearing of children—is not bound by necessity to the inheritance or bequeathal of a human world. To inhabit such a society—in which property (say, the kingdom) can be acquired and alienated irrespective of the "natural" bond between those in propinquity to the same maternal body—is to inhabit a world in which being someone's child does not guarantee that one will inherit a world or a livable life.

Indeed, elective monarchy is a form of social life that seeks to radically sever the inheritance of the world from the natural fact of having children and therefore from the sexual division of labor in general. It thus aims toward, and portends, a radical diremption of nature from the social sphere tout court. Such a system foresees and demands that the having of children be understood as no more than the having of property. Children themselves become a patrimony whose maternal origins are more or less irrelevant.

In this way, an elective monarchy does nothing more than make explicit—at the level of "state" organization—what is structurally implicit in modern forms of civil society. As the notion of private property first surfaces most fully in Roman law, for example, it presents a configuration of social life wherein that society's coherence is rooted in the relative self-sufficiency of the individual citizen—and where living as an "individual," as a legal persona, means to be entitled to property, to what is one's own, to a sphere of possession.[25] In other words, what binds together the society—as a collective of such "individuals"—is its protecting and enforcing the right of individuals to hold property. By the same token, it is in holding property, in taking possession without regard to "natural" bonds, that one is understood to be an individual person, a legal being. Similarly, what an elective monarchy like Shakespeare's Denmark implies—what Claudius's accession makes clear—is that dominion over land and property means that all property can be legitimately acquired and alienated, expropriated and appropriated, irrespective (in principle) of one's shared relation to a maternal body.[26] The state structure becomes simply the means through which this legitimacy is bestowed or recognized—as is the case in *Hamlet,* where the legitimacy of Claudius's accession is granted by the "better wisdoms" of the councilors, to which Claudius refers in his opening address (1.2.15–16).[27] In other words, the state here functions as that which enforces and protects the rights of certain individuals to acquire and hold property—indeed, the kingdom itself can only be held in this manner, since Claudius's holding of it depends on this prior "state" approval.

By establishing the social sphere itself as a certain collaboration, let us posit, between state structure and civil society, as the only thing capable of legitimating the inheritance and bequeathal of a human world (property, a kingdom, laws, social norms, and protocols), a system of property rights effectively seeks to strip "natural" kinship of its power to determine social bonds and generational devolution. In *Hamlet,* the "state" would thus correspond to the law represented in the councilors' "wisdom," insofar as their approval appears to legitimate and protect Claudius's power to inherit and bequeath, whereas the court itself—Claudius, Polonius, and the rest—appears rather more like a "corporation" or some other kind of property-holding entity.[28]

And this means, moreover, that such a system of property rights, or private property, seeks to supplant the care of the dead as the primary claim of culture for itself—that is, as the primary way in which the difference between culture and nature can be said to belong *to* culture. Indeed, by replacing care of the dead as *the* cultural assertion par excellence, property rights effectively render the "natural" family unit increasingly irrelevant to the broader social context of which it is a part. For, if care for the dead is no longer the most essential way in which society stakes a claim for itself, then the "natural" family itself is no longer essential to the constitution of the social. In this light, I would propose that we read *Hamlet* as auguring something like the demise of the "natural" family as a significant social category.

Although the play shows the lingering social force of Gertrude's maternal bonds to those around her, it also reveals that force to be increasingly anachronistic or insufficient as a category for understanding Hamlet's predicament.[29] Where property rights replace care for the dead as the organizing claim of the social for itself, the "natural" family—in which maternal generation appears as essential to social bonds—has no necessary relation to anything outside itself.

In such a situation, the family can only appear irredeemably incestuous, doomed to close in on itself in an antigenerative spiral. So we watch Hamlet and Laertes (whom Hamlet calls "brother" [5.2.240])—both born to families of power and estate, both the living end of their bloodlines—struggle to see who can be buried the deepest in the grave of the young Ophelia, from whose "fair and unpolluted flesh" one can expect at best an offspring of "violets" but no children (5.1.232–33).

{7}

Has this fellow no feeling of his business . . . ? (5.1.65)

Other consequences ensue. Deauthorizing the care for the dead as the primary work of culture has a way of laying bare, retrospectively, the work of mourning that "natural" filial or familial ties had compelled and made possible. The protection of property rights shows, precisely by replacing it, that care for the dead had *also* been a work of mourning, a way of continuing to live with the "natural" inevitability of loss. And, for this reason, the new primacy of property rights has the effect of rendering the work of such mourning itself a thing of the past.

Because we now know that this relation to the dead—for example, as "natural-born" son—is no longer authoritative in a broader social-political context, mourning becomes an entirely subjective, personal problem. Indeed, care for the dead can only appear as a personal idiosyncrasy—one that alienates the would-be mourner from the new social order. This is, certainly, how Hamlet's behavior now appears to his very own mother:

> Good Hamlet, cast thy nighted colour off
> And let thine eye look like a friend on Denmark.
> Do not for ever with thy vailed lids
> Seek for thy noble father in the dust. (1.2.68–71)

Following Gertrude's words, we might also understand the advent of a form of social life organized around property rights as the declaration that the dead have no *ongoing* hold on us, that we can be done with them and can dedicate ourselves wholly to the world of the living once they are interred. The dead must be buried, and *"yet"*—Claudius says in his opening speech—"so far hath discretion fought with nature / That we with wisest sorrow think on him / Together with remembrance of ourselves" (1.2.5–7, my emphasis).

Obviously Claudius does not, and cannot, suggest that his brother's body should not be buried and his life should not be remembered—any more than he can later stomach the stench of Polonius's body beneath his stairs. Rather, Claudius's early speeches are significant for the way in which they seek to *limit* the claims of the dead on us—to contain, therefore, death's (or nature's) own power within the domain of social life.

"The survivor," says Claudius, is "bound / In filial obligation for some term / To do obsequious sorrow"—but this "term," he goes on to say, implies a foreseeable terminus (1.2.90–92). (Incidentally, of course, all of this is entirely consistent with the aim of a murderous act—hence Claudius is an authoritative voice for these thoughts. For murder not only aims to accomplish the termination of the victim's life, and thereby the trouble that the victim's life *is*, but also attempts to show that death can be something dealt by a human agent, not just by nature or fate. This is why, as the ghost says, murder is "unnatural"—"most foul, strange and unnatural" [1.5.28]. To freely perform a murder is to demonstrate, or at least to try to demonstrate, that death's hold on us is not absolute; *we* can give death, too, and thereby turn it from loss to gain, from necessity to freedom.)

Of course, if care for the dead can be *completed* by the living, can be over and done with, then such care cannot serve as the *ongoing* affirmation of culture by itself that, as I tried to elaborate earlier with reference to Hegel and Vico, provides family life its reason for being. At best, the blood-related family would reconstitute itself periodically—at funerals—and then disperse. And eventually, of course, the time between reassembly and dispersal would shrink to the point of oblivion.

Claudius's first words on the stage, therefore, might be heard as symptomatic of a deep struggle between, on one hand, the system of individual property rights represented in his election and, on the other, the centrality of the *ongoing* care for the dead—the work of mourning—in the constitution of our social bonds.

This struggle is played out in a variety of domains in *Hamlet,* for example in Hamlet's verbal bouts with Claudius, in the ghost's complaint from beyond the grave, and in the dumb show and *The Mousetrap.* But the clearest manifestation of this struggle can be seen and heard in the tension between two competing notions of what a grave site *is*—to whom it belongs and how it comes to belong to that person—for reasons I will try to make clear. It therefore seems virtually inevitable that *Hamlet* must finally lead us to, and *into*, the grave—just as Hamlet must, finally, traverse the bones of his forebearers in order to return from the sea to the land of his birth.

_~

Is the site of interment, fundamentally, that to which the living are teth-ered because of a testimonial bond between the deed of burial and those whose living relationship to one another is determined by that deed? Or, is the grave itself—and, indeed, that which it ostensibly houses—nothing more than a piece of property, an austere marker that independent own-ership, a tomb of one's own, is the condition of belonging to any collec-tive at all?

On the one hand, in the graveyard scene of *Hamlet* the grave site and its contents are figured therein as nothing more than private property—a bit of terrain, by definition to be appropriated and expropriated. Indeed, the expropriation—or exhumation—of skulls is the required "spade-work" for a proper burial; the terrain must be cleared of other "prop-erty" before it can be made one's own. So, one by one, the skulls are tossed back up—"There's another!" (5.1.96).

What strikes Hamlet and Horatio, observing the gravedigger at work, is first of all the disjunction between the gravedigger's task and his jovial performance of it. "Has this fellow no feeling of his business," marvels Hamlet, "a sings in grave-making?" (5.1.65–66). Horatio's parabolic re-ply—that "custom hath made it in him a property of easiness" (5.1.67)—underscores that the exhumation carries no weight of ritual performance; it is nothing more than a menial task, carried out with a whistle and a song (5.1.61–64). Thus, correspondent to the levity of the gravedigger's song, skulls fly upward as if rendered lighter by their bald anonymity. To watch the gravedigger work is to see plainly that these buried bones are not "individuals" but truly nothing more than pieces of nature—or, more precisely, natural remains of a former proprietor that need to be evacu-ated to make room for a new owner.[30]

"That skull had a tongue in it, and could sing once," cries Hamlet in the first of many attempts to restore some modicum of individuality to the first skull tossed up by the gravedigger. "How the knave jowls it to th' ground" (5.1.74–75). Hamlet's speech throughout this scene is notable not solely for its (previously noted) reduction of individuals to "dust" ("Imperious Caesar, dead and turned to clay") but also for the extent to which it, conversely, aims to *restore* some sense of individuality to the nameless remains, to bring them back into the community of the living. And, not coincidentally, Hamlet restores this individuality by imagining them all to be landowners—politicians, lawyers, landlords—whose (imagined) individuality is bound up with their having been possessed of property and, consequently, with their relative nobility vis-à-vis the "peasant" gravedigger (5.1.136). "Why, may not that be the skull of a lawyer? . . . Why does he suffer this mad knave now to knock him about the sconce with a dirty shovel, and will not tell him of his action of battery? Hum" (5.1.96–101).[31]

Thus, the skulls of property owners are rendered, to all appearances, nothing more than pieces of property themselves—props of nature that are nearly indistinguishable from the earth in which they lie. And the earth, too, has been appropriated by the living, who now have a claim on it; the soil appears here not as that which occasions the care for the dead but rather as that which reflects the entitlements of the living. Indeed, the question initially debated by the gravedigger and his companions—namely, whether or not Ophelia shall receive a "Christian burial"—concerns both the rites to be performed as well as the location of the grave, the consecrated ground in which it is carved out. "If this had not been a gentlewoman she should have been buried out of Christian burial," they conclude, making clear that Ophelia's grave, and the rites that accompany her burial, are manifestations of her family's nobility and estate (5.1.23–25).[32] Thus far the grave appears as nothing more than owned land—a site to which certain people are entitled and from which others can be evicted. If we have some social being or standing insofar as we *own*, insofar as we hold possessions, then we are finally beholden to that which we possess. We reveal ourselves in this way, too, to be nothing more than plots of the earth. As Hamlet puts it, discoursing on the skull he imagines as belonging to, not coincidentally, a lawyer, "The very conveyances of his lands will scarcely lie in this box, and must th'inheritor himself have no more, ha?" (5.1.108–10).

Trying to radicalize the denaturalization of the social sphere by making individual property rights constitutive of our sociality only serves to throw the individual back, more basely than before, into the "nature" he now *is*—as owner of the earth and thus as what is proper to it.

When all is said and done, we property holders inherit no more than the solitary graves we furnish for our own occupation. Indeed, if the grave maker is right in asserting that his activity is the most enduring form of world making ("'A gravemaker.' The houses he makes last till doomsday" [5.1.58–59]), then real estate in which to be buried is the dearest bequeathal and inheritance there is.

{8}

Swounds, show me what thou't do.
Woo't weep, woo't fight, woo't fast, woo't tear thyself,
Woo't drink up eisel, eat a crocodile?
. . . Dost come here to whine? (5.1.269–72)

What does care for the dead look like when the act of interment is confused with, or replaced by, the act of taking up possession and residence?

Following Ophelia's corpse in the procession of what Hamlet calls "maimed rites" (5.1.208), Laertes complains, twice: "What ceremony else?" (5.1.212, 214). "Must there no more be done?" (5.1.224) he repeats, before grudgingly allowing Ophelia's body to be lowered into the ground. His are not the worries of a pious Christian (since pious Christians tend not to call priests "churlish" and tell them that they will rot in hell, as Laertes does at 5.1.234–35); rather, they express Laertes' anxiety over the fragility of his own nobility, his own property rights—particularly in the wake of Polonius's "obscure funeral," held with "[n]o trophy, sword, nor hatchment o'er his bones, / No noble rite, nor formal ostentation" (4.5.210–12). Laertes, thus, demands to know what is to be *done* in response to his loss.

Not one to sit still for long, Laertes seizes the very next provocation to do *something*. That provocation comes in the form of Gertrude's attempt to steal the last word on Ophelia's life by binding her at least at a rhetorical level to Hamlet, calling her "Hamlet's wife"—"I thought thy bride-bed to have deck'd, sweet maid, / And not have strew'd thy grave" (5.1.238–39). Of course, the mere suggestion that Ophelia might be, or might have been, closest to Hamlet immediately provokes Laertes to reclaim the burial as *his* deed, to reclaim *his* social bonds. "Hold off the earth awhile, / Till I have caught her once more in mine arms," he cries leaping into the grave. "Now pile your dust upon the quick and dead, / Till of this flat a mountain you have made / T'o'ertop Pelion or the skyish head / Of blue Olympus" (5.1.242–45).

Not to be outdone by this performance, Hamlet at this point discloses himself to the assembled mourners, struggles with Laertes, and leaps with him into the grave. Refusing to call Laertes by name (although he has just introduced Laertes for Horatio's sake in confidence at 5.1.217), Hamlet demands to know "*what* is he whose grief / Bears such an emphasis" (5.1.247–48, my emphasis)—as if the "what" were meant to echo one of Hamlet's earlier questions: "What's Hecuba to him, or he to her, Hecuba / That he should weep for her?" (2.2.553–54). As with the player king's recitation of the Hecuba and Priam story, the question opened here—by drowning the stage with tears and amazing the very faculties of eyes and ears—is: what, exactly, is the relationship between the one who publicly grieves and the one who has died?

What is the relation between the tears of the living and the dead for whom they weep? Does the *act* of grief denote grief truly? If not—and, of course, there is no way to tell—then why perform or act in this way?

Before offering my own response to this, let me quickly say what I suspect is *not* the issue here. Although I can certainly understand the temptation of many astute readers of the play to see these hysterics as revelatory of both Hamlet's and Laertes' love of the dead Ophelia, I do not think that what is on display here, in these histrionic leaps, bounds, and speeches, is grief pursuant to desire for Ophelia.[33] That is not to say that there is not genuine grief and love for the dead Ophelia; there may well be. Rather it is to say that love, and therefore grief, do not lend themselves to authentic *display* at all, because performative displays of this kind always carry, without regard to "true" intentions, the seeds of inauthenticity and betrayal. As such, there can be no purely authentic declaration of love; nor, therefore, any genuine performance of grief. As more tangible evidence for my claim here, however, I point to the simple fact that although Hamlet and Laertes *declare* that they want to be buried here and now with Ophelia, neither of them wind up underground just yet. Yes, love is represented elsewhere by Shakespeare (and by Shakespeare's guide in this, Ovid) as being a relation that forbids one lover to bury the other; lovers, in principle, must be entombed together. But this seems like the conclusion of a different drama, not of *Hamlet*.

After all is said and done, Hamlet and Laertes pull themselves back out of the grave. They let Ophelia be buried. And they live to fight again, over another more petty matter—namely, their swordsmanship. There is a livable future here, however brief or meaningless—"Let Hercules do what he may, / The cat will mew, and the dog will have his day" (5.1.286–87).

So, what needs explanation here is the meaning of the sheer histrionic display, of the hyperbolically dramatic character of Hamlet's and Laertes' actions over and in Ophelia's grave. What on earth are they up to? What is at stake here? My own answer is a simple one, as empty as it is meaningful: honor.

Honor, to venture a definition, now appears as the way individuals are recognized as socially significant, precisely when participation in a social sphere itself has been, or is being, emptied of all deep significance.[34] Put differently, the pursuit of honor or nobility becomes *the* most important thing that an individual can pursue when that society has been reduced to nothing more than a field of play on which the recognition of honor is bestowed (typically as a pretext for increase of property). Honor and nobility are the recognition one gains for oneself when there is nothing more to be gained beyond such recognition. This is why one pursues it with abandon—because in such a horizon, there is truly nothing to lose and everything (in a sense) to gain.

The pursuit of honor has, therefore, a kind of endemic absurdity. Indeed, anyone familiar with early modern and modern critiques of aristocracy—from More's *Utopia* to *King Lear*'s Edmund, to Hobbes's "state of nature," to the French revolutionaries—will recognize right away that "honor" signals nothing more than a *base,* transparent grab for power and property. Such critiques reveal nobility to be nothing more than a show, a display.

Nobility itself, like wealth and property, is a reward for honorable service—it is the means by which one can receive or inherit something of value without having to leave behind anything of value. Now, Hamlet himself is not entirely above such sycophancy. Indeed, his willingness to play the game is signaled not only in his acquiescence to the empty obedience demanded of him by Gertrude and Claudius at the opening of the play but more starkly in the way he speaks of Rosencrantz and Guildenstern, after sending them to their deaths—as if their failed attempt at honorable service to the king was proof of their "baser nature" (5.2.60).[35] From this point of view, it makes perfect sense that Hamlet and Laertes would regard nobility and honor as, in the end, crucial. For, without it, it is not clear they have any livable life open to them at all.

So, they fight—first, over Ophelia's body and grave and then again at court, ostensibly in order to satisfy the king's wish to see gentlemen play with swords. That, for Laertes, honor and nobility are at stake in both scenes is plainly clear—not only because he says so at 5.2.242 and because of the laughable lines assigned to Osric on Laertes' behalf but also because the audience knows that Claudius has pushed Laertes into the poisoned swordplay with very precise rhetoric. "Laertes," he goads, "was your father dear to you? / Or are you like the painting of sorrow, / A face without a heart?" (4.7.106–8). Now, whether or not Laertes "really" grieves for his father is, again, not the point. The point—as Claudius knows full well—is Laertes' inheritance, his nobility. Therefore, what he *does* in response to his father's murder is for the sake of his inheritance; his future social life is at stake. "What would you undertake," tempts Claudius, "to show yourself in *deed* your father's son / More than in words?" (4.7.123–25, my emphasis). To repeat, Claudius is not asking for some sort of naively "authentic" form of grief from Laertes; on the contrary, he explicitly asks that this "deed" be a show—a phony wager to engage Hamlet in swordplay in order kill him. "If this should fail," says Claudius, "[a]nd that our drift look through our bad performance, / 'Twere better not essay'd" (4.7.149–51). The play's the thing; and Laertes must play along. His hysterical grave leaping at Ophelia's funeral follows subsequent to this set of instructions from Claudius. In fact, Ophelia's death is announced to Laertes by Gertrude in the very next lines.

What is perhaps more surprising than Laertes' efforts to appear noble by proposing the swordfight to Hamlet—through Osric's preposterously pretentious testimony to Laertes' nobility (5.2.105–32)—is Hamlet's quick acceptance, uttered in the "tongue" of noblesse that Osric here attempts to speak: "Let the foils be brought, the gentleman willing, and the King hold his purpose, I will win for him and I can; if not, I will gain nothing but my shame and the odd hits" (5.2.172–75). Hamlet plays the game, accepting the rules—fully intending to win, it seems: "Since he went into France, I have been in continual practice. I shall win at the odds" (5.2.206–7). Honor and nobility turn out to be the least disgusting social principles open to Hamlet, and therefore he grabs the chance.

In the same breath, however, Hamlet confides to Horatio, "Thou wouldst not think how ill all's here about my heart" (5.2.208–9). Hamlet, of course, does not elaborate much except to say that "[i]t is but foolery" (5.2.211), as if referring to both the swordplay and his own misgiving. So, it comes down to this: whether fighting with Laertes in the grave, or bandying swords with him at court, Hamlet does nothing more than play around.

This can be put more formulaically. To be honorable, Hamlet must outstrip—and, in this sense, disown—his own previous deeds with each new endeavor. Honor, paradoxically, now means having to continually outperform not only others but also oneself—and, for this very reason, honor means having *to continually separate oneself from one's own deeds.* Thus, the prerequisite for being noble—for playing around in this way—is "madness" or an "antic disposition," a continual self-alienation without end.

> What I have done
>
> . . . . . .
>
> . . . I here proclaim was madness.
> Was't Hamlet wrong'd Laertes? Never Hamlet.
> If Hamlet from himself be ta'en away,
> And when he's not himself does wrong Laertes,
> Then Hamlet does it not, Hamlet denies it.
> Who does it then? His madness. (5.2.226–33)

What this apology seems to suggest is that *nothing Hamlet does* should be counted as *the* deed of Hamlet's life, the action on which he stakes his social existence, his defining moment. Indeed, being honorable now means *never letting a single deed define socially who one is.*

Disinheriting oneself of a singularly defining or meaningful history is the price of honor. Shakespeare's hero does not claim his deeds and misdeeds in the manner of the Attic tragic hero. Rather, he says in the third person before all in the open court, "Hamlet does it not, Hamlet denies it" (5.2.232).

⁓

Self-alienation—the disavowal of any abiding relation between oneself and one's deeds—therefore appears to be the upshot of Hamlet's predicament. The mania with which this self-alienation is manifested throughout the play in Hamlet's speech, through the disavowal of his own words and deeds, is clear enough. Consider, as only two initial examples, the gratuitousness with which he gets Polonius to agree that "yonder cloud" looks "like a camel," only to then compel him to agree that it is "like a weasel" and then "like a whale" (3.2.367–72), and the grammar of his self-abuse at the end of the second act: "Am I a coward? / Who calls me villain . . . // who does me this? // . . . Why, what an ass am I!" (2.2.566–78). The fact that this madness, or "antic disposition," appears so much a part of Hamlet's *character*—rooted in the language scripted for Hamlet by Shakespeare—has tempted many philosophically minded readers of the play to focus on Hamlet's individuality as, to use Harold Bloom's phrase, "the grandest of consciousnesses as it overhears its own cognitive music."[36]

However, in light of our analysis thus far, we are in a position to suggest that Hamlet's self-alienation, his "madness"—we might as well call it his subjectivity—manifests itself in the way it does only in light of a certain set of social conditions, only in light of the crises into which principal determinations of generational devolution (above all maternal ties and property rights) have fallen. That is, his subjectivity is how the "disinheritance" in the play—the impossibility of either living with or living without "nature" (matrilineal descent), on the one hand, and living with or without "property rights" (the problem of nobility, of Claudius's election), on the other—gets borne, made actual and dramatic, in flesh and blood.

Let me quickly assert that I am not suggesting that Hamlet's "madness," his subjectivity, is reducible to being a mere effect or symptom of the disinheritance of social norms into which he is born. Had Horatio, say, been born in Hamlet's place, no doubt a different drama would be on display. In other words, I take seriously Hamlet's insubstitutability, his uniqueness—what Hegel calls "the formal inevitability of [his] personality"—as itself determinant of the way things unfold. However, rather than take Hamlet's "uniqueness" as the soul of the tragedy Shakespeare composed, I want to suggest that Shakespeare has left a tragedy that is in a sense more dialectical, ironically, than Hegel himself seems to have recognized.

For the problem brought to light by Hamlet's self-alienation is neither *only* Hamlet himself—as Hegel would have it when he writes that Shakespeare's characters appear to us as "the finest examples of firm and consistent characters who come to ruin simply because of this decisive adherence to themselves."[37] *Nor* can we conclude that the emptiness of "nobility" produces in every nobleman the same self-destructive "disease" on display in Hamlet, although we have to recognize something socially symptomatic about Hamlet's behavior in order to recognize him at all.

Rather, the problem lies in getting at what the relationship is, exactly, between, "the formal inevitability of [his] personality" and the fact that his predicament is socially recognizable to us at all; that is, what the relationship is between the unprecedented character of Hamlet himself, his fate, and the social conditions of disinheritance I have been trying to outline.

Put more directly, we still need to understand what makes Hamlet's fate *dramatic*. If *Hamlet* were only the dramatic genealogy of the origins of the loss of authoritative social conventions, then Hamlet himself—his uniqueness, his passions—would not matter. But that cannot be right. for Hamlet's significance to the *drama* can hardly be overstated. But if this were only the sad story of Hamlet himself—*his* own ruin—then why would *we* be moved?

{9}

If a do blench . . . (2.2.593)

Up until this point, I have been trying to lay the groundwork for getting at this question by means of a summary delineation of Hamlet's disinheritance. I have proceeded in this way for the sake of trying to clarify for myself, and hopefully for the reader, the terms of this dialectic between Hamlet and the disinheritance of the world into which he was born.

However, I confess that now I sense that this approach encounters an insuperable limit, or something for which it cannot account. And this limit is, I propose, anticipated by the elementary question that I posed at the outset regarding our affective response to Shakespeare's play. For, an affective response to a dramatic representation implies a certain relationship—although perhaps not a dialectical one—between an individual and a collective, between the protagonist and his singular fate and *other*s to whom that fate may or may not turn out to be moving.

Thus, the relationship between the singular being, Hamlet, and the terms of his disinheritance is not to be grasped so much dialectically as dramatically. We need an account of what makes Shakespeare's play *dramatic,* if that is what we think it might be. What Herder observed more than two centuries ago remains the case: we still have no philosophical account that does for Shakespeare what Aristotle did for Sophocles—to find words "for the . . . feeling prevailing" in his drama.[38]

With this in mind, let me briefly pick up a thread I left hanging a moment ago regarding Hamlet's self-alienation. Because Hamlet himself, for the sake of honor (that is, out of social necessity), acts "inauthentically" —by disowning his own words and deeds, by following his "antic disposition," by claiming himself to be mad—he tends to suspect others of the same sort of inauthenticity. In alienating himself from himself he also alienates himself from others.

This is perhaps clearest in his interlocutions with Ophelia and with Gertrude, most likely because it is in these relationships that some authenticity is to be desired—and, therefore, is most sorely missed when absent. So, when Ophelia's answer to Hamlet's request that he be "remembered" by her is to return his "remembrances" back to him, Hamlet's response is to immediately disown his prior actions (3.1.86–92). "No, not I. / I never gave you aught" (3.1.95–96). If Hamlet seems "mad" to Ophelia in their exchange, it is only because he mirrors *her* self-alienation in disowning his prior actions. Like Hamlet, Ophelia acts "honorably" in disowning her ties to Hamlet to obey Polonius and maintain her family's nobility and estate.

Where self-alienation is the very structure of selfhood—as appears to be the case in a society structured by displays of honor as generative of worldly inheritance—love can only be affirmed through its denial and undoing. "I did love you once"; but then again, "I loved you not" (3.1.115, 118–19). The other's words and deeds, therefore, are not to be believed under any circumstances—hence radicalizing one's own equivocation is perhaps the only "authentic" way of claiming the general inauthenticity of social bonds and human relationships. "What should such fellows as I do crawling between earth and heaven? We are arrant knaves all, believe none of us" (3.1.128–30).

Just as Hamlet and all men are not to be believed, neither is Ophelia— nor any woman: "God hath given you one face and you make yourselves another" (3.1.114–45). Knowing this, Hamlet is in no hurry to get to his mother's chamber—putting off Rosencrantz's, Guildenstern's, and Polonius's entreaties on her behalf. "I will speak daggers to her, but use none," he reflects, "My tongue and soul in this be hypocrites" (3.3.387–88). With his impulse to kill his mother firmly in check (although it is perhaps ultimately redirected toward Polonius), Hamlet sets about turning Gertrude's honor to shame. Her honor, of course, lies in that she is queen—or, more precisely, that she *is still* queen following her husband's death and Claudius's accession. And she attempts to put Hamlet in his place by reminding him of what she is: "Have you forgot me?" she demands (3.4.13). Hamlet's retort—"You are the Queen, your husband's brother's wife" (3.4.14)—is, of course, what he wants to underscore to her. For the "step from this to this"—from one brother to another—signals to Hamlet that his mother's honor (her position as queen) is inseparable from her shamelessness. "You cannot call it love," he tells her, thereby accusing her of selling herself, her body, for her title. Gertrude does not deny the accusation. And Hamlet does not doubt the validity of his accusation any more than he has faith in the honesty of Gertrude's words. He does not expect, or get, a grand confession. The obscurity that Gertrude sees in her own soul mirrors what the rest of us see in her as well.

Nevertheless, what Hamlet seems to desire here is significant for our purposes—for he seems to desire from his mother not a verbal confession but rather an involuntary, affective response to the "counterfeit presentment" he shows her—something closer to a kind of confession in her looks. "O shame, where is thy blush?" (3.3.81).

Knowing that Rosencrantz and Guildenstern are lying to him when they claim to be in Elsinore only to visit him, Hamlet chides them: "You were sent for, and there is a kind of confession in your looks, which your modesties have not craft enough to colour" (2.2.278–80). The involuntary self-disclosure—the "confession in your looks"—appears to Hamlet, and to us, as authentic; it appears (if it does) as the uprising of the body's nature from within, and out of, social artificiality. We know Rosencrantz and Guildenstern were lying; and we know their bodily affect to be truer than their words.

This, of course, is not to deny that a better actor—a more sophisticated socialite—than Rosencrantz could turn color on cue. Witness, moments later, the veteran first player reciting the Hecuba and Priam speech, which is followed by Polonius's complaint: "Look whe'er he has not turned his colour and has tears in's eyes. Prithee no more" (2.2.515–16). As I have suggested elsewhere, an ancient precedent for this scene is Plato's *Ion*.[39] Socrates asks Ion, "When you sing a pitiful episode about Andromache or Hecuba or Priam, are you at that time in your right mind, or do you get beside yourself?" (535b–c).[40] Ion responds with his own account of his spoken performance: "What a vivid example you have given me, Socrates," he says, referring to the story that the first player will recite in *Hamlet* two millennia later. "When I relate a tale of woe," Ion continues, "my eyes are filled with tears; and when it is of fear or awe, my hair stands on end with terror and my heart jumps" (535c).[41] So, affective responses are not the sole property of the "audience"—they can belong to the performers, too, as part of their mad enthusiasm.

However this does not stop Hamlet from hitting on the idea, of entertaining the possibility—probably as a result of his encounter with Rosencrantz and Guildenstern, followed by the first player's performance—that the "play's the thing / Wherein I'll catch the conscience of the King" (2.2.600–601). In other words, Hamlet places his bets not on the veracity of the performance of *The Mousetrap* or on the veracity of the representation of his father's murder. On the contrary, he *doubts* the ghost's word and proposes the play in order to "have grounds / More relative than this" (2.2.599–600). Rather, the "ground" he seeks is the authenticity of Claudius's involuntary response, his "turning colour"—"I'll observe his looks; / I'll tent him to the quick. If a do blench, / I know my course" (2.2.592–94).

The strategy, it seems, thus goes something like this: if human words and deeds are *required*—by the social principles of honor, nobility, and property rights that animate those words and deeds—to be inauthentic and disownable, then social life is irredeemably theatrical, false, dissembling. However, accepting the theatricality of social life tout court—like accepting that subjectivity is duplicitously performative—has a hidden side, or a latent possibility. That possibility lies, as it were, in the "natural" affects that human words and deeds seem capable of eliciting—a blush, a tear, goose bumps, a bodily shiver.

The possibility—and it is never more than a possibility—is that this theatricality has a definite and detectable limit in the "natural," affective response of those who witness the performance, insofar as that response is not *itself* theatrical, mimetic, feigned.

In other words, if one is truly moved—if one feels shame, for example—then the authenticity of that response will be manifest in the undeniability of the blush.

Moreover, where that natural affect—the blush or tears—is observable, and therefore shared, it might immediately make of itself a (potential) ground for commonality. Indeed, whereas the *social* dimension of theatricality turns out, as we have seen, to be the emptiness of the performative—the self-alienation of every subject from herself and others—the *affective* dimension of the theater reveals itself capable of instituting its own nascent sociality; namely, the sharing of a "natural" affect.[42] The scene thus shows itself potentially capable—on its own, through its very spontaneity—of reconciling the natural and the social in a way that lets the latter be born from the former. This occurs through a displacement of the task of suturing nature and sociality away from the action of the play—its content, its plot—to its formal relationship to an audience, through their affective response. The "success" of the gambit will, therefore, depend on the potential for such a displacement.

Shakespeare, correspondingly, does not script for us Claudius's affective response at the operative moment. It therefore remains a great exegetical puzzle for interpreters of the play. And Hamlet himself does not seem fully satisfied with the "truth" the scene provides, saying only that he'll "take the ghost's word for a thousand pound" (3.2.280–81). However, the play-within-the-play is perhaps significant precisely for its inconclusiveness. That is, it does not require us to name *how* Claudius was moved or indeed if he was moved by the play at all. Rather, Hamlet asks us to suppose that his royal audience at watching *The Mousetrap might* be moved and that his affect would manifest itself in a natural response of his body that would be recognizable as such. And, moreover, if Claudius is moved—*if* he "do blench"—then he is *implicated* in what he is watching.

Indeed, if he is moved, then he is guilty in some fundamental way—his affective response would itself, by itself, bind Claudius to a past he would no longer be able to disown but would have to answer for.

That is, Hamlet aims to stage nothing less than a test for the power of tragedy itself. To see if it still works.

For what was tragedy if not a formal occasion by means of which a natural reaction—shared tears, a collective shiver of the spine—*might* immediately disclose the *social* stakes of our affective response to what we see before us, that is, to what we represent to ourselves dramatically?[43] Aristotle, of course, tied *katharsis* to plot as irreducible to its dramatic enactment, but is not the actual enactment of tragedy ("the play's the thing") also an ulterior attempt to close the diremption of nature from sociality—an attempt to let the latter derive from the former, through spontaneous affect?

In Shakespeare's theater, the only possible "answer" to the question of whether tragedy still works will lie in something wholly unpredictable, unscriptable—his audience's affective response, as a measure of self-recognition.

Shakespeare, after all, does Hamlet one better in not scripting Claudius's response for us, in not making his reaction merely a part of the story. For Shakespeare does not reduce the affective dimension of the theater to a poetic principle—like plot. His drama is more radical than Aristotle's philosophy in this regard. He leaves the stakes of Claudius's response *for us* to judge and perform—for us to work out among ourselves. In this way, Shakespeare compels *us* to gauge the relationship between individual action and a collective, affective response without any prior, prescripted criteria with which to make the judgment.

There is no transcendental or categorical ground for recognizing *ourselves* in the fate of Hamlet—no ground for our sociality, that is, beyond the contingency of *Hamlet* revealing to us something of ourselves, something constitutive in our past that we cannot deny. "The play's the thing" wherein our conscience might be caught precisely because there is no more substantial ritual or practice that could do the trick. Because it performs it into being, collective self-recognition has no other ground than the actuality of the drama itself.

CHAPTER THREE

On *King Lear*

... World, world, O world!
But that thy strange mutations make us hate thee,
Life would not yield to age. (4.1.10–12)

N O OTHER PLAY BY SHAKESPEARE opens with a more firmly established and inheritable world; yet, no other play finishes with a more profound sense of social, ethical, and worldly loss, as if by the drama's end the inheritance and bequeathal of our sociality were neither desirable nor possible.

If *Hamlet* throws the inheritability of patrimonial or matrilineal principles of social organization and generational devolution into crisis, then that drama nevertheless promises, at least, the future custodial duties implied by a military occupation. Whereas Fortinbras will have others to invite to his coronation, *King Lear* can close with no such ceremony. The "great world" is worn "out to naught" (4.6.136–37).

"The theme of *King Lear* is the decay and fall of the world," wrote Jan Kott in his celebrated commentary.[1] The question before us is not whether the world depicted in *King Lear* is inherited or inheritable; we already know it is neither. The question, rather, is whether we are able to understand this disinheritance, the dramatic retrospective of which *King Lear* stages for us, as a past that might still offer insight into the conditions of our lives together.

{2}

Where nature doth with merit challenge. (1.1.53)

Generational devolution is the necessity with which *King Lear* begins.
The value of the kingdom—with its natural resources, established so-

cial duties, traditional routines, material wealth and attendant prerogatives—appears at the outset to depend on its being bequeathed and inherited. What is the kingdom worth, as an occasion for our dramatic investment, if it is not transmissible?

Because the kingdom is secure, undivided, whole—fantastically so,
such as it has never been elsewhere in Shakespeare—the anxiety at the
outset, in contrast to *Hamlet's* disjointed Denmark, does not concern
the "state" or condition of the social world that is to be divided and bequeathed. On the contrary, the sovereign unity of the worldly inheritance
in question is what permits it to be divided so neatly and cleanly. ("Know
that we have divided / In three our kingdom" [1.1.37–38].) Lear has se-
cured the value and integrity of the dowry for which he is, as its sole ex-
ecutor, responsible. The problem that orients the drama from the outset
is therefore not that there is little of worth for the father to give his daughters, since everyone gathered knows the precise value of what has been
divided and bequeathed—the calculations have been exact. "Equalities
are so weigh'd that curiosity in neither can make choice of either's moi-
ety" (1.1.5–6).

Likewise, the kingdom having been "divided . . . in three," there remain
no doubts regarding the identity of the inheritors: Lear has assembled his
daughters and their respective suitors so as to leave them "answered"
(1.1.48). The kingdom—which encompasses the natural world ("shadowy
forests . . . champains rich'd . . . / plenteous rivers and wide-skirted
meads" [1.1.64–65]) as well as the trappings of "rule" and "cares of
state"—is to be inherited by, and equally divided among, the children of
its sovereign patron, the king. The inheritors along with the quality of their
inheritance are fixed and resolved.[2] So, although Cordelia may stand to inherit a "third more opulent," it can be fairly said that the kingdom has
been divided "equally" so as to avoid future strife between its inheritors.[3]

Thus, the troubles that one might imagine for a scene of bequeathal—
for example, the contestation of the will or eventual disputes over the
value of whatever is to be inherited—are not on the horizon at the outset
of *King Lear*.

What remains a puzzle for those gathered to witness the opening scene
is the simple *act* of bequeathal. *How*, exactly, is the *entire* worldly inheritance in question to be transmitted while its proprietor, the king himself,
still lives—given that Lear will still depend, for his own survival, on some

residue of what he here bequeaths?[4] Everyone knows *what* Lear will transmit, and to *whom,* but no one can yet say what the deed itself will entail, what the "darker purpose" will sound and look like (1.1.36). Rather than take the transmission of the natural and material world for granted—for example, by focusing as might be expected on a struggle among its inheritors or on a discussion of the estate's worth and measure—the play's opening gambit focuses our attention on a different set of questions.

How is the whole kingdom—"rule, / Interests of territory, cares of state" (1.1.49–50)—to be taken up by its inheritors while Lear still lives and breathes? Can it be done? What will constitute its being done?

Strictly speaking, of course, the death of Lear—the sovereign proprietor—is the most essential precondition for the completion of the kingdom's bequeathal. After all, it is in the first place Lear's own mortality—the reality that, for all his power, he is still a natural creature, a mere mortal—that necessitates the passage of the kingdom to those who survive him, if the kingdom itself is to prove durable and worthwhile at all.[5] As such, only Lear's demise can serve as the fullest confirmation that this passage has been completed.

By the same token, it is the (quite natural and routine) presumption that Lear's daughters will outlive him that makes of Lear's demise the precondition of their full inheritance of the kingdom. The noncoincidence of their natural life spans (which the very fact of bearing and bringing up children makes plain) compels the act of bequeathal; and this in turn means that Lear's "act" ought to appear to correspond to that form of social devolution that Claudius simply called "nature"—namely, the fact that children generally live to bury their fathers.

Lear's advanced age, increasingly visible against his daughters' vitality and vigor, makes the inevitability of their inheritance *seem* to encroach. And perhaps it is this appearance that spurs Lear to act as if he could fully anticipate his own death as well as his daughters' survival. Or, perhaps, it is as if Lear strives to make his death a *part* of his life by living as if already dead, crawling "unburdened toward death." In any event, the fact that Lear's death might be believed imminent because he is "old" (2.4.147) or that the kingdom's inheritors might be divined because he has three daughters does not change the essential reality of the matter: only Lear's actual death can effect the kingdom's division and inherited continuation.

Death is, after all, an incessant demand that nature makes on generational devolution and cultural transmission. Worldly life and social organization are made inheritable in part through nature's reclaiming our ancestors, who thereby leave the world to us by giving themselves to us as *our* dead.

Indeed it is this demand that our dead make on us—namely, that we demonstrate that they belong to *us* and not merely to nature or to the earth—that gives cultural life an essential purpose: to bind the living and the dead and thereby orient us between past and future through the ritual practices of caring for our dead.[6]

Our children cannot fully take up the world until they can set us down. "The younger rises when the old doth fall" (3.4.27).

~

So, strictly speaking, Lear himself ought not live to see the act of inheritance accomplished. For Cordelia, Regan, and Goneril to inherit their father's world—for the form of social life that sustains and binds them to prove more lasting than their father's pulse—Lear would have to display more than "the infirmity of his age;" he would have to actually die. Lear's hubristic aim, therefore, stands as a challenge to nature and her demands. Lear not only wishes to live to see his kingdom inherited; he also wishes to enact that inheritance himself.[7]

> . . . tis our fast intent
> To shake all cares and business from our age,
> Conferring them on younger strengths, while we
> Unburthen'd crawl toward death. (1.1.38–41)

I presume that the emphasis in this last phrase should fall on the verb "crawl." Lear wants to survive, for some period of time, the enactment of his daughter's inheritance, performed by his own act of bequeathal. Of course, were this possible it would require Lear to survive as something other than a mere mortal; he would need to approach the status of Hobbes's *deus mortalis* rather than merely possess a more ancient "divine right" of kings.

For, what could be more godlike than demonstrating, by one's own actions, that one can survive the social necessity of one's demise? Whereas nature would accomplish his daughters' inheritance of Lear's kingdom only through Lear's death, Lear would accomplish this inheritance by his very own *doing*.

His performance seeks to accomplish for itself an inheritance that only nature could permit and thereby to accomplish an overcoming of the natural precondition for that inheritance.

Lear's hubris, we should be clear, is not that he imagines himself to be immortal. He knows he will die and that his death is, as Northrop Frye once put it, "the debt he owes to nature."[8] The fragility of his bodily life imposes itself on him, and on everyone around him, with relentless insistence. His hubris thus does not take the form of a challenge to nature's claim *on him* as a mortal man; rather, it takes the form of a challenge to nature's claim on the conditions of sociality, nature's constitutive role in the generational transmission of inheritable practices, goods, and territories. Lear is simply denying that his death is a necessary precondition for the devolution of one generation to the next.

In this sense, Lear seeks—by means of his own authority and power—to place himself above, or outside, the very conditions of his own power and authority. His constituted power would, thereby, exceed that which constitutes and sustains it. Lear's power would reveal the form of social life on which his power depends—the generational devolution of the kingdom itself, rule, care of state, interests of territory, and the various ritual practices that give shape to the social life of the realm—to be inessential for the exercise of that power. The kingdom itself, *that* form of sociality, would thus appear relatively devalued at the very moment of its purported bequeathal.

Consequently, even as Lear's hubris takes root in his desire to live to see his kingdom inherited by his descendents, his actions here cause us to suspect that, were he to succeed, he would reveal his power as king to be detachable from the transmission of the kingdom, from *its* desirability.

All this leads us to our first tragic impasse: Lear's power to accomplish the inheritance of the kingdom through his own deed *turns out at the same time to depend on throwing into question the kingdom's inheritability and our investment in it.*

⁓

After all, Lear's success in accomplishing that which only nature could allow to unfold would, in effect, signal that his power is more durable than his kingdom's transmission—since that inheritability, as we have seen, would still depend on the natural death of Lear himself and its sequential priority to his daughters' deaths.[9]

Lear's success would therefore mean that sovereign power—figured now as borne by a *deus mortalis*—is more durable than the generational devolution of worldly life. And, by being more durable, it is this *sovereignty* that would prove more worthy of our sociopolitical investment than the institutions, practices, and rituals that once bound one generation to the next.[10]

In light of this, we ought to hear Lear's subsequent challenges to nature herself, shamelessly addressed to the elements on the heath during the storm, as the bald manifestation of a form of madness—we can also call it "modern sovereignty"—that is presaged from the very start.

Lear's vocal defiance of the wind, bellowed as if to see who can gust the hardest—"Blow, winds, and crack your cheeks! rage! blow!" (3.2.1) —should now appear as the inevitable encounter between nature and a sovereign who, while admitting bodily mortality and natural fragility, refuses to cede to nature the authority to make social life inheritable.

Challenged thus, how is nature to answer? Stripped of her authoritative place in the inheritance of the kingdom, how else is nature to appear to us but as mere "elements" (3.2.16), the "enmity o' th' air" (2.4.211), as harsh and indifferent to the living that she afflicts as to the dead that she absorbs?

Where such as Lear rage, nature can do nothing but bluster.

Rumble thy bellyful! Spit, fire! spout, rain!
Nor rain, wind, thunder, fire, are my daughters:
I tax you not, you elements, with unkindness;
I never gave you kingdom; call'd you children,
You owe me no subscription: then let fall
Your horrible pleasure; here I stand, your slave;
A poor, infirm, weak, and despis'd old man.
But yet I call you servile ministers,
That will . . . join
Your high-engender'd battles 'gainst a head
So old and white as this. . . . (3.2.14–24)

{ 3 }

I will forget my nature. (1.5.33)

In denying the necessity of his natural death for the survival of the form of sociality that he has anchored and embodied in his life, Lear aims to make generational devolution possible without nature's help, without relying on natural processes to accomplish or make possible the inheritance of sociality and worldly life.

But this is of course an aim of patrimonial forms of sociality more generally. What we have in *King Lear*, as commentators have long observed, is the representation of patrimony's most radical claim and a vision of that claim's dramatic fallout: namely, that the "natural" devolution of generations—the begetting of children who survive the death of their forebearers—is not bound by necessity to the inheritance or bequeathal of a human world.[11] Lear endeavors to demonstrate that a certain form of social life—organized, as he says, around "rule, interest of territory, cares of state" (1.1.49–50)—can provide on its own for generational devolution, can provide a future *for* that sociality and its participants, independent of the demands that nature might make on it. ("Crack nature's moulds, all germens spill at once" [3.2.8].)

In *King Lear*, this defiance of nature's role in generational devolution does not only take the form of the attempted demonstration that one can survive the necessity of one's demise in the bequeathal of a livable social life; this challenge to nature unfolds as well through a denial that natural birth, natural generation, and "increase" have social significance.

It should go without saying—and, in the play, it almost does go without saying—that the natural fact of maternity, the fact that we are "of women born," becomes all but irrelevant to the transmission of a patrimonial form of social life. The fact that mothers are almost never mentioned, and nowhere seen or heard from, in *King Lear* is symptomatic of the fact that the natural bearing of children is no longer regarded as relevant to the sustenance and transmission of a patrimonial sociality.[12] Mothers are nowhere to be seen in the play not because it is supposed that natural life might be generated outside of the womb. Rather, once lives are generated, the presence of mothers, reminders of our uterine origins, is no longer socially required.

Indeed, we might conclude that this betokens a form of social life that makes it impossible for a woman to appear socially as a mother; the fact of having borne a child no longer sustains a social significance or worldly role for that woman. If she is to appear and matter on the world stage, she must do so in some other way.

The orienting question of the patrimonial world in the play is therefore not the natural fact of maternity but the social acknowledgment of paternity. What needs social reckoning (from this perspective) is not the natural fact of giving birth, or of being born, but rather the worldly responsibilities that come with paternal acknowledgment. Shakespeare wastes no time making all this clear in the play's opening exchange among Gloucester, Kent, and Edmund. The natural fact of Edmund's birth—the fact that his mother "grew round-womb'd"—is only significant inasmuch she had "a son for her cradle ere she had a husband" (1.1.14–15). After all, acknowledging the natural "fact" of sexual reproduction is hardly a social challenge for Gloucester, who is shameless about admitting his blood ties to Edmund[13]: "[Y]et was his mother fair; there was good sport at his making." The trouble, rather, lies in the question of what, then, Gloucester is to do socially—that is, paternally—for his son, with his son? What does it mean that the "whoreson must be acknowledged"? (1.1.22–24).

Does the social acknowledgment of paternity entail anything beyond making public the fact of having had sexual relations with a child's fair mother?

We have already seen in Claudius a figure whose "election" portends a social structure in which property (say, the kingdom) can be acquired and alienated irrespective of the "natural" bond between those in sanguineous propinquity to the same maternal body. But whereas Claudius's position and authority—the mere fact that he can call Hamlet his "son" —remained tethered to his sexual proximity to Gertrude, Gloucester's paternal acknowledgment of Edgar and Edmund cannot be mediated or facilitated by his sons' shared maternal origins. Indeed, it appears that they did not have the same mother. So, although Edmund's mother may have afforded him his natural life, it is nonetheless transparently obvious that there would be no livable social existence, no inheritance of land, title, and role for Edmund without Gloucester's admission of paternity.

With his natural origins relegated thus to a mere "fault" (1.1.16) of sexual pleasure, the irreversibility of Edmund's birth—or, "issue" as Kent puts it (1.1.17), further obscuring Edmund's natal origins—leaves Gloucester, even more than Claudius, in the social position of *both* mother and father; he is the primary caretaker of Edmund's being in the world. The patrimonial world of *King Lear* requires Gloucester to relate to his sons without being able to rely—as Claudius still could—on the duty and obedience a son owes his mother.

Of course, as Edmund knows full well, children born into a fully patrimonial world do not really owe a father any duty whatsoever, beyond empty obedience.[14] Children merely attend their father's death, behaving more or less well in order to receive his land and monies. On the face of it, Edmund's life at the start of the play thus looks something like Laertes' life at Elsinore. Edmund simply obeys his father, or "lord," but without being assigned any significant duty to carry out as a result of this obedience; he offers his "services" and promises to "study deserving" (1.1.29, 31) but is not asked to specify what such service and deserving would entail, exactly. As with Laertes' sojourns in Paris, Edmund's time is occupied with little more than vaguely defined comings and goings. ("He hath been out nine years, and away he shall again" [1.1.32–33].)

Apparently the best a father can hope for is a son who, like Laertes, waits patiently for his father's death instead of actively seeking his murder—preferring, say, "drabbing" with Parisian whores to the active plotting of patricide.

But, of course, if this is true then there is really *no* fixed and binding social, ritual, or ethical duty—beyond empty obedience and patience—that would compel Edmund to simply wait for his father to die.

Indeed, *why* wait? Why should Edmund not, as if inspired by Lear, bring about more quickly with his own *deed* an outcome that nature would only bring to pass more slowly, namely, the death of his father? Why should Edmund not *accomplish his own inheritance* rather than "[s]tand in the plague of custom, and permit / The curiosity of nations to deprive" him? (1.2.3–4).

These are, of course, the questions that are both posed and answered with cold, murderous calculation in the letter that Edmund forges and attributes to his brother, Edgar. "This policy and reverence of age makes the world bitter to the best of our times; keeps our fortunes from us till our oldness cannot relish them" (1.2.47–49). And, as he reads the letter purporting to plot his murder, Gloucester is stung by its message because he recognizes in it nothing he can refute. He cannot denounce the *letter* as base or illegitimate; indeed, Gloucester accepts its authenticity, because the letter speaks the truth. From his sons' point of view—given that they each stand to "enjoy half his revenue" as soon as Gloucester dies (1.2.53–54)—there is nothing for them to gain by allowing their father to live, except for whatever value his life itself holds for them.

What must terrify Gloucester as he reads the letter is the realization that he cannot count on his sons' love as a "bond" that might transcend the value of what Gloucester's death would mean for his sons—given, that is, how patrimonial inheritance defines their relationship. The best that Gloucester can do is hope for some kind of love, fearing its loss not because he would lose his sons' "affection" but because that so-called love is all that would prevent his sons from contriving to hasten his death.

Edmund's ruse—the forged letter, his feigned loyalty to his father—is designed to make plain to Gloucester that the measure his sons' love for him is merely the number of breaths they allow him yet to take. ("Nature," cries Gloucester in response to this thought, "finds itself scourg'd by the sequent effects. Love cools . . . and the bond crack'd twixt son and father" [1.2.109–14].) Filial "love"—now bereft of any explicit duty or obligation—can be shown by nothing more than the mere respect for a father's natural, bodily life; that is, by a refusal of murderousness.[15]

If Gloucester is loved by anyone at all, it is as a mere man, not as a father. We will have occasion to return to this thought when we consider Gloucester's late scenes with Edgar.

_~_

"Why bastard? Wherefore base?" (1.2.6).

In the absence of a clear social significance for "natural" maternity, the fact of bearing children out of wedlock can hardly scandalize. And, in fact, no one in the play really questions Edmund's "nobility" or his claim to his father's inheritance. The Earl of Kent—the play's veritable spokesman for old-fashioned social values—calls Edmund "proper" at the very outset, declaring "I must love you, and sue to know you better" (1.1.30).[16] Edmund has his father's acknowledgment, too, and his "love"—"Our father's love is to the bastard Edmund / As to th' legitimate" (1.2.17–18).

We should therefore hear in Edmund's celebrated critique of the difference between legitimacy and baseness not a radical subversion of a firm social division between himself and Edgar. Such a division does not exist; Edmund and Edgar are for all intents and purposes social peers.

Instead, we ought to hear in his words—"Well then, / Legitimate Edgar, I must have your land" (1.2.15–16)—a darker suggestion, namely, that the disappearance of the difference between legitimacy and baseness signals the removal of any number of ethical or social obligations toward one's peers, one's brother, one's father, one's companions. In such a world, one's peers, one's brothers, one's father, one's lovers, one's comrades become indistinguishable from one another, as it were: all now appear equally base, equally legitimate. And if this is the case, no human life *need* have— pursuant to any binding social or ethical structure—any particular value to Edmund except in relation to his own desires and ambitions. "Let me, if not by birth, have lands by wit: / All with me's meet that I can fashion fit" (1.2.190–91).

Hence, what Edmund is marking in his speech when he sneers, "Fine word, 'legitimate'" (1.2.18) is that nothing more than a dead word, an empty term whose social or ethical meaning has been lost, prevents him from being *self*-legitimating. We can therefore understand Edmund not, as many astute readers of the play have proposed, as a villain whose motives are inherently wicked.[17] Instead, we might understand Edmund's deeds—the betrayal of his father and brother, his instrumental deceptions of Regan and Goneril—as motivated by nothing more than his desire to take possession of that which he deems good for him to acquire.

Edmund is motivated, plainly and simply, by what Hobbes will later call "felicity." Edmund is no Iago; he is not willing to sacrifice his own life or well-being for the sake of ruining another (any more than he is willing to sacrifice his life to save or help another).[18] Rather, he roams the world stage as the embodiment of the new "individual" that Hobbes will describe a generation or so later—a being devoid of ethical bearing, because constitutively bereft of given or inherited social-political bonds. (Indeed, Shakespeare's fool seems to be anticipating Hobbes's dictum "Homo homini lupus" when he declares, "He's mad that trusts in the tameness of a wolf . . . [or] a boy's love" [3.6.18–19].) Edmund is, rather, driven by pure conatus and impulse; he is at war with everyone but himself and views those closest to him (his father and brother) as mere obstacles to his own advancement. So, when given the chance, he does not hesitate to betray his father and take his title and properties.

> This seems a fair deserving, and must draw me
> That which my father loses; no less than all. (3.3.25–26)

In understanding Edmund as Shakespeare's prescient mise-en-scène of the Hobbesian individual, however, we should not forget that Shakespeare dramatically positions Edmund in a very precise way—namely, between brother and father, between sister and sister. For Hobbes's "individual," by contrast, there are no such *dramatic possibilities;* the state of nature that Hobbes describes is a state in which there are no existent social, familial, political, or ethical bonds—drama is therein foreclosed from the very start.[19] The modern "individual" that Hobbes philosophically concocts lacks a family, just as she lacks political ties generally. We should, writes Hobbes in a memorable phrase, "consider men as if but even now sprung out of the earth, and suddenly (like mushrooms) come to full maturity, without all kind of engagement to each other."[20]

What Hobbes's mythologeme—the ahistorical, atemporal "Bellum omnium contra omnes"—cannot and does not account for, of course, is how "individuals" might come to appear in this way, that is, how they might have *come to seem to us as apolitical creatures.* Whereas Hobbes presupposes as an ontological given the "maturity" of willing, desiring, moving "individuals" within a "state of nature" that has no history, Shakespeare offers in Edmund (as he had, similarly, in Richard III and in Jaques, Rosalind, and Oliver), a dramatic retrospective of that individuality—its debut. Edmund's words and deeds teach us how—at what cost, with what fascination and charm, to what ends—inherited familial bonds, social ties, political allegiances, and loyalties can be systematically undone and rent asunder.

Edmund's betrayal of Gloucester thus instructs us, avant la lettre, that Hobbes's apolitical individual did not sprout like a "mushroom," fully formed, lacking a family. Shakespeare's drama invites us instead to bear witness to this new creature and acknowledge that this "whoreson" individual, is, just like all of us, of woman born; like any of us, he can lie, seduce, and betray.

For him, there is no social bond, no kinship tie, no ethical relation whose severance he cannot survive, flourishing in fact by its very destruction.

"*I* grow, *I* prosper" (1.2.21, my emphasis).

~~⋰~~

With all of this in mind, we can now return to the story of Lear and his daughters by means of an instructive contrast with the subplot of Gloucester and Edmund.

By striving to outlive the *social necessity* of his own demise, and by endeavoring to survive his daughters' inheritance of the kingdom, we might understand Lear as striving to remove the temptation or the need for his daughters to kill him in order to accomplish for themselves their own inheritance. The "future strife" that he seeks to prevent might be, in the first place, his own assassination or violation.

Of course, as we know, Lear fails to prevent his own undoing at his daughters' hands. Indeed, the rest of the drama grapples with this failure, which reveals Goneril and Regan to be as impatiently murderous, as covetous and individualistic, as Edmund. Yet we still need to understand the reasons for, and the contours of, Lear's failure.

Lear's goal, of course, is frustrated almost as soon as it is announced. In the immediate wake of his disastrous exchange with Cordelia in the opening scene, Lear winds up compromising his initial plan to realize the full bequeathal of the divided kingdom by retaining, with calamitous results, "the name and all th' addition to a king" (1.1.136). In this way Lear turns himself into, as Goneril says, an "[i]dle old man, / That would still manage those authorities / That he hath given away!" (1.3.17–19). However, on my reading, retaining the name and authority of king is an unintended error that Lear makes as a result of his falling out with Cordelia; his initial ambition was, as he himself claims, to fully "divest" "all cares and business" along with "rule, interest of territory, cares of state" (1.1.49–50).

Now, if I have been right in concluding that Lear's aim is to outlive the social necessity of his own demise by accomplishing through his own action his daughters' inheritance of the kingdom, then a question arises. Assuming Lear *could* survive the accomplishment of his daughters' *full* inheritance of the kingdom—that is, supposing that he could outlive his wholesale self-divestment of "rule, interest of territory, cares of state," which would leave nothing for himself—then what would be the condition of that survival? What was to be his livelihood, once he had "given all" (3.4.48) away? Could he save nothing, would he give them all?

Here we move closer to an understanding of the play's opening scene; that is, to the problem of why Lear should have confused the act of bequeathal with the question of his daughters' love for him.

{4}

Is it the fashion that discarded fathers
Should have thus little mercy on their flesh?
Judicious punishment! 'twas the flesh begot
Those pelican daughters. (3.4.72–75)

In light of what we have just said regarding Gloucester and Edmund, I propose that we now return to Lear's gambit in the opening scene of abdication in a manner that diverges from critical orthodoxies.

In accomplishing the most radically "patrimonial" performance of all by denying nature a role in generational devolution, by accomplishing his daughters' full inheritance while he still lives, Lear would not only have demonstrated himself to be the embodiment of a new kind of sovereign, a *deus mortalis*. In divesting himself fully of rule, interest of territory, and cares of state, he would also—by the same token and only in this manner—have succeeded in *overcoming* his patrimonial (kingly, proprietary) relation to his daughters, leaving himself before them as nothing more than an "unaccommodated man" (3.4.109).[21]

By denaturalizing generational devolution, by denying the natural necessity of his own death for the transmission of the sociality that sustains his life, Lear would have realized nothing less than *his own renaturalization*. He seeks to remake himself—by sovereign act, as it were—into a mere man.

I am tempted to state matters thus: by means of a self-divestment that only a *deus mortalis* could accomplish, Lear attempts nothing other than to give birth to himself. He wants *to bring about and at the same time to undergo* his own reentrance into the world as a natural creature, "un-burthen'd," naked and without title, helpless and infantile, wholly ex-posed to the care others might bestow and the harm they might inflict.

A preponderance of critical opinion suggests that we grasp Lear's re-moval of his clothes during the storm and his identification with Poor Tom—"unaccommodated man is no more but such a poor, bare, forked animal. . . . Come; unbutton here" (3.4.109–12)—as a sign that, follow-ing his humiliation at the hands of Goneril and Regan, Lear has *learned* through his suffering something that he did not know at the play's outset; namely, that he is a mere mortal, "the thing itself" (3.4.109), and not a god.[22] I am suggesting, however, that Lear had strived to tear off his clothes from the very start—and that this was precisely what the self-divestment of the opening scene was meant to do. His self-divestment was meant to reduce him to the status of a mere man, above all in the eyes of Cordelia. He wanted to strip himself of accommodation to see if he would then be accommodated. To see if he would be loved, offered "mercy" (3.4.73) when he was no longer king but instead a mere man.

For the sake of testing (*really* testing) his daughter's love, Lear longs to divest himself of the paternal-sovereign authority that Gloucester dreads being stripped of for fear of losing his sons' love.

Whereas Gloucester naively believes that sons should love their fathers because they are patrimonial-paternal figures, Lear organizes the scene of the kingdom's division according the opposite presumption. He knows full well that, while he remains king, he cannot be loved as a mere human being—though he can be harmed as one. Just as he knows that any dec-larations of love that he receives while king—including those he will re-ceive in the opening scene—are not to be trusted; such declarations are nothing more than confirmations of his patrimonial position and power. They are not a loving acknowledgment of *him*, the white-haired, aging, and ailing man.

The truest test of filial love and acknowledgment is not to be found in any rhetorical test, therefore, but in whether or not his daughters will—without being legally, ethically, or ritually bound to do so—take his ag-ing body into their homes, tolerate its inevitable failings, care for his nat-ural life, and let him crawl unburdened toward death.

Now, I am not for a moment presuming that Lear supposes Goneril and Regan would "really" love him, or care for him, in this way. On the contrary, I understand Lear's hastily improvised plan to keep a "reservation of an hundred knights" (1.1.133) and "the name and all th' addition to a king" (1.1.136)—the plan B that he announces precisely when he realizes that his disinheritance of Cordelia means that he will have to be "sustain'd" by Goneril and Regan—to be a recognition that the latter probably do not really care whether he, as a mere man, lives or dies. Lear knows that he cannot turn himself over to their care entirely without (for safety's sake) mitigating his exposure, without remaining more than a mere man (hence, "the name and all th' addition to a king").[23]

I am, however, claiming that Lear is at his most sincere when he declares, in his rage, that he had hoped to live out his days with Cordelia; indeed, it is as if the frustration of *this* wish were the source of his anger:

> Peace, Kent!
> Come not between the Dragon and his wrath.
> I lov'd her most, and thought to set my rest
> On her kind nursery. . . . (1.1.121–24)

In thinking to set his rest on Cordelia's kind nursery, I imagine that Lear wished, finally, for at least the chance to receive love as himself, a mere man. He wanted to be loved not as king—for the love a king receives is mere empty obedience, an obedience that we now know is only a hair's breath away from murderousness. Lear wished rather to be loved as only a natural creature can be loved—cared for, that is, in his own circumstance of bodily frailty, neediness, and helplessness.

Lear needed therefore—by means of his sovereign power—to set a limit to his sovereignty, to show that he was not reducible to the power that he wielded. Lear longed to use his sovereign authority and patrimonial position in order to create, by his own doing, the conditions of possibility for what he fantasized might be the purest, most disinterested form of love possible. Not the love of a mother for the child she has borne, compromised as it is by the natural demands of instinct and maternal nourishment, nor the love of a lover, tainted by the vicissitudes of sexual desire, but rather the uncompromised love of a daughter for an aging father who has already given her all he has to give, who has already offered her all she could ever hope to receive, who has indeed shown himself to be quasi divine—never more so then when he strips himself of that divinity, returning to earth in a weakened, hence lovable, form.[24]

"Upon such sacrifices, my Cordelia," Lear will later explain, "the Gods themselves throw incense"—for "such sacrifices" make possible conditions for being loved that not even nature or gods can furnish (5.3.20–21). Lear's first thought upon being arrested and taken to prison—and, thereby, well and truly stripped of worldly entitlements, rights, and recognitions—is in fact that now he might at last achieve these conditions. Prison will finally provide the test of—and therefore the opportunity for—Cordelia's love of him as the natural creature he has turned himself into:

> . . . Come, let's away to prison;
> We two alone will sing like birds i' th' cage
>
> . . . .
> . . . so, we'll live,
>
> . . . . . .
> . . . and we'll wear out
> In a wall'd prison, packs and sects of great ones
> That ebb and flow by' the moon. (5.3.8–19)

Lear's desire might thus be considered as follows. He regarded the conditions of possibility for being *loved* as a *natural* creature—the most desirable form of sociality imaginable—to be something that nature alone could not bestow. That is, he understood human lovability not as a divine gift or natural *given* but as a condition that has to be artificially made, painstakingly achieved as the culmination of a human life's work. He understood the accomplishment of those conditions—of that loving sociality—to be something that he, and he alone, could achieve by design and purpose. Indeed, that achievement would be the final end and scope of a denaturalized patrimonial sociality—the fullest sovereign accomplishment imaginable.[25]

I understand the question that motivates Lear to be something like this: *"If my throne, my patrimonial accomplishments, my territorial acquisitions and social authority do not finally yield me this love, then what are these worth?"*

⤋

Yet, precisely for these same reasons, the love from Cordelia that Lear desires to make possible could *only* come about by means of the demonstration of an uncontestable patrimonial power—the very demonstration of which, again, Lear's enacted inheritance of his daughters was intended to provide.

Hence, it will turn out that Lear could only achieve the conditions under which he might, finally, be loved in a pure and disinterested way by destroying the conditions under which such love can be avowed.

Thus we are provided with our second tragic impasse: Lear could only be loved, as a mere man, as a human father, by first proving himself capable of what only a *deus mortalis* could perform. Only by dehumanizing himself could Lear become human again; he could make himself into a lovable natural creature only by behaving monstrously, in defiance of nature's claims.

Only by demonstrating that he could outlive the necessity of his natural demise could he finally crawl toward death.

Only by showing his power to be uncontested and incontestable could he once again render himself helpless and powerless.

{5}

Tell me, my daughters . . . (1.1.48)

What does one do when confronted with an incontestable power, with absolute sovereign power consolidated in an individual person?

If one is shrewd, of course, one flatters them.

Lear's opening demand—"Which of you shall we say doth love us most?" (1.1.51)—is obviously not an occasion for his daughters to tell him "how they really feel." That is, he is not asking them to communicate some "message" or "content" to him. Their "obedience" is what is expected; but since obedience here does not entail any prescribed duty or task, what is required is a performance that shows the very hollowness of that obedience (1.1.278). This is why Lear requires that they formally recognize his absolute power, his a priori supremacy, in the language of recognition appropriate to such power—flattering speech.

What makes flattery appropriate here is simply that flattery, to invoke J. L. Austin's well-known category, works "performatively." Flattery does not merely "describe" the one who is flattered, nor does flattery "refer" simply to some meaning or content that the flatterer wishes to communicate. Rather, flattery—the paradigmatic instance of which is telling an-other "how much" one loves him—is a locutionary act, a doing that es-tablishes, alters, or reifies a certain relationship between the speaker and the addressee.

To be sure, telling a father, a king, how much one loves him is an ex-emplary instance of this sort of speech because affective bonds, like love, are particularly "empty" of speakable meaning or import. This is not to say that genuine bonds or sentiments of love do not exist; it is simply to say that such sentiments do not lend themselves to authentic locutionary *performance* at all, because—as Shakespeare reminds us over and over—such displays always bear, without regard to "true" intentions, the seeds of inauthenticity and betrayal. Thus, the act of telling a father, a king (or, for that matter, a lover or a friend), how much he is loved is necessarily empty because the "meaning" that the locution claims to bear does not make itself available to speech. Nothing could be less meaningful than telling another "I love you"—except, perhaps, telling him *how much* one loves him.

So what is Lear asking for? And what are Goneril and Regan *doing* when they tell him how much they love him? In one sense, they are sim-ply turning the very *act* of telling Lear how much they love him into the *content*, the matter at hand—namely, by showing that the "meaning" of their speech lies only in its very performance. And if this performance is, as I just suggested, also the demonstration of the "hollowness" (1.1.154) of "what" is declared, then what Regan and Goneril are doing is perfor-matively revealing their own emptiness as speakers—letting their mere speech take *their* place before absolute power, as it were.[26] They become mere speakers of speech, hollow vehicles for the self-showing of flattering discourse. In this way, they reveal the "power" in question to be that which only recognizes, and is recognized by, self-emptying speech of this sort. Indeed, such incontestable power might be defined as that which can require its subject to perform in this self-evacuating way and need hear only this sort of speech.

Such a sovereign would therefore be unable to recognize self-revelatory speech, to hear language as expressive of the passions and uniqueness of the speaker herself. For, it is deafness to *her* that allows the king's ears to be tuned to flattering music alone.

So, what shall Cordelia speak, if she is to make herself heard? "Love, and be silent" (1.1.62) arises as the first thought, or response, to her predicament.[27] If her love is genuine, and thus unspeakable, then her only course of action is passive silence. Come what may. As Cavell nicely states it: "To pretend publicly to love, where you do not love, is easy; to pretend to love, where you really do love, is not obviously possible."[28] If her love is indeed "more ponderous than her tongue" (1.1.78) and therefore cannot be made into the "empty" content it must become if it is to satisfy the demands of flattering discourse, then anything Cordelia speaks here can only betray that love. Indeed, even the slightest word from her—"nothing" (1.1.89)—will compromise her.

How might we interpret what Cordelia ends up saying? We might be tempted to understand Cordelia's speech in this scene—the fact that she opens her mouth at all—as a betrayal of that unspeakable love or as a sign of her limitations as a lover of her father. She is unfaithful to the silence that she herself regards as love's most faithful consequence.

Of course, it can hardly be said that her betrayal is unprovoked. Lear, after all, demands that she, like her sisters before her, "Speak" (1.1.86)—and in making such a demand Lear is, in effect, blackmailing his daughters by insisting that they speak flatteringly or not at all. This should be obvious from the outset, insofar as Lear does not ask *if* his daughters love him. On the contrary, what they must do by speaking, if they are to satisfy his demand and thereby affirm his power over them, is hardly up to them.[29]

By responding to Lear's demand as she does—by saying "Nothing, my lord" (1.1.87)—she perhaps wants to say, or means to say, "I can *say* nothing, my lord." Perhaps she wants to communicate to him her silence—to say to him that there is nothing she can *say*. Instead, she says literally "*nothing*"—and thereby betrays her silence with the word that she thought would merely indicate it. In fact, she says "nothing" twice—as if for emphasis, opening her mouth to repeat herself precisely when loving demanded silence.

If Cordelia's love were genuinely unspeakable, only her absolute silence—a kind of passive resistance, as it were—would have safeguarded it, given it a chance to be perceived for what it is. But her word—"nothing"—nullified that chance. All that remains for her, having spoken, is to explain her remark—to drag it, ungainly and inappropriate, into the public light by disclosing what she means.

Yet just because Cordelia speaks does not authorize us to conclude that she does not "really" love Lear. However, it might well show us that we do not yet know what form of "love" it is, what loving implies for her. She explains further:

> Unhappy that I am, I cannot heave
> My heart into my mouth: I love your Majesty
> According to my bond; no more nor less. (1.1.91–93)

What is jarring here, of course, is Cordelia's brusque invocation of her "bond"—a word that must strike Lear like a hammer—as if she were bound to her father by nothing more than filial obligation and duty. The question, of course, is, *what* bond? *What* duty and obligation? None has been mentioned, and "how" Cordelia is bound to Lear—*how* she loves him—is precisely the matter that, in principle, was to be decided once and for all by the scene.

To make fuller sense of her response, I propose that we depart somewhat from the interpretations suggested thus far in order to hear again the subtle precision of Cordelia's logic in this speech.

"Love," in her words, is proposed as nothing more than the name one gives by metonymic extension to the sheer natural fact of geniture and propagation. "You have begot me, bred me, lov'd me" (1.1.96).[30] Cordelia is, scandalously, claiming to be bound to Lear by nothing more than mere blood, mere nature. "No more nor less" (1.1.93).

Indeed, on close inspection, the sequence that derives love from begetting and breeding looks, outrageously, like an assertion of *maternal* propagation, as well as a paternity suit (or a demand for recognition that he *could* be her father). As if Lear is here said to be naturally responsible for bringing her into the world.

Cordelia thus calls Lear to acknowledge, *before* his patrimonial accomplishment can be completed, that he is, like she herself, a natural creature. And she calls him to affirm, or to deny, that this shared nature is constitutive of their relation to one another.

Moreover by speaking in this way, Cordelia makes plain that her very birth, her ongoing life and the resulting breath that she draws to speak to Lear all, call Lear to either acknowledge or refuse, before anything else, his own *paternity:* that "'twas [his] flesh begot / Those pelican daughters" (3.4.74–75).

Indeed, it is precisely *this* definition of "paternal care"—namely, as "propinquity and property of blood"—that Lear invokes in rage when he disinherits Cordelia a moment later (1.1.113–14). His rage itself shows us that the first effect of Cordelia's claim to be bound to Lear by breeding and begetting, by nature alone, is to force Lear to confront his paternal bond as a natural fact. Her words return him to the very same feminine-maternal claims and demands of nature that the scene of inheritance, and his patrimonial act, sought to deny.

{6}

I marvel what kin thou and thy daughters are. (1.4.189)

What, to now pose anew the traditional question, are we to make of Lear's vehement rage in reaction to Cordelia's claim? And why should this rage, and the madness it manifests, devastate the inheritability of Lear's world?

I would like to offer two responses to these questions.

First, because the scene of inheritance that Lear has contrived requires, and itself performs, a refusal of the claims of nature, there is no way for that performance to include Lear's acknowledgment of a natural bond— say, the fact of "breeding and begetting" Cordelia—from within its enactment. As we have already seen, it is the social significance of "breeding and begetting" that patrimonial forms of social devolution are meant to supersede.

Thus Cordelia's brief words, with their simple "truth" of procreation, throw the entire patrimonial world—the king himself, his kingdom, its bequeathal, its desirability and durability—into a crisis from which it never fully recovers. And she sets this crisis in motion by doing nothing more than challenging Lear to acknowledge a series of facts that he cannot deny without exposing himself as mad: namely, the fact that she exists, that she is his natural daughter, and that her natural existence is itself proof of his own natural being.

For Lear to deny these facts would mean not only denying his social relation to Cordelia—that he owes her a dowry, say, or has taken responsibility for her material well-being and upbringing; it would also mean denying his own natural origins (that he was himself begot) along with hers (that he begot her). At stake in Lear's response to her words will therefore be *both* his denaturalized patrimonial relation to Cordelia *and* his natural paternity, the fact of having fathered her.

After all, Cordelia is baldly implying that her inheritance should follow from a certain fact of the matter—that she is his daughter by blood—rather than by any patrimonial accomplishment or sovereign decree. In this way, she ties her worldly inheritance to a demand that her father recognize his natural paternity, that he recognize paternity itself as primarily natural, and that this recognition constitute their bond to one another.

This demand is not one that Lear can accept, however, without utterly undoing the very performance that he has just undertaken, without foreclosing the sociality that he has spent his life trying to achieve. To acknowledge, as Cordelia would have it, that the "bond" of breeding and begetting *defines* their relationship would be to foreclose the emergence of any *other* form of "love," of any other form of human attachment or social bond, between them. For Cordelia's claim would impose natural limits on love—on the very scope of human sociality—by making "love" *follow* "begetting and breeding," as if the latter were the necessary preconditions of the former.

What is blasphemous therefore, from Lear's perspective, is that Cordelia would make natural geniture and blood ties determinant for generational devolution. Love, as Cordelia speaks of it, could never be free and disinterested. Rather, love would be, as she says, a "duty" that derives directly from natural birth, from the force of "natural law" that here asserts itself against Lear's "positive law."

Worse still, Cordelia dashes Lear's most deep-seated desire. For Lear understands now that Cordelia will never love him as a mere man. (He returns to precisely this thought when he is reunited with Cordelia toward the end of the play, saying: "I know you do not love me" [4.7.73].) Cordelia says, in essence, that she could *never* love or be bound to Lear as anything other than as a "child" (4.7.70) to her natural father; he is for her no more and no less than the creature whose life and breath are physical preconditions of her own. She will merely "return" to him "those duties back as are right fit" (1.1.97).

Although I can understand the temptation to see in Cordelia's early speeches a "confession" of love that Lear hard-heartedly fails to recognize, I see nothing in her actual words *to Lear* that might lend itself to this interpretation. (Lear does not, I presume, hear Cordelia's first asides to the audience.) Cavell, for example, says of Cordelia that "all her words are words of love; to love is all she knows how to do," and he calls this "the cause of the tragedy of *King Lear*."[31] The problem, however, is not that Cordelia "loves" Lear; rather, the problem is that "love" as "bond" implies certain terms through which she communicates this bond ("begetting" and "breeding"), and the "right" ("as . . . right fit") to which she attaches that love.

Indeed, Cordelia even goes so far as to say that she could never love *any* man freely and disinterestedly. Any eventual husband would merely "carry half [her] love with him," as if a mode of human loving that did not follow entirely on the sheer fact that she was "begot" and "bred" were unthinkable for Cordelia (1.1.102). "Love," as she articulates it, is never free and disinterested; such love is merely the name of a social bond that one honors, habitually and ritually, as a debt owed to one's natural origins.[32]

⁓

We can therefore understand Cordelia's response as posing to Lear the terms of a drastic choice. Either he can acknowledge the natural fact of begetting and breeding as determinant of their relationship and make any patrimonial inheritance dependent on that prior fact, thereby in essence reducing the patrimonial world he has built to a mere moment of natural necessity. Or he can deny her claim. And this denial would constitute not only a destruction of both his natural and social bonds to Cordelia but a rejection of nature's claim on the sociality that he seeks to institute.

The hyperbole with which Lear chooses the latter is breathtaking.

Invoking the supernatural, Lear alienates himself from nature, calls on gods of the underworld, and disinherits Cordelia by disclaiming the very fact of having fathered her.

> Let it be so; thy truth then be thy dower:
> For, by the sacred radiance of the sun,
> The mysteries of Hecate and the night,
> By all the operation of the orbs
> From whom we do exist and cease to be,
> Here I disclaim all my paternal care,

Propinquity and property of blood,
And as a stranger to my heart and me
Hold thee from this for ever. . . . (1.1.108–16)

Lear, it should be underscored, disowns not only Cordelia, his "some-time daughter" (1.1.120), but *all* . . . paternal care, / Propinquity and property of blood"—in effect denying any relation between his patrimonial position and mere blood ties. Or, more precisely, he not only disclaims his paternal bond to *her*; he also rejects the claim of natural procreation on generational devolution tout court.

And if Lear refuses to recognize the claim of nature that Cordelia makes, and that she herself (in her bodily presence) *is* ("She is herself a dowry" [1.1.241]), on the generational devolution and form of social life he seeks to institute ("we / Have no such daughter" [1.1.262–63]), then Cordelia likewise refuses to regard the worldly inheritance that Lear was offering as itself constituting a loving bond, a meaningful form of human attachment. ("[F]or want of that for which I am richer, // . . . I am glad I have not, though not to have it / Hath lost me in your liking" [1.1.230–33].)

Patrimonial inheritance is as meaningless to Cordelia as natural, quasi-matrilineal, devolution is to Lear. The resultant rift between Lear and Cordelia (" nor shall ever see / That face of hers again" [1.1.263–64]) expresses the incompatible demands of these two social principles, which come to stand in tragic opposition to one another because fidelity to one principle involves the breach of the other. What becomes clear, as a result, is that neither is capable of sustaining and facilitating the worldly inheritance of the kingdom at issue. This constitutes our third tragic impasse.

✦

If Cordelia objects that there be no patrimonial scene of bequeathal without an explicit acknowledgment of natural begetting—and therefore that there be no denaturalized renaturalization, as Lear had dreamed—then Shakespeare permits us to measure the validity of Cordelia's claim only by seeing it refused. The value of the natural bond between generations—the value of natural "increase" (1.4.288) itself—is to be gauged only by how fearfully it can be repudiated.

I say "fearfully" not only because of what such a repudiation would entail, namely the suspension of natural growth and propagation, but because Lear frighteningly claims for himself this power to adjourn nature. As if he could halt and cease natural geniture by sheer force of will and decree. Having denied the natural begetting of one child, he likewise forswears the natural generation of the others; thus, Goneril receives his malediction:

Hear, Nature, hear! dear Goddess, hear!
Suspend thy purpose, if thou didst intend
To make this creature fruitful!
Into her womb convey sterility!
Dry up her organs of increase,
And from her derogate body never spring
A babe to honor her! . . . (1.4.273–79)

Lear shows Cordelia, with no regard for the destructive cost of this display, what he shows Goneril: that she is not loved in the way that she believes herself to be loved, as a natural creature, fruit of his loins. Cordelia thinks that she is his daughter, no more no less, and that her birth, her natural existence, is itself an insuperable claim on him. But Lear will prove Cordelia wrong, repudiating even her claim to be naturally begotten, calling her a "wretch whom Nature is asham'd / Almost t'acknowledge hers" (1.1.212–13), just as he will later deem Goneril "degenerate" (1.4.251) and she and Regan "unnatural hags" (2.4.280).

Lear will curse, as no natural mother could do, Cordelia's very birth and deny its meaning for him—in the name of a fantasized love that he now knows to be impossible.

"Better thou / Hadst not been born than not t' have pleased me better" (1.1.233–34).

For the sake of the bond he wished to establish with her, Lear will sever the only extant bond between them. To preserve the condition of possibility for an impossible sociality, the "love" he dreams of, Lear will destroy the only love he has.

You say you are bound to me by nature alone?

That to you I am merely, and will never be more than, your natural father?

And that the gifts I have to bestow upon you merely follow, like day

*does night, on your mere breeding? You would reduce my life, my gifts,
and the love I bear you to a debt owed to nature?*

"[T]hou art my flesh, my blood, my daughter; / Or rather a disease
that's in my flesh, / Which I must needs call mine" (2.4.223–24).

*But you forget that, more swiftly than nature is able, I can withhold
my gifts and take back what nature once bestowed. I can deny nature her
due.*

If I am not free to bequeath, then I am free to disinherit!

"Thy truth then be thy dower!" (1.1.106)

{7}

But goes thy heart with this? (1.1.105)

At all appearances, we can now grasp the tragic structure that results
from the play's opening scene; that is, we can see how Lear and Cordelia
are brought into conflict through the collision of two competing, incompatible demands and principles. We have thus provided a preliminary understanding of the question of the vehemence of Lear's rage in response
to Cordelia's speech: his rage expresses a tragic collision, an irreconcilable
difference, between their principled positions.

And yet our understanding remains only preliminary. For if what is
"tragic" here is merely the incompatibility, and therefore the unsustain-
ability, of Lear's and Cordelia's respective principled positions—in the
abstract, so to speak—then we still have not accounted for the way in
which Shakespeare makes this tragic predicament *dramatic* as concrete,
individual fates. Even if we might be interested, in theory, in whether a
society organizes itself in matrilineal or patrimonial terms, it is not yet
clear what our investment in Lear and Cordelia is. why do we care, if we
do, about *them* and their relationship?

After all, *our* dramatic investment in the scene does not just lies, I
would wager, in the collision of patrimonial inheritance with natural geniture as abstract principles of generational devolution; we do not regard
Lear and Cordelia as mere spokespeople or representative voices of competing ideal forms of social life. Rather Lear and Cordelia are, for us, in-
tensely particular beings, acting passionately and interestedly; both are
not only "free artists of themselves" but also possess unmistakable forms

of self-consciousness as manifested in their asides, speeches, and solilo-quies.[33] And they are, we might furthermore agree, two individuals who "really" love one another, in spite of everything else—even if they under-stand and express their "love" for one another, their reciprocal bond, in radically different ways.

But perceiving Lear and Cordelia as individuals who act and suffer only begets further questions. Suffering and frustrations may well be our shared lot in life, but how can such sufferings and frustrations matter for those who are not directly touched by them? How, without falling back on a notion of shared natural purpose, can we care about others' pains and reversals other than through "accidental sympathy with the frustra-tion of another's will?"[34]

I shall begin to approach these questions by suggesting that the tragic drama in *King Lear* arises more deeply from the fact that neither Lear nor Cordelia manages to separate from *themselves* the social principles or "truths" that they purport to express and uphold; they therefore fail to keep their attachment to, and identification with, these "truths" from be-ing the sole ground of their relation to one another in the opening scene. (Hence the righteous frigidity of Cordelia's answer: "So young, my Lord, and true" [1.1.107].) Cordelia is unable to answer Lear in the way that she does—subverting his patrimonial ambitions by reasserting the fact of her (and his) natural origins—without at the same time injuring Lear himself, without rejecting *him* and not merely his claim. By the same to-ken, Lear cannot repudiate the claim of nature on the patrimonial social-ity he wished to accomplish without at the same time rejecting Cordelia herself, for her "claim" is not detachable from her being; indeed, she pre-sents herself to Lear *as* that claim, as nature's claim on him, when she gives her answer.[35] ("*You* have begot *me*, bred *me*, lov'd *me*" [1.1.96, my emphasis].) That this injury is done during what Cordelia must know is meant to be a supreme expression of love for *her*, Lear's "joy" (1.1.82), only underscores Cordelia's incapacity to separate her rejection of his pat-rimonial claim from her rejection of Lear himself as well as Lear's inabil-ity to show his love for Cordelia as anything other than a "more opulent" inheritance.

"But goes thy heart with this?" implores Lear, as if struggling to catch sight of some difference between Cordelia herself and her stated position, as if trying to discern *her* passion from the passion of her attachment to this "truth." To no avail: "Ay, my good Lord," comes the cool response. "So young," he tries again, "and so untender?" (1.1.105–6). I take Lear's use of the word "untender" to be an overture to Cordelia, an attempt to confess to her his own tenderness and vulnerability, his own hurt feelings. Because Cordelia refuses to acknowledge herself as being "tender," as being "made of penetrable stuff" (to steal Hamlet's phrase), she appears to Lear here as hard-hearted. To his confession, Cordelia again offers nothing but the truth of her principle: "So young, my Lord, and true" (1.1.107). In failing to acknowledge the injury she has caused him, and indeed in repeating the injury by mockingly reiterating Lear's very words only in order to emphasize her own word "true," she immediately finds that this "truth" is all she has left. "Thy truth then be thy dower" (1.1.108).

Or, more precisely, she has reduced herself to her truth: "She is herself a dowry" (1.1.241).[36]

Both Lear and Cordelia therefore identify themselves in word and deed—consciously, willfully, purposefully—with a principled form of sociality, with a theory of generational devolution as such; they offer their "individual" speeches to one another as mere expressions of those social principles.

Correspondingly, they fail to look for spontaneously offered performances of loving recognition from each other; instead, Lear seeks to determine in advance *what* Cordelia's recognition of him should entail (namely, flattering speech in response to a sovereign power), just as Cordelia aims to determine the *way* in which Lear should recognize her "love" (namely, as pursuant to his being her natural father).

In trying to determine in advance *how* the other ought to recognize, *how* the other ought to "love," Lear and Cordelia thus betray their identification with abstract principles of love or recognition. They believe that loving acts *ought* to look and sound a certain way and that acts that appear to deviate from that norm are to be taken as unloving. They presume to dictate to one another the normative terms under which mutual acts of recognition will become recognizable as such.

Likewise, Lear and Cordelia believe that loving recognition should follow the furnishing of an adequate *reason* for that recognition. They mistakenly believe that they can offer another a cause, basis, or rationale for the other's love.

Because I am your father, a sovereign power, because "I gave you all"! (2.4.252)

Because I am your child, the fruit of your loins, because I know I am your "joy" (1.1.82).

What they fail to see is that they have nothing to offer one another, no "reason," except themselves—and that they themselves, by the same token, can only count as meaningful offerings by being received, loved, and recognized as such.

~

We might say that Lear and Cordelia imagine that they have the "right" to be recognized or loved in such and such a way ("as . . . right fit" [1.1.97]). So, just as Cordelia supposes that the mere fact of having been "begotten" endows her with the right to be recognized as a natural child, so, too, Lear imagines that his patrimonial bequeathal *entitles* him to be loved and recognized in a predetermined way—hence, his repeated complaint of having "thankless" children (1.4.298). So wholly does Lear reduce loving recognition to "gratitude," to something to which he is entitled and that he is owed, that his resentment at not receiving this loving thanks burns bright even as his wits begin to dim:

> . . . this tempest in my mind
> Doth from my senses take all feeling else
> Save what beats there—filial ingratitude! (3.4.12–14)

Through their presumption that they have the "right" to be recognized and loved in a certain way—that loving recognition should derive from and express an a priori abstract form of sociality whose rule and authority is to be merely confirmed through a predetermined form of recognition and love—Lear and Cordelia set themselves up for the tragic awakening that love and recognition are not "rights" to which one can be entitled.

On the contrary, it is only by actively loving and being loved—without being able to prescribe or regulate the "form" that loving should take—that one can come to seem "entitled" to anything whatsoever in the world.

That spontaneous acts of loving and being loved are the condition of any worldly rights and entitlements, and not the reverse, is something that can perhaps only be learned through the sting of finding oneself un-loved, rebuked, or put down, or, conversely, through the remorse or guilt that comes from having injured a loved one. For it is through such suf-fering—in the wake of failing to love or be loved—that one discovers that the very rights and entitlements one had held most dear have now lost their worth.

This is why, as soon as he feels himself unloved by Cordelia, Lear throws away his kingdom, his power, his life's work, his labor's invest-ment—effectively renouncing his deep investment in any form of entitle-ment by parting the "coronet" between Albany and Cornwall (1.1.139). After all, the entitlements he wished to bestow were, as we have seen, only meaningful to him so long as he thought that he might, by means of their bequeathal, bring about the conditions of possibility for being truly loved and recognized, as himself. In the absence of such loving recognition—in the wake of Cordelia's, and his own, hard-heartedness—worldly inheri-tance loses its meaning and value.

{8}

Take thou my soldiers, prisoners, patrimony;
Dispose of them, of me; . . . (5.3.76–77)

That the world we share—our practices, investments, riches, territories, and rights—can be made undesirable and unlovable is not necessarily a symptom of the inherent unworthiness of that world, any more than our love of the world is a sign of its "inherent" value. Rather, our love of the world we share and strive to make inheritable, whatever value it holds for us, is determined by our loving recognition of one another. As such, the bequeathal of a worldly inheritance or kingdom cannot, by itself, perform or take the place of that loving recognition. A parent cannot love a child by "giving them the world"; for the world's significance and meaning is itself, for child and parent alike, weighed and measured through loving acts that they perform, or fail to perform, without being able to rely for help on the mediation of an already shareable world. Love is irreducible to the sharing or bequeathing of the world, because the world only be-comes shareable in virtue of recognizing, or having been recognized by, one with whom it might be desirably shared.

In this sense, the loss of investment in the world—its disinheritance—is perhaps a sign, or tragic reminder, that our loving bonds to one another are entirely breakable and undoable. The most essential precondition for sociality, for generational devolution, can be shattered.

That everything we imagine to be most precious—our belongings, art works, cultic beliefs and practices, our laws and entitlements—can suddenly lose all significance and value is perhaps the clearest indication of what it means to fail to love or be loved, of how fragile our ties to one another are and how easily they can come undone. Our loss of interest in the world we share, its devaluation and disinheritance, might thus be a measure of our utter dependence on the loving recognition of others.

*

Lear's rage in disinheriting Cordelia and in casting off his crown and the consequent destruction of the kingdom he had spent his life building and strengthening, is difficult to watch, almost impossible to listen to; his self-pity is shameful. But Lear is disturbing not because he is a failure, senile, impotent, or unwell; that would merely make him pathetic and sad. Rather, Lear is disturbing because we cannot simply *pity* him, as we can pity the victim of an unpleasant fate.[37] His actions compel ethical reflection but without permitting pity to serve as the moral lens for such reflection.[38] Lear is disturbing to those of us who might still be invested in the worldly values he embodies—as, for instance, Kent clearly is (hence his valiantly doomed attempt to bring Lear to his senses)—because Lear fails *on purpose*. He is disturbing because of his willful, hard-hearted refusal, in the wake of his failure to love and be loved by Cordelia, to see his very own kingdom as worth rescuing and because he thereby compels *us* to look again at the world and reflect on our own investment in it.

Can *we* bear to see our shared world as less worthy of our love, our investment, our energy, and our commitment? Can we bear in the end to see Kent, the kingdom's most loyal subject and most deeply invested citizen, simply walk away from it all? Is this a conclusion that we can watch without reflecting on our own worldly investments?

More to the point, can we bear to confront that which could unmake our world in this way?

Or might we, like Lear, prefer now to bend our remaining energies toward anger, rage, destruction, bitterness, and madness? Might we, too, prefer to destroy and repudiate the world that we share rather than turn to face that which made us lose our investment in it?

"Is there any cause in nature that make these hard hearts?" (3.6.78–79)

Even after all this, we might still wonder: why does Lear and Cordelia's failure to lovingly recognize one another result in the kingdom's destruction, the world's disinheritance and loss of desirability? Might not this destruction simply be attributed to the fact that Lear was king—that is, to the fact he was uniquely well positioned to wreak havoc? Or might we simply understand his rage as, if not "the infirmity of his age" (1.1.292), then perhaps as a form of behavior that is typical of his character and personality? ("He hath ever but slenderly known himself" [1.1.293–94].) Is Lear's hard-heartedness the cause of the tragedy?

Readers of the play have often understood Lear's rage along these lines, I think, because such an understanding permits us, so to speak, to understand the drama as *their* tragedy and not *ours*. It allows us, in other words, to isolate Lear and Cordelia's fate from the rest of us and from the rest of the world. (This is, of course, what Goneril and Regan hope to do.)

But it seems to me that the actual sequence of events in the opening scene, and throughout the play, make this interpretation implausible. For the fate of Lear and Cordelia in the opening scene is not detachable from the fates of those around them. In fact, no prior attachment, kinship tie, political allegiance, or friendship survives the collision between Lear and Cordelia unscathed or undamaged. The opening scene—to say still nothing of what awaits us—unfolds as the exposure of any number of interpersonal divisions: father is rent from daughter, sisters from sister, king from subjects, subjects from other subjects, ally from ally. As we know, Lear's realm never recovers the stability, inheritability, or desirability that it held at the outset of the drama. Kent is banished, Burgundy is distanced, Cornwall and Albany are set up for civil war by having the kingdom split between them, Cordelia is abandoned by her sisters and leaves with France "without our grace, our love, our benison" (1.1.265). From this point onward, there is only further fragmentation and martial conflict.

Even more tellingly, none of the battles that follow—the battle between France and Cornwall, the struggle for Edmund's affection, the contest between Edgar and Edmund—approaches the ethical pathos of Lear's dis-inheritance of Cordelia. Indeed, these subsequent conflicts appear petty by comparison, barely worthy of our dramatic investment because they now seem like debased struggles between adversaries who have, as it were, nothing better to fight for or quarrel over. "This great world / Shall so wear out to naught" (4.6.136–37).

Perhaps this sheds light on the depravity of Regan and Goneril's competition for the loving recognition of a man who, we know, cares more for what these sisters can provide for him than he does for them. ("Neither," Edmund tells us, "can be enjoy'd / If both remain alive" [5.1.58–59].) Yet Regan and Goneril find they now have nothing else to live for but Edmund's love, nothing else worth killing for, nothing else worth killing themselves for. ("May all the building in my fancy pluck / Upon my hateful life" [4.2.85–86].) One sister thus murders the other before taking her own life—not for wealth or worldly power, as we might expect given that these sisters have split Lear's kingdom between them, but for the sake of Edmund's undivided attention. The other, likewise, sees no worth in her "soldiers, prisoners, patrimony" if she cannot, by bestowing them on Edmund, let "witness the world" that she loves him (5.3.76–78).

Regan and Goneril thus do die not for love; rather they die heartbroken, from the mere wish for love—they die pining. And because it was only a pining, a longing for love, it was only barely perceptible to us, if at all. In order to know what their deaths mean, what their lives meant, and whether or not they can be mourned, Albany issues the strange order to his men: "Produce the bodies, be they alive or dead" (5.3.230). In a macabre moment Albany, Edmund and the others drag Goneril's and Regan's poisoned and bloody bodies out into the public light, as if to decide what to do with them (consider, by way of contrast, the fact that Lady Macbeth's suicide does not require Shakespeare to show us her corpse for the meaning of her death to be plain).

No one, however, has anything to say about these dead inheritors of the kingdom.

"Even so. Cover their faces" (5.3.242).

The wars and quarrels that follow likewise lead to nothing more than the eventual recognition that there is, in fact, no remaining social world worth fighting over. How much has been lost, broken, undone since the play's opening! Abandoned on stage at the drama's close, neither Albany nor Edgar even wants to take up the "rule, interests of territory, cares of state" of the "gor'd state" that remains (5.3.320).

Again, in my view, this recognition comes most fully for the audience when Kent—whose words and deeds had always signified the possibility of significant ethical duty or meaningful worldly investment—simply walks away, with the enigmatic words: "I have a journey, sir, shortly to go; / My master calls me, I must not say no" (5.3.321–22). If I were a stage director, I would instruct the actor playing Kent to put on his street jacket at this point, walk through the audience toward the exit, and out the theater doors. Kent sees no reason to invest one single second more in a realm he had up until then staked his life defending. His and our dramatic investment alike is thereby depleted.[39]

Hence, whatever affective response we muster at the drama's close will be colored by this sense of exhaustion.

{9}

See better, Lear. . . . (1.1.158)

Even more perniciously (and here we get closer to an answer to why *we* might care about Lear and Cordelia and why the opening scene might disturb us), rights and entitlements *themselves*—that is, a shared sense that acts of social, filial, political, or friendly recognition can and ought to be prescribed, determined in advance—begin to appear as that which muddy or obscure the fact that acts of recognition are themselves the precondition of entitlements and rights. The very thing that loving recognition *enables*—namely, a sense of entitlement—is now seen as hampering or impeding such recognition, *blinding* us to love.

Appearing thus as obstacles, rights and entitlements can no longer be seen as self-sustaining, as being themselves of stable or enduring value. It is in fact no longer clear that rights and entitlements are anything at all *in themselves*, except perhaps forms of tragic blindness to the fact that acts of love and recognition remain stubbornly irreducible to the ritual, prescribed, normative "performances" that we routinely mistake, or substitute, for loving recognition.

Rights and entitlements are what we imagine ourselves coming to possess, acquire, or bear so that we may avoid facing what it means that—in order to be "entitled" to anything—we are utterly dependent on the loving recognition of others whose words and deeds we can never anticipate, prescribe, or control.

Because our love of the world—and therefore the inheritance and bequeathal of material wealth, ritual practices, formal words and deeds of recognition, property rights, territorial claims, and the like—is itself predicated on what it means to love and recognize others in ways that cannot be inherited or bequeathed, taught or cultivated, ritualized or codified, we learn that the assumed value of rights and entitlements, like all forms of worldly or social inheritance, cannot survive the failure to love or be loved.

Consequently, the value of the world as such—its inheritance and bequeathal—now collapses. The transmission of human sociality itself—the reproducibility of the conditions under which we live together—comes to a halt.

Shakespeare's tragedy leaves us not with a crisis in this or that historical or categorical *form* of social life or generational devolution but with the collapse of our belief that such forms bond us meaningfully to one another.

Consequently, if we are to "see better" (1.1.158) that loving recognition and social acknowledgment are not "rights" to which we are entitled by virtue of belonging to, or being members of, this or that form of sociality—if we are to grasp that such loving recognition is not reducible to inheritable, ritual modes and practices of social, familial, or political recognition—then we must "see" that our lives together are not made desirable, valuable, or lovable in virtue of those goods, practices, and rights we might inherit or bequeath.

The cost of "seeing" this, however, means that our kingdom, our shared world—the work of our hands, our ritual forms of speaking and acting, indeed our very language, along with our territorial claims and precious objects—now appears to us as less worthy of our love, our investment, our energy, and our commitment. So, too, we are required to see that it was never the case that worldly principles of generational devolution made our social life worthwhile. And that, therefore, when those principles are lost or damaged, we cannot simply await "new and better" principles to come along and save us, to bind us to each other in a happier or more durable way.

_~1_

But *how* is this to be seen? What gives rise to this insight? Is it an insight at all?

If my reflections here are not wrong, then worldly entitlements reveal themselves to have been forms of tragic *harmartia*—namely, structural failures to see how our dependence on another's love determines the desirability of any social life we might hope to have, bequeath, or inherit. Indeed, what the opening scene of *King Lear* shows us is that the inheritance of the kingdom itself—the transmission of our normative modes of worldly social life—can be unmasked as nothing more than an occasion for, and a further cause of, such blindness.

But once *this* blindness is revealed, what is discovered is not—as in Aristotle's reading of *Oedipus*—a "new'" understanding of how we might be bound to one another in ways of which we were "ignorant."[40] In contrast to the Greek tragic model, in Shakespeare's play, principled forms of sociality themselves, like the entitlements they presume to bestow, appear as precisely that which blinded us to their essential precondition: concrete, spontaneous, unpredictable acts of loving and being loved.

A different, much murkier, form of tragic blindness thus shows itself to be at work in Shakespeare's tragedy. Bringing it to light might help us to make sense of a traditional puzzle that *King Lear* has posed to interpreters.

The puzzle is that the entire tragic structure of *King Lear* seems to unfurl with ferocious speed in the opening scene. As we have seen, little more than one hundred lines into the play, the crucial failure(s) of recognition by Lear and Cordelia occur *at the same time* as their "transgressions" and their consequences—Cordelia's brief answers; Lear's raging disinheritance of her. The remaining "plot" of the play no doubt contains various further consequences of those initial misdeeds. But because, as I have just tried to argue, those misdeeds were *themselves* the expression of the crucial blindness or *harmatia* at issue, it is far from clear what more we *learn* about this blindness from the consequences that follows, other than what it means to live with the breach it opens. And, anyway, the primary "historical" or worldly consequences are already apparent:

Lear mad, Cordelia disinherited, Kent banished, allegiances divided, and so on.

Now, tragedies, we are generally told, are set in motion by specific deeds and transgressions—Oedipus's slaying of his father, Antigone's burial of her brother, the murder of Hamlet's father, or his mother's re-marriage—whose power, as Hegel puts it, "breaks forth only after the deed is done." This temporal delay or lapse between the deed and the "recognition" that follows is central to tragic structures as we tradition-ally understand them, even in the most recent scholarship: namely, as "plots" in which (to use Aristotle's own words) incidents "occur contrary to expectation yet on account of one another."[41] Indeed, the thought has been that it is precisely through this unexpected consequentiality that we learn something about the social, ethical, political, or personal stakes of the initial transgressions themselves. That is, the view that something can be *learned* from tragedy and that philosophical insight can arise through the experience of the "tragic" depends on this consequential separation of deed from recognition, which Aristotle calls "plot," and which, I think, Hegel has in mind when he repeatedly notes that "reality . . . stems from the action itself and results from it."[42] Tragedy, in sum, "teaches" us that philosophical insight—whatever we can learn about ourselves—is only available through "experience" (*Erfahrung,* to stick for a moment with Hegel's words), the turning around, or *peripeteia,* that follows on our misdeeds and missteps, on the "negativity" of our actions.[43] Troublingly, by contrast, *King Lear* stages for us a tragic predicament or plot structure in which there is no such delay. And therefore there is no further turn-around, no further experiential insight. The tragic blindness of Lear is not subsequently revealed ex post facto by means of a mythic or historical "reality" that "stems from [his] action itself and results from it." Rather his deed *immediately* expresses his blindness—as well as the meaning of that blindness—for all to see. (Hence Kent's quick response: "See better, Lear" [1.1.158].)

And because Lear's misdeed is thus not separable—historically, narra-tively, dramatically—from the manifestation of his tragic blindness, his disinheritance of Cordelia does not produce or lead to a "new" historical "reality" that "stems" from it. On the contrary, the tragic predicament Shakespeare offers does not, and *cannot,* unfold as narrative representa-tion of any such new reality.

I would therefore propose that we understand the tragedy of Shakespeare's *King Lear* as the unfolding *preemption* of any "new" reality. The precipitous collapse of tragic blindness and misdeed does not yield any ulterior insight about that collapse. The initial fall forecloses the emergence of any new history, new insights, or new revelations.

Murkier still—because this "fall" is asked to bear the full burden of tragic significance, without its meaning or significance being illuminated by a subsequent history or reality that follows—is the "historical" meaning of that fall, that initial misdeed, which stands to lose all retrospective clarity.

"But have I fall'n or no? // . . . Alack! I have no eyes" (4.6.56, 60)

{10}

. . . Get thee glass eyes;
And . . . seem
To see the things thou dost not. (4.6.172–74)

Shakespeare's tragedy might thus be perceived as the tragic undoing of whatever insights tragedies themselves might afford or might once have afforded.

We now stumble blindly onto terrain that allows us to retrace our steps not by means of a hindsight that would shed some light on a way forward. Instead we orient ourselves on this new ground—to the extent we can—by confronting as best we can our having been blinded. The late scenes (if they can still be called scenes) between Edgar, Gloucester, and Lear might be grasped as moods such a confrontation might take.

"You cannot see your way," Gloucester is told by the stranger on whom he leans. We might mock this stranger for his firm grasp of the obvious, except that he tells us everything we *can* know.

That Gloucester almost immediately names Edgar here—"O! dear son Edgar, // . . . Might I but live to see thee in my touch, / I'd say I had eyes again" (4.1.22–25)—makes of his failure to explicitly recognize Edgar when he takes him by the hand moments later another traditional source of bewilderment to interpreters and audiences alike. But perhaps we might take the procession that follows not as a denial of an apparent reality—namely, that Edgar is phenomenally "there," holding him and leading him—but as a confrontation with what it means that there can be no "new" reality, and therefore no new beginnings or reconciliations, because *blindness* is itself the reality that Gloucester must now confront. His blindness portends no ulterior insight, for Gloucester cannot claim to apprehend if he is bereft of apprehension. ("Read," Lear challenges him; "What!" replies Gloucester. "With the case of eyes?" [4.6.140, 145].) If Gloucester is truly to confront his blindness, then he cannot "say that he has eyes again."

To recognize Edgar, or to be reconciled to him, under such conditions would be to deny the "reality" of the conditions under which that recognition would now take place.

In contrast to Oedipus, Gloucester does not come to know something "new" about the nature of his ties to others to which he had been blind. Gloucester's having failed to recognize Edgar at the beginning of the drama is itself the transgression for which Gloucester suffers; and the fact of that prior failure of recognition is the only insight the suffering yields. ("O my follies! Then Edgar was abus'd" [3.7.90].) Rather than signal a shift from ignorance to knowledge, therefore, Gloucester's blinding merely reveals his own folly but without leaving him any "new reality" to confront as a result of that revelation ("I have no way, and therefore want no eyes; I stumbled when I saw" [4.1.17–19].) To confess this to Edgar, or to try to start with him anew, would at best be a repetition of that acknowledgment—and would therefore offer no way forward at all.

Indeed, their predicament can be expressed in precisely this way: for Gloucester to recognize Edgar would be to deny themselves a new beginning.

If a "way" remains at all—and this is far from certain ("Know'st thou the way to Dover?" [4.1.54])—then its course follows the avoidance of recognition, reconciliation, forgiveness, or revenge. The "avoidance of love" is thereby not simply the description of a tragic deed—of a failure to acknowledge another.[44] Such avoidance turns out moreover to map the terrain on which we tread in the wake of tragic misdeeds.

That the avoidance of love can be *ongoing*—and, therefore, not confined to a deed, a moment of blindness, or suffered consequence—signals what it might mean that darkness and fog can, perhaps permanently, take the place of philosophical or experiential insight. The grotesque walk taken by Edgar and Gloucester is not, as Cavell has it, the "new" form taken by their relationship in its "present state"; it is what relationships look like once bereft of new beginnings, without a way to bridge past and future.[45]

～

What are we to do with another person if we cannot begin anew with him, if we cannot transgress anew, or be forgiven anew? What futurity might any relationship anticipate under such conditions?[46]

The dramatic problem that Shakespeare compels us to confront moves to a foggy terrain that must be groped, "seen feelingly," or leaped from toward we know not what—and on which, it seems, neither new beginning nor significant endings appear possible.

Nevertheless, for all that, Shakespeare does not suppose that we march this terrain alone. Isolation and solitude will in fact turn out to be a comfort for which we can, perhaps, only wish.

Thus, Edgar and Gloucester trudge alongside one another by fits and starts on ground that is no longer common. "Methinks the ground is even," says Gloucester; "Horrible steep," replies Edgar (4.6.3). But at the same time, they cannot shift to higher or lower ground in order to get a clearer perspective, or leave the ground behind altogether. Because there is no further insight to be had, nothing more to be learned, their procession cannot even take the form of an ordeal—after which some transformation or conversion might be effected.

Whereas blind, old Oedipus, at a certain point, parted with his children to march alone toward a mysteriously transformative, solitary death, Gloucester cannot shake Edgar. When the former pleads, after throwing himself forward and falling, "Away, and let me die"—he is told that his "life's a miracle" (4.6.48, 55). He will not be able to freely determine the end of his life's steps any more than he was able to determine their origin. ("Is wretchedness depriv'd of that benefit / To end itself by death?" [4.6.61–62].) Gloucester's loss of freedom and self-determination—his inability to leave his companion behind—means that he remains dependent, against his will, on a bond that is irreparably torn and rent.

It is generally presumed that the "great affliction" Gloucester wishes to "shake patiently" by leaping from "th' extreme verge" is simply his bodily life, his pains (4.6.36, 26). I would suggest, however, that the "affliction" of which he speaks and that he wishes to "shake" is not first and foremost his bodily life—a mortal coil to be shuffled off. Rather, the affliction here is above all the burden of living on with Edgar at his side. Gloucester's renunciation of the world, after all, includes the acknowledgment that this bodily life is fading fast—he knows he will die shortly.[47] But what he wants is to die having broken with Edgar—having severed ties with him, having freed himself, and therefore having, in some small measure, started anew.[48]

Hence, his instructions to Edgar—"Go thou further off; / Bid me farewell, and let me hear thee going" (4.6.30–31)-and his last words before leaping—"Now, fellow, fare thee well" (4.6.41).

We should not mistake the heartbreak we feel in watching Gloucester blindly leap, fall, and survive for the sickening feeling that accompanies the spectacle of a failed suicide. For, it is not Gloucester's death wish that has been thwarted; were he to be left lying there in peace, he would no doubt shortly expire. ("Away, and let me die" [4.6.48].) Rather, our heartbreak follows from the inescapability of his binding social condition—his tethers to Edgar. Gloucester discovers that there is no further leap into the unknown that he can take, for his arrival at that "verge" depended on Edgar's company and lead. Gloucester finds himself back where he started, helped to his feet by the very one he wished to flee.

Edgar's weak attempt to take on a new role at this point, to pretend that he is "someone new," perhaps typifies the most generous games we play under such circumstances. *I know you wished to leave me,* we say to the other, *just as I wished to leave you.*

We both would like, however briefly, to outlive this relationship that we have destroyed.

Because we know we cannot start anew by transforming our relationship, by reconciling and by starting over, we wish simply to live long enough to leave the other behind.

I cannot satisfy this wish, for either of us.

But I will do the best that I can. I will allow you to pretend.

And I, too, will pretend, again, to be someone else.

"I do remember now," says Gloucester, taking up his part, and his affliction, again:

. . . henceforth I'll bear
Affliction till it do cry out itself
"Enough, enough," and die. (4.6.75–77)

{11}

I know thee well enough. (4.6.179)

Relationships, Gloucester discovers, can be undone without being transformed or left behind. Our bonds to others can proceed bereft of futurity, seemingly without end. Together we endure our going hence, as our coming hither.

The series of "reunions"—for lack of a better word—that follow at this point in the play might be understood with this thought in mind. The mutual recognitions of Lear and Gloucester, and of Lear and Kent, are striking for the way in which, in each case, those recognitions unfold without offering any new future for those relationships. (I return to the late scenes between Lear and Cordelia momentarily.) What Gloucester and Lear recognize in one another is not (as, for example, Cavell has it) the discovery of an opportunity for self-reflective "insight"; still less do they perceive the possibility of a "new" confraternity. Lear's first reaction is not to deny that he knows Gloucester but rather to deny that this encounter will give rise to any new bond between them—"No, do thy worst, blind Cupid; I'll not love" (4.6.139).

The two men merely acknowledge, upon meeting, the debased conditions under which their shared recognition takes place. They recognize one another inasmuch as they recognize the *state* that the other is in. In kissing Lear's hand, Gloucester encounters only a "ruin'd piece of Nature" that, like himself, "smells of mortality" (4.6.136, 135). For his part, Lear focuses on the holes in Gloucester's head: "I remember thine eyes well enough. Dost thou squiny at me?" (4.6.138). Thus, like the two sick and aging men they are, they are left with nothing to talk about but their respective ailments and afflictions. They offer one another a general complaint about their worldly conditions as such: "When we are born, we cry that we are come / To this great stage of fools"—"Alack, alack the day!" (4.6.184–85, 183).[49]

⁓

Lear's recognition of Cordelia as his "child" likewise unfolds *as*—and not *in spite of*—his acknowledgment of the ongoing conditions under which that recognition takes place. It is for this reason, I believe, that Shakespeare stages it for us at a moment when Lear is awakening from sleep ("He's scarce awake; let him alone awhile" [4.7.51]):

> Where have I been? Where am I? Fair daylight?
> I am mightily abus'd. I should e'en die with pity
> To see another thus. I know not what to say.
> I will not swear these are my hands: let's see;
> I feel this pin prick. Would I were assur'd
> Of my condition! (4.7.52–57)

It is at this point that Cordelia speaks up, presenting herself to him as the first evidence of his condition, of his being alive and awake. ("O! look upon me, Sir" [4.7.57].) Lear's recognition of her is therefore inseparable from—indeed, it is the firmest proof of—the recognition of his bodily, worldly condition. Lear's conquering of his doubts about the world accompanies the overcoming of doubt about Cordelia's proximity to him; or, as Cavell has it, Lear accepts the world as it is by acknowledging Cordelia's place in it.[50] Coming to his senses—acknowledging the material conditions, the pin's prick, the strange battlefield tent, the unfamiliar clothes in which he is dressed—will mean facing her.

> I am a very foolish fond old man,
> Fourscore and upward, not an hour more or less;
> And, to deal plainly,
> I fear I am not in my perfect mind.
>
> . . . .
>
> Yet I am doubtful: for I am mainly ignorant
> What place this is, and all the skill I have
> Remembers not these garments; nor I know not
> Where I did lodge last night. Do not laugh at me;
> For, as I am a man, I think this lady
> To be my child Cordelia. (4.7.60–69)

Our understanding of this moment might be aided if we attend to the way in which this inseparability of Lear's recognition of Cordelia continues to unfold as a coming to terms with the (debased) conditions under which that recognition takes place. Hence, Lear's continued questioning—"Be your tears wet?" "Am I in France?" (4.7.71, 76)—as well as his persistent acknowledgement of his frailty—"I am old and foolish"

(4.7.84). Cordelia, for her part, does exactly what Edgar does for Gloucester to assure him of their shared condition. She provides no answers but merely helps him to his feet: "Will't please your Highness walk?" (4.7.83). Does this provide a way forward, however, or merely facilitate a shared trudge?

Shakespeare tempts us here with the possibility of forgiveness and new beginning in contrast to what he presents in Lear's recognition of Gloucester and Kent. The dramatic stakes of this temptation are palpable, almost unbearably so. (In fact, this temptation probably accounts for the long success of Tate's happy rewrite of the play as well as for the numerous critical attempts to find redemption in Cordelia and Lear's final encounters.) In a sense, this redemptive futurity should be what Lear's acknowledgment that Cordelia is his "child" signals—given that he had previously disclaimed all "paternal care, / Propinquity and property of blood" (1.1.113–14).

Yet even as he finally calls Cordelia his "child"—in fact, making her "weep" with joy at the achievement of this recognition, the very recognition she had desired from the outset—Lear holds onto his own injury. "Weep not: / If you have poison for me, I will drink it. / I know you do not love me" (4.7.71–73). Cordelia, it should be noted, does not interrupt her weeping to deny this—or even to answer this latest, explicitly desperate plea for loving recognition from her father. She does not return his recognition of her with the love he craves. She merely excuses his earlier transgression—"No cause, no cause" (4.7.75)—a Pyrrhic forgiveness, so to speak, since she has already won from him the admission that she is his child; that is, she excuses him only after he has already tried to make amends and suffered sufficiently. Her words merely indicate that Lear is no longer her master.

It is difficult to doubt Lear's abiding love for Cordelia. For this very reason, it is important to understand this love as precisely nontransformative and unredeeming. Indeed, that she remains his "joy" is essential to the foreclosure of transformative possibilities, to the preemption of new realities that we are tracking. Their reunion marks their failure to renew, alter, or transform their bonds to one another; they are back where they started.

One way to gauge this is to note that Lear loves Cordelia—and asks her forgiveness of him (4.7.84)—without, however, forgiving *her*.[51] Indeed, his injury at her hands is never mentioned between them. It would be comforting to understand this silence by invoking the obvious: namely, that because the very conditions in which Lear has been found are the clamorous effects of that initial injury, as of his own misdeed, there is hardly need to speak of it more.

And yet, if this were so—if all the harm had already been done—what would now be the harm of speaking of it? Indeed, if the injury were really *past*—over and done—would not this be the proper time for reflective hindsight, confession, and forgiveness, for recuperative healing?

But, far from restoration, it is Lear's infirmity and ongoing need for a doctor that Shakespeare depicts. There is, in fact, a peculiar moment in the context—never commented on in the critical literature, so far as I can recall—when Cordelia appears ready to open her mouth, to address the history Lear has lived. But the doctor stops her with these words:

Be comforted, good Madam; the great rage,
You see, is kill'd in him: and yet it is danger
To make him even o'er the time he has lost. (4.7.78–80)

We might consider the doctor's words as expressive of a diagnostic ambivalence that has afflicted our own understanding of the play. We, too, would like assurance that Lear's relative calm at this point—the fact that he is not ranting, tearing off his clothes, or running away from his companions—is evidence that "the great rage" is over.

" . . . and yet . . ." Shakespeare leaves us a word of caution. What has been "lost" by Lear cannot yet be accounted for *as a loss* and therefore still poses a present "danger."

Recall, too, that when Kent, in this same context, tells Lear, somewhat optimistically, that Lear is "in his own kingdom" (4.7.76)—expressing the belief that past losses can be recouped, kingdoms restored—Lear takes the remark as "abuse" (4.7.77).

Henceforth, no one—not even Cordelia—will speak with Lear of what has happened. It is as if past injuries cannot be named without inflicting them again. Something in the nature of the affliction itself forecloses its own healing.

... I would not see thy cruel nails
Pluck out his poor eyes; nor thy fierce sister
In his anointed flesh rash boarish fangs ...

. . . .

... but I shall see
The winged vengeance overtake such children. (3.7.55–65)

"See 't shalt thou never," spits Cornwall. "Fellows, hold the chair / Upon these eyes of thine I'll set my foot" (3.7.66–67).

The singular cruelty of Gloucester's torture arises from the way in which it combines the infliction of a wound that, while not mortal, cannot be healed with the simultaneous and explicit foreclosure of the possibility of revenge, punishment, or forgiveness of that action.

The blinding of Gloucester makes permanent the condition of bodily helplessness that was temporarily accomplished by his bondage and thereby extends his defenselessness indefinitely. It is as if the torture secures not only the doing of bodily harm—the binding of Gloucester's arms, the plucking of his beard, the gouging of his eyes—but also the indefinite prolonging of this helplessness, beyond the scene of torture, and even beyond the lifespan of the torturer(s).

Significantly, torture is experienced by Gloucester not only as a cruel violation of his bodily integrity, his physical autonomy, and his capacity to fend for himself. The production of Gloucester's helplessness also destroys his ethical orientation in the world—wrecking his trust and faith in others, in inherited ways of interacting with them, and in meaningful ways of making sense of his worldly relationships.[52] Indeed, the bodily helplessness and suffering that his blinding brings about—"all dark and comfortless" (3.7.84)—immediately leads Gloucester to issue a cry for help ("Give me some help!" [3.7.69]), a cry addressed above all to his son Edmund ("Where is my son, Edmund?" [3.7.84]). Because his body is no longer able to act in a self-determined way in response to his injury, he is compelled to appeal to others, first of all to his son—required to test their love for him by asking them to perform deeds for him. He not only finds himself at the mercy of what others might henceforth do to his bodily integrity; he is also forced to discover just what, if anything, others will do *for* him, on his behalf—to test what ethical obligations, if any, others will fulfill in relation to him.

"Edmund, enkindle all the sparks of nature / To quit this horrid act" (3.7.75–86). But, as it happens, vengeance is the inherited ethical principle that is eradicated first. Gloucester imagines revenge, to borrow the definition given by Hannah Arendt, to be "the natural, automatic reaction to transgression."[53] Yet, he immediately learns that ethical possibilities, of which revenge is one, are spirits that do not come simply because one calls on them. Such responses do not unfurl like natural processes; they do not kindle like natural sparks. In fact, the would-be avenger is revealed as an accomplice to the very violation that he is called on to avenge. ("Out, treacherous villain!" come Regan's piercing words. "Thou call'st on him that hates thee; it was he / That made the overture of thy treasons to us, / Who is too good to pity thee" [3.7.86–89].)[54] If, as we have seen, *Hamlet* is a revenge tragedy that arises from the crisis into which the act and principle of revenge, as an ethical principle and tragic possibility, has fallen, then the puncturing of Gloucester's eyes turns out the lights on the theater of revenge once and for all.

As if through a total inversion of Oedipus's self-mutilation, Gloucester learns—immediately upon suffering the consequences as a bodily infliction—that his relationships and bonds are not what he thought them to be. The act of blinding is thus collapsed into the moment of "insight" or recognition; the tragic reversal accompanies the misdeed by teaching Gloucester what he did not know. Here again—perhaps paradigmatically—we perceive Shakespeare's collapse of tragic misdeed, blindness, and insight as the foreclosure of further insight, "recognition," or "reversal."[55]

So, too, punishment and forgiveness are foreclosed along with revenge. After all, Gloucester is deprived of the capacity to punish Cornwall, who lies dead at close of the scene, or Regan. And if there is truth to Hannah Arendt's axiom that "men are unable to forgive what they cannot punish," then Gloucester is robbed of the chance of releasing himself and others from what has been done to him.[56] In a matter of seconds, Cornwall's gesture—"Lest it see more, prevent it. Out, vile jelly" (3.7.82)—not only robs Gloucester of his sight, but also of the possibility of meeting that transgression with a gesture or deed of his own, whether punitive, vengeful, or forgiving.[57] Not only is Gloucester's relation to Cornwall, Edmund, and Regan undone; the futurity of all of his relationships has been punctured. There is available to him no worldly recourse—legal, ethical, civic, fraternal, paternal, or other—that would furnish a meaningful response to what he has suffered.

If one desires to ease this suffering, or even merely to keep the old man company for its duration, then this cannot be done not as father and son but only as strangers. We do not learn the name of the "first servant" who rises to "help" Gloucester before Cornwall can put out his second eye; we know only that his actions precede those of a "second" and "third" servant, who "fetch some flax and whites of eggs / To apply to his bleeding face" (3.3.105–6). In similar anonymity, Gloucester walks alongside not his son, Edgar, but a beggar—the "poorest shape / That ever penury, in contempt of man, / Brought near to beast" (2.3.7–9)—and together they form a pair of mere natural creatures exposed equally to the harm and care others might afflict.

_~_

Strikingly, Shakespeare's staging of the torture of Gloucester places the victim, rather than the perpetrators, at center stage. The "reasons" for which Gloucester is tortured—whatever we take those reasons to be (Cornwall's "wrath" [3.7.26], Regan's sadism, the discovery of a traitor's secret)—are almost immediately supplanted, dramatically, by the fact of the violation itself. By shifting our attention away from the aims and means of the perpetrators, Shakespeare seems to ask us to regard the scene in relation to the victim's bodily vulnerability and ultimate helplessness.[58]

The body's natural vulnerability to either the provision of care or the doing of harm has sometimes appeared as the "given fact of the matter" for ethical and political thought. At the origins of Christian ethics, Augustine's reflections on sin and ethical violence rest on the observation that our flesh is vulnerable to willful violation and degradation. Thomas Hobbes, in a very different vein, supposed that the natural "equality" of human beings—against which politics appears and to which it must respond—is in fact nothing grander than our shared vulnerability to being killed by another.[59] In her recent work on contemporary forms of violence, Adriana Cavarero goes so far as to suggest that bodily vulnerability is in fact defined by the "tension generated by this alternative" between injury and care ("di ferita e di cura"), "as though the null response—neither the wound nor the care—were excluded" in relation to a vulnerable body. In her view, bodily vulnerability implies, and is defined by, the alternative of harm or care inasmuch as they characterize different responses to this vulnerability—"as though the absence of wound and care were not even thinkable."[60]

In addition to this general vulnerability—shared even by the armed and the strong at all moments of life—no one, continues Cavarero, can pass through life without also being exposed, for a time, to the doing of harm or the provision of care as radically defenseless or helpless (inerme).[61] We are born in precisely this way, of course; and it is likewise the natural condition of our infancy and old age, our moments of sleep and illness. The "natural" given of such helplessness—the fact that no life can avoid being helpless, at least for a time—is perhaps the condition from which our ethical sense of the body's "dignity" or wholesome integrity typically arises inasmuch as we are revolted and horrified by infanticide or the random carnage of "innocents" disfigured or blown apart by bombs.

Something of the ethical valence that we attach to the tension, or alteration, between the provision of care and the doing of harm thus depends on the givenness of bodily helplessness—on the natural fact of its unavoidability. We are born helplessly exposed to the care or harm others might perform and depend for our relative independence on whatever care we receive. Without being able to understand this helplessness as natural, would we be able to distinguish in the same way, with the same conviction, between the doing of harm and the provision of care?

Scenes of torture nevertheless introduce a measure of bewilderment into any ethical orientation that is grounded in the "natural" condition of helplessness. For the torturer does not prey on helplessness as a natural given, as does the abuser of children or infants, but rather produces that helplessness circumstantially, through artificial means and techniques. ("Bind fast his corky arms" [3.7.29].) Similarly, torture is a human activity whose point is not just to inflict or cause suffering and pain under conditions in which such infliction might have, finally, some given "limit" or horizon—for example, the death of the tortured, or human mortality.[62]

The horror *specific* to torture, inasmuch as it can be distinguished from other forms of violence or abuse, does not lie solely in the violations as such nor in the exploitation of a natural defenselessness or mortal limit. It also lies in the demonstration that this helplessness can be artfully accomplished by recreating the helplessness of our infancy for the sake of exploiting the fact that our dependence on others is an essential condition for any independence or autonomy to which we might aspire. By exploiting his victim's enduring dependence on others, the torturer turns the very conditions of his victim's (fragile) independence and autonomy against him.

Where helplessness is produced by human art, and as new techniques of unilateral power are refined, any residual appeal to harm and care as definite *alternatives* finds itself called on to account for a circumstantial helplessness whose "naturalness" is no longer fully clear. This is not to imply that the difference between harm and care disappears, any more than it is to claim that natural helplessness can be avoided or fully denaturalized over the course of a bodily life. On the contrary, we might even wish to say that, by exposing us to unilateral power, scenes of torture serve to magnify our remaining affective perception of the distinction between doing harm and providing care. We may well continue to perceive what we take to be a natural, infantile helplessness even on the face of the torture victim.

And yet in the wake of torture "care" finds itself distinguished from "harm" not by its "good," "life-preserving" effects—or by the way in which caring acts do not exploit the conditions of dependency that make our independence possible but seek instead to foster the other's independence. Confronted with the victim of torture, "care" appears hemmed in by a perhaps insuperable limitation: although one might endeavor to "care" for a specific bodily injury that the victim of torture has suffered (the way that the nameless servants tend to Gloucester's bloody eyes with flax and egg whites), one cannot assuage or ameliorate the *fact* of having been tortured, of having been *made* helpless by another. One cannot "care for" or "tend to" the exploited dependency under which the tortured suffers or has suffered; one might help another to live with the betrayal, but the wound opened by the betrayal cannot be closed.

Even if we grant ameliorating effects to the "flax and whites of eggs" fetched by Cornwall's servants to "apply to [Gloucester's] bleeding face," can the care the servants provide do anything more than respond to conditions that they, unlike Cornwall, did not create—and moreover cannot, by their caring actions, remake? (3.7.105–6). For all this, torture is not only a "misdeed," crime, or transgression that alters or transforms a given condition or state by breaking a prior norm, law, or boundary. For "crimes" or transgressions invariably serve to show, retrospectively, the force and endurance of whatever normative state was broken, whatever boundary transgressed. By the same token, such crimes can only be grasped as "criminal" ex post facto: no deed can be criminal, disobedient, or "new" prior to its being done.[63] (Unless, of course, we follow Cavarero in understanding "torture" as a crime against the human condition at its ontological level—in which case the "transgression" loses much of its sociohistorical valence).[64]

Cornwall's torture of Gloucester is, however, neither criminal nor even a misdeed in this sense. The act itself demonstrates that, because no "law" was broken, no "law" can orient or furnish a response.[65] Torture —as lawless, unilateral, and sovereign—makes its own laws, conditions, protocols, and so forth. In fact, Cornwall distinguishes his torture of Gloucester from both lawful punishment and criminal misdoing in precisely this way: "Though well we may not pass upon his life / Without the form of justice, yet our power / Shall do a court'sy to our wrath, which men / May blame but not control" (3.7.24–27).

What kind of deed is Cornwall doing if it is neither criminal nor lawful, that is, if it is neither a deed sanctioned and foreseen by established natural or man-made conditions nor a transgression of human or natural laws? Can his actions and their outcome be regarded as significant if they do not lend themselves to our understanding through the tragic-poetic categories of plot, reversal, recognition, or insight or through their correspondent ethical principles, such as revenge and forgiveness?

By understanding Gloucester's torture as a suffering that collapses retrospective insight and blindness, and therefore as an affliction that perhaps does not lend itself, philosophically or historically, to any new or further insight or meaning, we might see Gloucester's torture as exemplary of the drama from which it arises. For, by putting the poetics and philosophy of the tragic into crisis—that is, by revealing that there are deeds we can perform from which no historical meaning, no bridge between past and future, can unfold—Shakespeare's drama compels us to change not only our poetics and philosophy of tragedy but also, correspondingly, our understanding of our very activities as human beings.

{13}

Is this the promis'd end?
Or image of that horror? (5.3.263–64)

Shakespeare transforms our understanding of ourselves in what we take to be the form of a drama, *King Lear,* by staging the tragic undoing of our sense of the tragic and by unveiling the blindness inherent in the self-conception of ourselves as agents that classical tragedy furnished. Although this means that we can no longer fully rely on corollary categories for understanding tragic events—such as suffering, or reversal, or recognition—we may nevertheless still be guided, like Gloucester, by a "feeling insight" into our own affective response to what we witness.

However, if this is to guide us at all, we must consider Shakespeare as having displaced the classical question of *how* we respond affectively to what human beings can do to one another. For our answers to the question of "how" we respond affectively to our social, political, and dramatic actions and their representations—via our inherited notions of pity, fear, sorrow, or grief—all take for granted the "fact" of a possible affective response. The question "how" we are moved, in other words, presumes that we are moved and movable.

King Lear, however, stages a crisis in this proximity of affective response to the understanding, transformation, and transmission of our sociality, kinship ties, political allegiances and other abiding relationships. Because *King Lear* is not the representation of a tragic misdeed that forces a self-induced transformation of our bonds to one another, any affective response we might have must be divorced from an understanding of, or insight into, that transformation. We might still be moved by the disinheritance of the world that we have witnessed, but we are increasingly unable to say *how* or *why* and therefore remain unstirred by our own response. ("O! you are men of stones" [5.3.257].)

We watch Lear bear Cordelia's body onto the stage, but our understanding of what we are seeing remains questionable, along with our affective response to this sight. "Is this the promis'd end? / Or the image of that horror?" (5.3.263).

Cordelia's death must signal the end, the antigeneration, of the kingdom. ("No, no, no life! // . . . Thou'lt come no more / , Never, never, never, never, never!" [5.3.305–8].) Lear has, in fact, survived the necessity of his own demise—but not for the reasons he anticipated at the outset. He now bears the weight of his world's collapse in his arms. Surely this is what Albany perceives here: "Fall and cease" (5.3.264). But the apprehension of the mere fact of this fall and cessation, of her death and the world's disinheritance, remains divorced from a shareable response to, or insight into, what we apprehend. We look, perhaps in vain, to our hearts for some clue as to what this portends—"Break, heart; I prithee, break!" (5.3.312).[66]

In testing *if*—not *how*—we are still moved by what we can do to and with one another, Shakespeare forces us to make sense of the actions we have witnessed by confronting the inadequacy of our inherited ways of responding to misdeeds and suffering.

If what we have seen ourselves perform leaves us bereft of insight and affective comprehension into those deeds, how are we now to see ourselves?

CHAPTER FOUR

On *The Tempest*

"Hell is empty
And all the devils are here." (1.2.214–15)

W HAT CARES THESE ROARERS for the name of King?" cries the
boatswain over the sound of the storm at the beginning of *The
Tempest* (1.1.16–17).

Together with Lear's address to the thunder and wind on the heath, the
boatswain's words in the face of the roaring sea can be understood to
demonstrate the indifference of nature to human society and authority:
the "direct exposition of the . . . violent confrontation of nature with the
social order."[1] This diremption of nature from sociality, however, is not
a discovery or insight brought to light through a tragic deed and consequent "reversal." Shakespeare's storms do not teach us a lesson that we
do not already know; rather, they reveal the diremption of nature from
culture to be the ongoing horizon of our interpersonal struggles and interactions.

The fracturing of the ship's crew is occasioned by the battering winds
and waves but it is not caused by these elements. The fury of nature's
claims ("these roarers") is as undeniable as it is socially insignificant.
("We are merely cheated of our lives by drunkards" [1.1.55].) Just as the
storm in *King Lear* merely provides Regan and Goneril the opportunity
to shut the doors on their father, so too, the tempest reveals cracks in the
ship's social structure that existed well before the storm. "Remember
whom thou hast aboard," Gonzalo implores, to which the boatswain
replies, "None that I more love than myself" (1.1.19–20). The contest
underway, as the boatswain and his mariners understand perfectly well,
is not to decide if authority resides with nature or with human beings;
rather, the question is whether any natural or human *nomos* can hold

together those on the ship. "Let's all sink wi' th' King," offers Antonio; "Let's take leave of him," returns Sebastian (1.1.62–63).

The ship will be wrecked. But they will not go down together. "We split, we split," cries out Gonzalo, referring to his companions as much as to the boards beneath them, "Farewell, brother!—We split, we split, we split!" (1.1.59–61).

{2}

. . . I will plague them all,
Even to roaring. (4.1.192–93)

In the aftermath of the tempest, Prospero's first words in the play assure us, and Miranda, that no one was drowned. "There's no harm done." His words are hypnotically soothing: "No more amazement: tell your piteous heart / There's no harm done." Miranda is unconvinced ("O, woe the day!"), but Prospero insists, repeating: "No harm."

"I have done nothing," he continues, "but in care of thee" (1.2.14–16).

Yet, beneath our stupor, a worry remains: can we distinguish the provision of care from the doing of harm? Does Miranda—do we—have a way to suture nature and sociality that would permit us to say what is good or beneficial, to know what a "good life" or a desirable end might be? Prospero has just demonstrated his own artistic mastery over nature; namely, his power not only to "put the wild waters in this roar" but also to assure that there is "not so much perdition as an hair / Betid to any creature in the vessel" (1.2.2, 30–31). As Shakespeare makes clear throughout, Prospero's "art" is the exploitation of an alienation from nature—the most radical overcoming of the claims of nature that we have yet encountered.

—I have bedimm'd
The noontide sun, call'd forth the mutinous winds,
And 'twixt the green sea and the azur'd vault
Set roaring war: to the dread rattling thunder
Have I given fire, and rifted Jove's stout oak
With his own bolt; the strong-bas'd promontory
Have I made shake, and by the spurs pluck'd up

The pine and cedar: graves at my command
Have wak'd their sleepers, op'd forth, and let 'em forth
By my so potent Art. . . . (5.1.41–50)

Our challenge, therefore, is not to discover the source of Prospero's "art"; it appears more powerful than nature because it expresses an estrangement from and denial of nature's claims. The challenge, rather, is to ask after the social consequences of this "art," the interpersonal, concrete, and dramatic stakes of the diremption of nature from culture.

By presenting from the outset this diremption in an extreme, hyperbolic fashion, Shakespeare forces us to confront, once again, limit situations between human beings for whom authoritative social bonds—kinship ties, civic relations, economic dependencies, political allegiances—have long ago unraveled. *The Tempest* asks what it is to live with, to have long endured, this disinheritance.

✒

Seeing this depiction clearly requires the initial acknowledgment that Prospero's "art" also appears to take a rather specific form: the "torment" of others. He torments, to varying degrees, everyone in the play, including his daughter. The island itself is a scene of torment, a domain in which Prospero's power—a power that appears to owe nothing to nature, and everything to his "art"—is unilaterally, incontestably sovereign.

Through techniques of his own (which result from "secret studies," and his "neglecting wordly ends" [1.2.77, 89]) and through the exploitation of those he has forcibly enslaved (those whose sole activity, "toil," profits him), Prospero fashions artificial conditions under which the "experiences" of others—both their suffering of events themselves and their affective response to these events—are divorced from any activity or agency proper to them. In this way, all are rendered helpless to prevent, avenge, undo, or oppose what is done to them. "My high charms work," Prospero declares, "[a]nd these mine enemies are all knit up / In their distractions: they are now in my power; / And in these fits I leave them" (3.3.88–91).

Moreover, by detaching their experiences from anything that they themselves might do or say in response to what they undergo, Prospero effectively denies to others conditions under which they might, by their interactions, inherit, alter, or transform the social bonds that tie them to others. His activities systematically deprive others of a worldly, historical, and social life, first of all by stripping others of their capacity to act and react in a self-determining fashion. We might understand the island itself as an apt figuration of this deprivation. It is a radical experiment, we might say, in the possible consequences of the disinheritance of the world.

~

"Hast thou," Prospero demands of Ariel, "perform'd to point the tempest that I bade thee?" (1.2.193–94). Correspondent to sovereign command, Ariel describes his instrumental role in the torment of the ship's mariners and passengers. On Prospero's orders, Ariel created for the men the illusion that they were drowning.

The significance of the torment, as he tells it, lies not in the technical details of the waterboarding—such as the quantity of "bold waves" poured down upon the men or the length of time for which they were submerged (1.2.195–206). The point of the exercise, rather, lies in the response that it produces in its sufferers and in its spectators. Thus, Prospero inquires of Ariel if any of the men remained unbroken by the procedure: "Who was so firm, so constant, that this coil / Would not infect his reason?" (1.2.207–8). "Not a soul," Ariel informs him, "[b]ut felt a fever of the mad, and play'd / Some tricks of desperation. . . . // With hair upstaring,—then like reeds, not hair" (1.2.208–13).[2]

With regard to the technique itself, it is no doubt significant that—like the "cramps" and "aches" with which Prospero "rack[s]" the "bones" of Caliban or that he later inflicts on the shipwrecked Italians by means of the invisible Ariel—Prospero's simulation of drowning leaves behind no visible marks or wounds on the sufferers. The infliction of the suffering—although no doubt felt or experienced inasmuch as it is capable of provoking our horror and pity—is not reified or legible as a historical fact. What the inflictions leave behind, if anything, are grounds for denying its having occurred at all.

The torments that Prospero performs become an "insubstantial pageant faded." They "[l]eave not a rack behind" (4.1.155–56).

"But are they, Ariel, safe?" asks Prospero. "Not a hair perish'd," confirms Ariel (1.2.217). If anything, the observer would have now to regard the tormented castaways as apparently well cared for; freshly bathed, so to speak, and dressed in newly laundered clothes. "On their sustaining garments not a blemish, / But fresher than before" (1.2.218–19).

As we know, it is a hallmark of certain tormenting practices—to some of which we give the name "torture" (or, at least, we debate the aptness of the appellation)—to frustrate the visible detection of inflicted harm, and, even, to offer professions that great care has been provided. At work in such practices is not a simple trompe l'oeil nor a conventional deception designed to mask or hide the "truth" of the injury under the "disguise" of care. More troublingly, we are confronted with the artificial production of "living conditions" under which torment and care can be mistaken for one another. As we know, after all, humane journalistic or scientific investigations into "truth claims" regarding such practices can be frustrated, in advance, by the sophistication of artistic illusions typical of the practices themselves. This sophistication—the refinement and realization of "new" artistic practices—calls to be understood in relation to its transformation of our very capacity to judge whether "living conditions" are decidedly beneficial or harmful.

We might therefore conclude that such practices unfold, vexingly, as the blurring of any perceptible difference between harm and care—not only for observers but also potentially for the sufferer herself. The harm inflicted by such acts calls, further, to be understood as damage done to our inherited ways of distinguishing—ethically, historically, medically, psychologically, bodily, and so forth—harm from care, the beneficial from the injurious. The natural clarity of the "good life," as distinct from other living conditions, comes to appear illusory.

Indeed, the fact that we are dealing with a simulation of drowning—both for observers, as well as the sufferers—means that we are confronted with an activity whose "reality" (by which I mean the "reality" of the suffering that this simulation brings about, which we take seriously) unfolds as a challenge to "historically consequential reality." That is to say, the "art" of the torment includes, within its process, a negation of the irreversible consequentiality of our actions. It denies that its performance is, or could be, a criminal transgression because it denies being a historically consequential deed at all.

As a result the pity and terror we feel for those who suffer finds itself unexpectedly estranged from the "reality" of pitiable and terrible events.

This estrangement leaves the one who feels pity and terror ignorant of who and what she is seeing; she is unable to articulate a relation between what she feels and the events that elicited these feelings. Such is our, and Miranda's, predicament at the outset.

> Be collected:
> No more amazement: tell your piteous heart
> There's no harm done.
> . . . .
> No harm. (1.2.13–15)

At the same time, Prospero nevertheless leaves others with the sense of undergoing "experiences"—of pain and pleasure, of loss and joy—that are eerily divorced from anything they themselves are doing or saying. What they are made to undergo deprives them, by the same token, of any way to grasp what they endure. The occupants of Prospero's island still feel "grief" and "torment," just as they hear music and see strange "shapes." They drink, feast, laugh, weep, and partake of spectacular entertainment. But the intensity of these experiences corresponds precisely to a detachment from the possibility of any active response to, or retrospective understanding of, what they are going through.

This intensity is artfully furnished, first, through the impairment or altering of our perception to a point at which our bodily and psychic experiences no longer seem narratable. ("These are not natural events; they strengthen / From strange to stranger" [5.1.227–28].) This "ecstasy" (3.3.108) that takes us out of ourselves—*The Tempest* offers, as a start, magic, spirits, trances, the infliction of physical or psychic pain, somnolence, music, masques, and charms—inhibits any historical, narrative, or retrospective understanding of what we have undergone. This is not to say that Prospero's "art," or "rough magic," generates mere illusion or fiction; rather, it produces a split between psychic and bodily experience, on the one hand, and consequential actions that might lend themselves to narrative accounts and historical judgment, on the other.

In light of this, let us proceed in a manner analogous to Shakespeare's play itself—by trying to discern the manifold interpersonal consequences of Prospero's "art," by examining what he does to the sailors, to Miranda, to the Italian rulers and their court, to Ariel, and to Caliban.

What foul play had we, that we came from thence?
Or blessed was't we did? (1.1.60–61)

"Both, both, my girl" (1.1.61) responds Prospero enigmatically to Miranda's demand for some interpretative understanding of her life story, which she is hearing for the first time and of which she has been ignorant. (["M]y daughter, who / Art ignorant of what thou art" [1.2.17–18].)

The bare bones of the story that Prospero has been telling his daughter are not hard to grasp. His brother, Antonio, with the help of Alonso, king of Naples, and his brother, Sebastian, contrived to usurp Prospero's dukedom in Milan—exiling Prospero and his infant daughter, Miranda, by setting them adrift at sea.

Like Miranda, we may find it taxing to "mark" the tale itself. (See 1.2.78–79, 87–89, 106.) For, unlike Miranda, we have already heard—especially from Shakespeare himself—other iterations of the same plot. We know how it goes, from Shakespeare's earliest plays onward: one brother betrays another, familial bonds are sundered; worldly inheritances and entitlements are lost, economic ties broken; political allegiances are forged only in the heated treachery of individuals who love no one but themselves; lives are forsaken, banished, and exiled.

Does our history comprise tragedies and betrayals that might someday fail to startle or surprise? Assuming our tragic history still manages to be moving to us, can it also bind us? Or does tragedy itself appear consigned to the archive?

Such is Prospero's—and Shakespeare's—dramatic dilemma, confronted with eager and hopeful newcomers like Miranda and ourselves: namely, to test what our investment in "our" story might now be.

⁓

"More to know / Did never meddle with my thoughts," says Miranda, betraying a near total lack of inquisitiveness into the historical and social preconditions of her present state (1.2.21–22). Whereas Oedipus felt compelled to know, at all costs, the story of his life, the Delphic injunction "Know thyself" cannot, on its own, inspire Miranda to be anything other than "ignorant" of who she is. Having been raised as she currently lives—denied relationships that she might transform or reshape—she cannot be sufficiently interesting to herself.

If Prospero is to help her to educate herself about herself (1.2.170–75), so to speak—if she is to come to be as invested in herself and others as he is in her—then he will have to find a way to reactivate the possibilities and meaning of human sociality for Miranda, for himself, and for the others.

Prospero's "art" calls to be understood in light of this ambition, of course. But how can this be accomplished? Can such a reactivation be realized through human art?

"The hour's now come," says Prospero, as if to finally turn the past into prologue, "[t]he very minute bids thee ope thine ear" (1.2.36–37). Like that of Miranda, our attention to the history that Prospero relates hinges on the possibility of its having a consequential, even an urgent, connection to the present state of affairs. "Hear a little further," says Prospero, "[a]nd then I'll bring thee to the present business / Which now's upon 's; without the which, this story / Were most impertinent" (1.2.135–38). Prospero is not offering Miranda a tutorial akin to those he delivers as her "schoolmaster" (1.2.172). The force and meaning of the tale itself is not detachable from the circumstances under which Prospero tells it and that it portends to illuminate. ("'Tis time / I should inform thee" [1.2.22–23].)

With Miranda, therefore, we listen with the expectation that the significance of "the present business" can be grasped through the historical retrospective Prospero will sketch—under the assumption that the present will, thereby, take its place within a narrative structure that might furnish for it a meaning and a context.

But this expectation presumes that "the present business" is itself an historical experience, a sequence of events whose meaning can be subsequently revealed through narrative recognition. And this turns out to be far from a safe presumption—not only because the present is still unfolding (in "real time," as The Tempest itself does) but also because of a more fundamental rupture, involving Prospero's *own* limitations as narrator and protagonist of the history he tells. Indeed, he does not finally complete the narration he himself began let alone provide for it the interpretive understanding that Miranda desires. "Know thus far forth" (1.2.177) he concludes, leaving unresolved the historical connection between past and present that he had promised at the tale's outset. And with these words, Miranda is put to "sleep" by Prospero's rough magic. "Here cease more questions" (1.2.184).

Before considering the "good dulness" that Prospero inflicts on others, and its connection to the cessation of critical inquiry, I wish to offer two hypotheses regarding Prospero's failure to make narrative sense of the relation between past sufferings and "the present business."

First: Prospero is forced to cut short the narrative in which he tried to connect past to present because of a crucial transformation in his own relation to the contingency of human events and actions. Past events— everything that happened between the loss of the Milan dukedom and his tutelage of Miranda on the island—constitute an experience that he underwent and *suffered*, "our sea-sorrow" (1.2.170). Prospero is a protagonist of that history precisely inasmuch as he underwent its unfolding without, however, being able to control or determine its end. As its sufferer, Prospero is able to offer an autobiographical account of this sequence of events, albeit only ex post facto, because those things remain formative experiences for him—pains and sufferings that resulted directly from his own actions (namely, his rapturous studies) and from the unpredictable actions of others (Antonio's betrayal of him).

By contrast, the shipwreck and "sea-storm"—"the present business" —constitute a set of conditions that he himself has brought into being as the product of his "art." Prospero is, so to speak, the *poietes* and demiurge of the present business; but he is not a sufferer of the events as they unfold.[3] Indeed, Prospero's immunity from the torment that he can nevertheless continue to inflict on others defines his position throughout the play. Experiences are, in "the present business," something that he causes others to undergo but that he himself does not have to endure in the same way.

Although this frees him to produce history as a work in progress, something whose end he foresees from the outset and that he brings about with practiced technique and skill, it also precludes him from narrating it *as something undergone*. As the "fabricator" of the sea storm, Prospero is thus denied any historical insight into the practical experience of it.[4] He cannot finish the tale for Miranda.

For the duration of the play, in fact, Prospero suspends his own experience of the historical sequence of events that, by his "art," he *makes* happen. He can be neither a narrator nor a protagonist of "the present business" because he is its maker, not its sufferer. His understanding of what is happening is akin to the technical "understanding" of the craftsman with respect to the artifact he makes; he "sees" in advance how the thing will turn out. For this reason, he is denied retrospective understanding or insight into what he has wrought.

Second, by exempting himself from the suffering that he continues to inflict on others—indeed, by showing himself capable of temporarily achieving this exemption by means of his "art," or "rough magic"— Prospero creates conditions under which suffering is experienced by others as *inflicted on them*. In this way, Prospero also creates conditions under which the "historical" experience of *others* is radically transformed. He manages to divorce their contemporary experience of suffering, agony, misery, and loss from their active participation in it.

This is why Prospero breaks off his narration to Miranda by putting her into an artificially induced stupor. ("Thou art inclin'd to sleep" [1.2.185].) Because Miranda is only able to experience her life as the passive suffering of conditions that she is helpless to transform ("O, I have suffered / With those I saw suffer!" [1.2.5–6]), she cannot have a historical understanding of her life. If anything, Prospero's opening tale only succeeds in emphasizing the extent to which historical understanding itself has been taken from Miranda along with her self-determination. "'Tis a good dulness, / And give it way: I know thou canst not choose" (1.2.185–86).

{4}

... thy brains,
Now useless, boil'd within thy skull! There stand,
For you are spell-stopp'd. (5.1.59–61)

Like the "sleep" forced on Miranda so, too, the "spell" or "distractions" that Prospero's "high charms work" on Alonso, Antonio, Sebastian, Gonzalo, and their attendants confine and imprison (5.1.8–10) their bodily and psychic lives by denying to them the capacity to make narrative sense of what is happening to them. "If in Naples / I should report this now, would they believe me?" (3.3.27–28).

What distinguishes the "monstrous, monstrous" (3.3.95) suffering that Prospero inflicts on the men, however, from the state of "dulness" in which he leaves his daughter is that in the case of the former this infliction purports to constitute a response to historical crimes of which these tortured men are guilty. "You three / From Milan did supplant good Prospero," speaks Ariel, announcing their guilt, "for which foul deed / The powers, delaying, not forgetting, have / Incens'd the seas and shore, yea, all the creatures / Against your peace" (3.3.69–75).

Whereas Hamlet devises the illusion of *The Mousetrap* in order to test his uncle's guilt, using it to gauge Claudius' affective response to the simulation he sees, Prospero transfixes his guilty usurpers with a theatricality that conflates the accusation, judgment, and subsequent torment into a single performance. If Hamlet instructs the actors "to suit the action to the word" (3.2.17) in their representation of the usurping brother—thereby delaying his own revenge—then Prospero bids Ariel and his "meaner ministers" to stage a spectacle in which revenge will be represented as having already been taken. Thus, we watch Alonso, Antonio, Sebastian, and Gonzalo—"all knit up / In their distractions" (3.3.89–90)—not in order to see if they, like Claudius, will "blench" at what they see. Rather, we watch them—along with Prospero—simply in order to see them suffer. Upon closer inspection, however, what Prospero undertakes at this point is neither punishment nor revenge. In contrast to the "theater of revenge" that characterizes so much English (and Greek and Roman) drama, the spectacle staged by Prospero does not offer, to borrow Hegel's definition, a "positive action" or "new infringement" that reacts to a prior transgression, "becoming part of an infinite progression . . . inherited indefinitely from generation to generation."[5] Revenge, as we saw in *Hamlet*, is after all a form of generational devolution. Vengeance is a deed done in fidelity to the dead and to past deeds; it is a "new infringement" that starts a new historical chapter only by reacting to what has already been done. But Prospero is not starting a new historical chapter by tormenting these men; his torture unfolds instead as the suspension of their historical existence—it "knit[s]" (3.3.89) them in indefinite "distraction" (3.3.90), "ling'ring perdition" (3.3.77), and "nothing but heart-sorrow" (3.3.80). It creates nothing less than hell on earth.

By the same token, the infernal torment inflicted by Prospero should not be confused with a form of punishment.[6] For to punish a crime is already, as Hegel and Arendt make clear, to turn the punishable deed into something over and done with, no longer identified entirely with its doer. In principle, punishment gives the criminal a chance to separate himself from what he has done, to leave the "foul deed" behind and be reconciled to us. But Prospero gives the men no such chance to free themselves from their foul deeds; quite the contrary, he chains them to their deeds without, however, avenging those deeds. As Ariel makes clear, the men are "[c]onfin'd together // . . . all prisoners . . . // They cannot budge till [Prospero's] release" (5.1.7–11). Before we come to Prospero's late claim, made only in the epilogue, to have "pardon'd" (7) we should look at what Prospero is doing as he holds these men—"confin'd," "distracted," "spell-stopp'd" (5.1.7, 12, 61). If he is neither punishing the men nor taking revenge on them, then what is Prospero doing by detaining them in this way?

Prospero stages for the "spell-stopp'd" men an invented drama in which Alonso will be represented as a tragic protagonist, who "picks the fruits of his own deeds."[7] Thus, Prospero convinces Alonso that his son has already been drowned as retribution for Alonso's own action.

> . . . for which foul deed
> The powers, delaying, not forgetting . . .
> · · · · · · · · · · ·
> . . . Thee of thy son, Alonso,
> They have bereft; and do pronounce by me
> Ling'ring perdition—worse than any death
> Can be at once—shall step by step attend
> You and your ways; whose wraths to guard you from,—
> Which here, in this most desolate isle, else falls
> Upon your heads,—is nothing but heart-sorrow
> And a clear life ensuing. (3.3.72–81)

To understand this "ling'ring perdition," it will be helpful to recall, first, what Prospero must already know—namely, that Alonso has feared his son "lost" from the moment he set foot on the island.[8] Nevertheless—however painful it would be to bear—the accidental drowning of Ferdinand would be an event that Alonso could mourn, a "loss" that he could come to recognize as such. Indeed, Alonso at length begins this work of mourning, declaring his son lost: "I will put off hope . . . // Well, let him go" (3.3.7–10).

Significantly, it is at precisely *this* moment that Prospero—whose timing, as we know, is impeccable—casts his spell over Alonso and the others. Just when Alonso has begun to fully mourn, Prospero will force Alonso to lose his son again.

Indeed, this time, Alonso will be forced—by Prospero's art, rather than by historical fate—to experience the loss of his son not as an act of nature or misfortune at sea but (in Prospero's artifice) as the direct consequence of Alonso's own actions.[9] "For which foul deed // . . . thee of thy son, Alonso, / They have bereft; and do pronounce / by me ling'ring perdition" (3.3.72–77). The loss will linger—"worse than any death can be at once" (3.3.77–78)—because it is perceived by Alonso as arising directly from his own "foul deed" (3.3.72). Alonso will now see himself as the one who accomplished what he had "mistaken" for a horrific accident, an act of nature. He is told that he himself sent his son to be feasted on by strange fish.

Such news cannot but leave Alonso irrevocably transformed. Indeed, his companions can hardly bear to see him thus reduced: "I' th' name of something holy, sir, why stand you / In this strange stare?" (3.3.94–95). We know this stare. It is the look of the tragic hero, caught in the moment of recognition that his own deeds have brought on him the calamity whose mystery he in fact had been trying to resolve.

But whereas Oedipus unartfully learns of having (really) killed his father only after having had children with Jocasta, Alonso is made to *believe* as an effect of Prospero's art that he has unwittingly put an end to the life he himself had brought into the world.

> . . . my son i' th' ooze is bedded; and
> I'll seek him deeper than e'er plummet sounded,
> And with him there lie mudded. (3.3.100–102)

{5}

Dost thou forget
From what a torment I did free thee? (1.2.250–51)

"Thou best know'st," Prospero reminds Ariel, "[w]hat torment I did find thee in; thy groans / Did make wolves howl, and penetrate the breasts /

Of ever-angry bears: it was a torment / To lay upon the damn'd, which Sycorax / Could not again undo" (1.2.286–91).

If this is to be believed, then Prospero has freed Ariel from eternal damnation. In return, he requires only that Ariel be his servant for "a full year" (1.2.250). The everlasting inferno is thereby transferred or redimensioned into the space and time of earthly existence. Instead of causing Ariel to "vent . . . groans / As fast as mill-wheels strike" (1.2.280–81), Prospero demands that Ariel sing for human ears. Whereas the witch Sycorax had "imprison'd" Ariel "into a cloven pine" (1.2.278, 277), Prospero compels Ariel to perform activities that come naturally to him: "[T]o tread the ooze / Of the salt deep, / To run upon the sharp wind of the north, / To do . . . business in the veins o' th' earth / When it is bak'd with frost" (1.2.252–56). Ariel's endless torment and imprisonment has been exchanged, we might say, for a sort of indentured servitude.

The greatest modification, of course, is that Prospero promises to free Ariel after a certain term—first a "full year" and then "after two days / will discharge thee" (1.2.298–99). We do not know if Sycorax had promised similar temporal limits for Ariel's imprisonment; we know only that the witch had "died, / And left thee there" (1.2.279–80).

Significantly, in reminding of Ariel of this history—a history in which Ariel, it should be emphasized, has never been "free" to act in a self-determining way (1.2.270–77)—Prospero effectively ties the conditions of Ariel's (eventual) freedom to Prospero's *own* survival. Because Ariel can only be freed if Prospero himself lives to set him free, Ariel is forced to invest his own life in Prospero's very being and continued vitality. Prospero's death would mean, as Sycorax's death had meant, Ariel's eternal bondage.

In contrast to Caliban, therefore, Ariel is not enslaved by means of brute force alone. Indeed, whereas Caliban knows that a stronger master could liberate him from Prospero's power (hence, the plot he hatches with Stephano and Trinculo), Ariel sees that Prospero has absolute and total power over him. In contrast to Caliban's subjection, Ariel's is not reducible to techniques of subordination. The unconditional nature of Prospero's power over Ariel on the island is no less so than Sycorax's infernal power had been. As was the case when Ariel was confined by Sycorax, his release now can only be granted by the one who can totally deny it.

Because the promise of freedom is inseparable from subjection to Prospero, Ariel's bondage itself becomes the precondition of any freedom to which he might aspire. ("But yet thou shalt have freedom" [5.1.96].) By the same token, because freedom can be promised to Ariel only by Prospero, we might say that Prospero's repeated promises to "free" Ariel are, in fact, the fullest manifestation of his unilateral, sovereign power over him (see 5.1.87, 241). Ariel is subjected to, and by, the promise of freedom. "Thou shalt be as free / as mountain winds: but then exactly do / All points of my command" (1.2.501–3).

In this sense, Prospero's power over Ariel appears wholly unconditional—coextensive with Prospero's very being. As Prospero's bondsman, Ariel is not held by "*a* power" that Prospero might represent or wield (such as magic, brute force, or legal authority) and that could be undone or opposed by "another power." Ariel is, rather, held in the grip of power itself—insofar as Prospero's power is, within the horizon of the play, insuperable and incontestable by anything other than itself.

Formed and shaped in this way by sovereign power itself, Ariel might thus be understood not as a "slave" or bondsman like Caliban (to whom I will come momentarily) but rather as the fantastical image of the "pure subject"—subjection beyond subordination. For Ariel is a being shaped and formed entirely by subjection to unconditional power, a being whose very appearance in the world as having been "shaped" in this way is itself "subject" to horizons granted by that shaping power alone.

Go make thyself like a nymph o' th' sea:
Be subject to
No sight but thine and mine; invisible
To every eyeball else. Go take this shape,
And hither come in 't. (1.2.301–5)

Students of the play might wonder why Prospero requires Ariel to "make" himself "like a nymph o' th' sea," given that Ariel will be "invisible / To every eyeball" but "thine and mine." Are we to understand Ariel's shape changing, his altered appearances and guises, as spectacles designed to give Prospero private pleasure? Are Prospero's commands thus to be understood as yielding for him gratification not only in the "work" that he makes Ariel do but in the total mastery of the form and conditions of Ariel's appearances?

Nothing precludes such an interpretation, but it strikes me as significant that in a play so obsessed with the bodily aspect and shape of its protagonists—Prospero's mantle, Caliban's "disproportion'd" shape, Ferdinand's and Miranda's appearances to one another—Ariel is nowhere described by Shakespeare as having an embodied "shape" or "form" independent of the ones attributed or assigned to him by Prospero.

I shall try to say something about the recognition of embodiment more broadly in the play in a moment. For time being I simply wish to underscore that, whereas others in the play are concrete, flesh and blood—as Ferdinand says of Miranda, "Nor can imagination form a shape, / Besides yourself, to like of" (3.1.56–57)—Ariel is a being deprived of any form not given by Prospero. The polyvalent semantics of *The Tempest* are not easily made univocal, of course, but perhaps we might understand the fact that Prospero uses a number of terms to refer to Ariel—terms that, like much of the play's language, oscillate between words that allude to the sea and the air ("spirit," "nymph o' th' sea," "bird," "chick")—to suggest that Ariel is not a being formed *by* subjection, which would imply a prior "being" that is subsequently "shaped" by power. Rather, Ariel is a being formed *as* subjection.

And if subjection is formative of his very being, we have to wonder if Ariel can "be" or "take shape" at all without being thus subjected.

Again, the imagery of Shakespeare's language is obviously open to multiple interpretations. However I understand the persistent identification of the experience of Ariel's promised freedom with the "elements" themselves—especially the thin air ("mountain winds" or the "auspicious gales" that will return Prospero's ships to Naples)—to provoke an unsettling question. Is there any substance to the freedom promised to Ariel?

Can the experience of absolute freedom be formative? If not, can it be subjectively experienced at all?

Is it, perhaps, an experience approximate to radical abandonment?

{6}

The fringed curtains of thine eye advance,
And say what thou seest yond.
What is 't . . . ? (1.2.412)

Ariel has no naturally given shape, no singular, innate bodily form. Caliban is, by contrast, a flesh and blood creature with a particularly enigmatic shape that is the topic of some discussion in the play.

If subjection to power is formative of Ariel's very being, then Caliban is a being whose subjection by Prospero has failed to be fully formative; Caliban's shape and appearance were naturally formed, as it were, in his mother's womb. (According to Prospero, Caliban is a "freckled whelp hag-born" [1.2.283], a "mis-shapen knave" whose "mother was a witch" [5.1.268–69].) Whereas Ariel's subjection shapes his very embodiment, Caliban is identified as a monstrosity resistant to wholesale reformation. Indeed, it is Caliban's innate resistance to reformation that, according to Prospero, constitutes his monstrosity. "Abhorred slave, / Which any print of goodness wilt not take, / Being capable of all ill!" (1.2.353–54).

Caliban's appearance on the world stage raises a series of questions about what, exactly, the recognition of a "human shape" entails. How, and under what conditions, is such a shape recognizable in socially inherited ways—as human, animal, gendered, ethnically marked? What is the relationship between the recognition of a human shape and the sort of social existence that might follow such recognition? The relationship between embodiment and the recognition of the "human" (or "animal," "woman," "man") is, of course, central to the action of The Tempest generally. Shakespeare's development of this problematic deserves a few words here. We might say that the play stages—or requires in order to be comprehensibly staged at all—nothing less than a new phenomenology of materiality, perception, embodiment, visibility, physical sensation, and so on. Nearly every scene in the play offers some challenge to our inherited ways of grasping what we see—from spirits and harpies whose material "shape" is (like old Hamlet's ghost) "questionable" to ethereal music and sounds ("no sound / That the earth owes" [1.2.409–10]) and other assorted insubstantial pageants.

It is easy to relegate these aspects of the play to the historical practices of the theatrical milieu in which Shakespeare worked—increasingly characterized at the time The Tempest was first performed (1611) by "masques" and elaborate new visual techniques for dramatic representation. However, such relegation avoids the larger question it begs: namely, what compelled the development of such techniques and stagecraft? What made new representative strategies necessary or desirable? And what made such techniques successful—that is, appreciated by audiences?

These "theatrical" questions correspond, I would suggest, to the broader dramatic question with which we concluded the chapter on *King Lear.* How are we now to see ourselves?

What insight into our lives together, our shared activities, or into our modes of interpersonal recognition is afforded by the form and content of our drama? Indeed, what modes of bodily and social recognition are *presumed* or *made possible* by the ways in which we dramatically interact?

If the figure of Caliban has been particularly troubling for directors and critics of the play alike, then it is perhaps because of his special insistence that these questions be addressed. Let us try, therefore, to see if we might begin to offer something approaching an articulation or understanding of Caliban's embodied appearance. Can we say who or what it is that we see?

⁓

Before taking another look at Caliban, it will be helpful to observe that the play itself could be approached as the unfolding presentation or debut of these flesh and blood creatures on the world stage, one by one or two or three at a time. This is how Shakespeare structures the drama in the wake of the opening shipwreck. First we see Miranda (who will encounter, with us, the rest of them), then Prospero, then Caliban, followed by Ferdinand, before Alonso, Sebastian, Gonzalo, Antonio, Trinculo, and Stephano. This procession might be said to challenge us—as it challenges Miranda—to gauge our apprehension of each new arrival in relation to our prior apprehensions of others.

Consequently, the criteria for recognizing each new arrival—as phenomenal, embodied beings—are revised and reinstituted with each new embodied appearance. Each new bodily appearance on the world stage —inasmuch as it is not like any other embodied being ever before seen— thus requires a revision in the very manner in which bodily form or appearance is to be understood or recognized.

It is as if *The Tempest* unveils a world stage on which arrive a string of newcomers, each of whom—because they are all endowed with a corporeal shape like no other—compels us to construct a new conceptual framework to replace the one we had erected to grasp the appearance of the preceding one. Indeed, it reveals those earlier conceptual frameworks to be constructions that we erected as responses to whatever we had seen. Every new arrival therefore embodies a challenge to our phenomenological capacities of recognition—as if something *unrecognizable* or *not yet* recognizable attended every new bodily appearance.

This challenge is explicitly marked at many points. Recall Prospero's admonition to Miranda: "Thou think'st there is no more such shapes as he, / Having seen but him and Caliban: foolish wench! / To th' most of men this is a Caliban, / And they are to him angels" (1.2.481–84). Or Miranda's speech to Ferdinand:

> I do not know
> One of my sex; no woman's face remember,
> Save, from my glass, mine own; nor have I seen
> More that I may call men than you, good friend,
> And my dear father: how features are abroad,
> I am skilless of . . . (3.1.48–53)

Or Prospero's exchange with Miranda, as Ferdinand first comes into view:

> *Prospero:* The fringed curtains of thine eye advance,
>   And say what thou seest yond.
> *Miranda:* What is 't? a spirit?
>   Lord, how it looks about! Believe me, sir,
>   It carries a brave form. But 'tis a spirit.
> *Prospero:* No, wench; it eats and sleeps and hath such senses
>   As we have, such. This gallant which thou seest
>   Was in the wrack . . .
>
>   .   .   .   .
>   A goodly person . . .
>
>   .   .   .   .
> *Miranda:* I might call him
>   A thing divine; for nothing natural
>   I ever saw so noble. (1.2.411–22)

And, finally, near the play's conclusion:

> *Miranda:* O, wonder!
>   How many goodly creatures are there here!

> How beauteous mankind is! O brave new world,
>   That has such people in 't!
> *Prospero:* 'Tis new to thee. (5.1.181–84)

Now, in each of the scenes that I have just cited, Prospero frames the terms and conditions of Miranda's apprehension and recognition of embodied beings—of herself, as of others. For instance, he leads Miranda to the recognition that Ferdinand is not a "spirit" but a "gallant" who "eats and sleeps and hath such senses / as we have." In this way, Prospero presents Ferdinand's "goodly person" and upright, bodily humanity as being similar to Miranda's own embodiment. He thus leads Miranda to affirm her *own* embodied humanity in virtue of her apprehension and recognition of *his*. Miranda's recognition of her own body as human—as of her own "sex" as "woman" (3.1.49)—is thereby bound up with her extension of a similar recognition to others.[10] We might even derive from this—somewhat adventurously and provisionally—an axiomatic theory of recognition. By recognizing in others whom we encounter a bodily existence and "such senses as we have," we establish and affirm the sociality of an embodied "we" that facilitates and sustains inheritable modes of *socially* recognizing bodily life forms (as "human," "goodly," a "man").

There is a catch, however. Such "mutual" recognition is not symmetrical nor even necessarily reciprocal. For it is also conditioned by the fact that acts of bodily recognition occur between relative (or even absolute) newcomers and those who encounter these newcomers on their arrival. The incarnate creatures that populate the world stage are not all dropped there at the same time, after all. Some were born before others; some have been around a while. Prior to her encounter with Ferdinand, Miranda had seen no other embodied being except Prospero and Caliban. Likewise Caliban, having seen only Prospero, Miranda, and Sycorax, does not know how to recognize Trinculo and Stephano (like Miranda, he initially takes them for "spirits"). By contrast, Ferdinand, having "eye'd" "full many a lady" (3.1.40, 39), encounters Miranda in light of those prior visual encounters. Prospero, we can presume, has seen them all before.

With this in mind, let us gingerly expand our axiomatic theory of recognition, before taking a closer look at Caliban.

The conditions under which an embodied newcomer is "recognized" as "one of us" in a socially inheritable way—as, say, human, male, female, androgynous, ethnically distinct, tall, short, sensate, or alive—are invariably characterized by the fact that one of the parties is always, so to speak, "newer" to the world stage than the other. We might even venture to point out that this is because embodied beings capable of recognizing and being recognized are *born*—hence born *of*, and *to*, someone else who precedes them. Moreover, this connection between embodied being and natality presumes a constitutive horizon in which newcomers encroach on existing networks of relations that have no determinable limit—since such networks are themselves constituted and renewed by the very arrival of each newcomer.

One last corollary to this might be the following. It obviously is possible for an embodied being to recognize, or to be recognized by, another bodily creature in such and such a socially inherited way (as a human being, for instance) *for the very first time.* Inasmuch as we have a social life at all, each of us, at some point in our lives, begins to recognize—and to be recognized by—others in socially inheritable ways. But such "first times" are conditioned by the fact that they presuppose a preexisting plurality of others for whom such "first times" have already occurred. Social forms of recognition, which turn a plurality of "born" creatures into some socially inheritable form of life (a family, a people, a race, or humanity itself), presuppose not only the preexistence of other "born" creatures of varying shapes and sizes but also an indeterminable number of prior acts of social recognition.

Because our ritualized, codified acts of recognition are the manner in which inheritable, social conditions for living of various kinds—family units, ethnic groups, the "human race"—are transmitted from one generation to the next, our inherited modes of recognizing other embodied beings are always preceded and conditioned by other—prior—acts of recognition.

This is, again, why the very criteria for recognizing each new arrival are continually revised and reinstituted with each new appearance.

~

With this in mind, let us envision an extreme situation. Let us suppose that the conditions of generational devolution—and, therefore, of inherited modes of social and bodily recognition—come to a halt. Suppose that, correspondent to such a predicament, one were to find oneself expelled from the social world into which one was born—forcibly banished or exiled from all human company, bereft of all prior social bonds and familial ties. Now, if were one to be cast out alone—sent away, for instance, to a life of solitude on a deserted island—then social and bodily "recognition" would cease to be a problem, for there would be no one to recognize or be recognized by. To make matters more dramatic, then, let us suppose instead that one were to be similarly banished to that same island—but this time in the company of another castaway, although not a castaway who was a contemporary or prior acquaintance. Let us suppose that one were cast out alongside an absolute newcomer, an infant "not / out three years old" (1.2.40–41)—an embodied being who has yet to recognize herself, or any another embodied being, in any socially inherited or formal manner.

> . . . and, i' th' dead of darkness,
> The ministers for th' purpose hurried thence
> Me and thy crying self. (1.2.130–32)

Such are the circumstance under which the banished Prospero "cares" for Miranda.

If our provisional theory of bodily recognition is at all plausible, then we might understand these circumstances as providing Prospero the chance to fully circumscribe or determine the conditions under which Miranda will socially recognize all the embodied beings she comes to encounter.[11] He will be able to craft and determine the conditions under which she encounters others for the first time, framing the very way in which she apprehends them as bodily creatures—and thereby anticipating the socially inheritable ways in which she might recognize others and bind herself to them.[12] What is perhaps a structural feature in scenes of parent-infant recognition is, so to speak, distilled and radicalized in this context.

In this way, Prospero acquires nothing less than the sovereign power to fully determine the social life that his daughter will inherit—he selects the embodied beings to whom she shall be bound as well as the formal modes of recognition that will do the work of binding. Hence, he presents to her eyes the vision of Ferdinand, framing his appearance as human, endorsing their engagement and wedding. Likewise, Miranda's bodily recognition of the other shipwrecked men unfolds as the success with which Prospero is able to make social life "new" to Miranda. Prospero is able to do this, under the circumstances of his exile on the island, moreover, without regard for the sociality of which he himself had been the inheritor. Rather than expose her to the contingency of the world stage—with its unpredictable newcomers and unforeseen bodily encounters, along with its culturally inherited modes of recognition—Prospero raises the curtain for Miranda on a theater within whose confines he can circumscribe not only which bodily creatures she will see but also the conditions under she will recognize, and be recognized by, them. This "brave new world" is not a horizon of born creatures that Miranda encounters, as it were, in contingent and unpredictable ways; it is, rather, produced by Prospero's "art."

"Art" or sovereign acts of creation thus come to appear as an essential moment in the "natural" devolution of generations. Indeed, Prospero is able to accomplish the most realized form of patrimonial bequeathal we have yet encountered. He creates for Miranda the very conditions of an inheritable social world without depending on the natural fact of natality in order to accomplish this inheritance. For, although he obviously does not literally give birth to the men she encounters, he fully determines the conditions under which they will "appear" bodily to her and be socially recognized by her. Prospero fashions a "brave new world" that is, indeed, "new" to Miranda.

There remains only one "given" that unsettles the framing of Prospero's "art" in this regard: Caliban.

{7}

This is a strange thing as e'er I look'd on. (5.1.289)

Caliban is native to the island, a "freckled whelp hag-born" that the witch Sycorax "did litter here" (1.2.283, 282). As the island's sole embodied inhabitant "honour'd with / A human shape" (1.2.283–84), Caliban appears as the inheritor of the territory by matrilineal descent. "This island's mine, by Sycorax my mother," Caliban tells Prospero, "[w]hich thou tak'st from me" (1.2.333–34).

Although Caliban's claim to ownership is instituted retrospectively, in virtue of Prospero's expropriation of territory, it is nevertheless clear—

prior to any question of property rights—that Caliban, as an indigenous presence, constitutes the only embodied life form whose appearance and whose deeds Prospero is unable to fully choreograph.[13] Whereas the embodied appearances of the shipwreck's survivors are circumscribed for Miranda by means of Prospero's art, Prospero cannot compose or design Caliban's appearance for Miranda. ("'Tis a villain, sir, / I do not love to look on," says Miranda [1.2.311–12].) The sheer fact of Caliban's bodily life, formed by maternal birth, imposes a limit—a natural given, or a claim for nature's insuperability—with which Prospero must contend. ("A devil, a born devil, on whose nature / Nurture can never stick" [4.1.188–89].) Likewise, inasmuch as Caliban's laboring body furnishes the material conditions of Prospero's and Miranda's existence, he appears to them as a necessary condition for their own bodily survival—reminders, as it were, of nature's claims on them. ("[A]s 'tis, / We cannot miss him: he does make our fire, / Fetch our wood, and serves in offices / That profit us" [1.2.312–15].)

So, Prospero encounters Caliban as a natural given, a necessity with which he must contend if he is to manage the claims of nature at all. And it is worth remembering that Prospero never contemplates the destruction of Caliban—he does not, and perhaps cannot, imagine "doing away with him" or "doing without him."

Perceiving Caliban as an embodied being endowed with a "human shape," Prospero appears to have initially offered Caliban socially inheritable rights pursuant to this bodily recognition. We are told, for instance, that Prospero treated Caliban with "human care" and "lodg'd" him in Prospero's own cell (1.2.348). Moreover, Miranda and Prospero "took pains" to "make" Caliban speak and taught him "each hour / One thing or other" (1.2.356–57). So far, so good, we might say. The perception of a naturally born "human shape" appears to have borne with it the bestowal of concomitant "social rights" to shared housing, nourishment, "human care," and education.[14] Indeed, we might conclude that *because* Caliban was perceived by Prospero to be endowed with a "human shape," Prospero extended to him "human care," tenderness, and affection. ("[T]hou strok'st me, and made much of me" [1.2.334].)

So, what goes wrong between them?

Caliban "seek[s] to violate" Miranda's "honor" (1.2.349–50). Prospero "prevent[s]" (1.2.352) him. Although it remains unclear precisely at what point, Prospero intervened in the course of the sought violation. Whether only Miranda's "honor" was preserved (inasmuch as she was not impregnated) is not specified, but there is little doubt regarding Caliban's desire.

> O ho, O ho! would't had been done!
> Thou didst prevent me; I had peopled else
> This isle with Calibans. (1.2.351–53)

What resists reformation in Caliban, and maybe in us all, and hence what makes us monstrous is desire. It is the autonomy of Caliban's desire that Prospero cannot abide and which he and Miranda curse. ("Abhorred slave, / Which any print of goodness wilt not take, / Being capable of all ill!" [1.2.353–55]; or, again, "A devil, a born devil, on whose nature / Nurture can never stick; on whom my pains, / Humanely taken, all, all lost, quite lost" [4.1.188–90].)

We might say that it is desire as such—as innate, natural impulse or conatus—that Prospero curses. Inasmuch as desire is resistant to reformation, to Prospero's "art," it marks a limit of his sovereign power. Inasmuch as Caliban's desire represents a "natural" impulse, something over which even Caliban himself does not have control, it represents an intrusive claim of nature on social life. Inasmuch as desire is unreformable—neither regretted nor ceded ("would't had been done!")—it cannot be simply tamed nor eliminated.

However, it would probably be more correct still to say not that Prospero cannot abide desire as such (which would also mean not abiding his own desire) but that Prospero cannot abide desire as it appears in the person of Caliban. He cannot abide *Caliban's* desire. Most obviously because it stands opposed to Prospero's own desire. And, therefore, he cannot abide Caliban or be reconciled with him. At best, he can acknowledge the fact of Caliban, which is where he ends up: "[T]his thing of darkness I / Acknowledge mine" (5.1.275–76).

We might say that Prospero thereby reduces Caliban to the *fact* of Caliban's desire. He comes to see the human being, Caliban, as nothing more than a necessity, a dark thing to be acknowledged *of necessity*, as a claim of nature, a foreclosure of freedom. This, I think, is how we might begin to understand Caliban's enslavement.

Because Caliban's enslavement is indefinite (in contrast to Ariel's servitude) and because Caliban is repeatedly characterized as unreformable by nature, we can see Caliban's enslavement as the only social form of recognition available to the "fact of Caliban" (the fact of his desire, of nature's claims on him and on Prospero and Miranda, of their bodily necessities). Slavery *is* the way that he is acknowledged; his enslavement is the way those "facts" get admitted.

The particular awfulness of Caliban's slavery, moreover, lies in this: because it follows from an acknowledgment of *him* as a fact of life, as desire, as natural necessity, it forecloses for Caliban any *other* form of social (or loving) recognition besides that of a slave. *He is reduced to his natural givenness, to a mere fact of life.*

Caliban is not only forced to perform slavishly—by laboring to provide for the material conditions of the master's life. The "fact of enslavement" also attaches itself to Caliban's very being, even determining the manner in which his singular body itself will be perceived by others—as "filth" (1.2.348), "a thing most brutish" (1.2.359), part of a "vile race" (1.2.360), "hag-seed" (1.2.367), "a born devil" (4.1.188), a "tortoise" (1.2.318), a "monster" (2.2.31).

~

It remains unclear whether Caliban's enslavement precipitates changes in others' perception of his bodily life. Is the debased perception of Caliban's bodily life—the fact that he appears to some like a "fish" or a "tortoise"—the practical upshot of his enslavement?

So far as I can see, this ambiguity cannot be cleared up by reference to a clear perception of Caliban's body that neatly precedes his enslavement—given the point in time at which the play opens. After all, once Caliban is enslaved and forced to labor and sleep outdoors, his body itself is bound to appear to others differently.

Consequently, Prospero's mistreatment of Caliban cannot be straightforwardly contested by another who, stumbling on the scene, might challenge Prospero by demanding, *how can you treat this man this way? Can you not see that he, like you and I, is endowed with eyes, hands, organs, dimensions, senses, affections, passions?* For any such reference to bodily life as the given, final ground of social rights and recognition only begs the prior question of how social recognition is bound up with the perception of embodiment. Just as the initial perception of a bodily life determines the form of social life available to that creature, so, too, bodily life is in turn shaped by the concrete conditions of the social existence available to that body.

Indeed, matters are made more complex still when we consider that Caliban's body—like that of all embodied beings—is aging ("with age his body uglier grows" [4.1.191]), is subject to illness and pains and injuries, and therefore is itself in constant deformation. Caliban's maltreatment at Prospero's hands results in further deformations—(he is whipped [1.2.347] and side stitched and racked with cramps [1.2.327])—whose distinction from natural birth defects is increasingly imperceptible. (When Trinculo, stumbling upon the prostrate Caliban, initially mistakes him for a "fish," he corrects himself by attributing his malformation to injury: "[T]his is no fish, but an islander, that hath lately suffered by a thunderbolt" [2.2.36–37].) "He is," Prospero concludes, "as disproportion'd in his manners / As in his shape" (5.1.290–91).

If social recognition is bound up with the perception of a bodily life but at the same time bodily life is deformed or transformed by the social conditions under which bodies are constrained to live—adversity, abuse, toil, and so forth—then is there any way to neatly separate bodily recognition from social recognition, such that the one could be said to function as the precondition of the other?

~

Our inherited ways of socially recognizing bodily creatures—as human, animal, gendered, or ethnically distinct—are not only ways in which we name whatever being we see before us. Because, as we have seen, our acts of social recognition are subject to revision in the face of each new bodily appearance we encounter, it might be more accurate to understand such "names"—human, animal, woman, Caucasian—as marking nothing more than our perception of a natural born creature with a given "form" whose bodily life and social existence are, however, open to radical transformation or deformation.

If bodily life forms are, to varying degrees, continually transformed by the ways in which they are socially recognized, and if, at the same time, social recognition is bound up with how one's embodied being is phenomenally apprehended, then perhaps we might regard forms of social recognition both as heralding and tracking ongoing modifications in the very ways in which we apprehend embodied life and as initiating metamorphoses in the bodily lives of individuals or entire species.

We might go one step further by suggesting that our inherited modes of socially recognizing embodied life—human, animal, male, female— portend and imply the transformation and deformation of natural bodily life forms in ways that are both natural, such as through aging, and nonnatural, such as through injury and surgery.

At the same time, our inherited modes of socially recognizing embodied life continue to presuppose, at some level, a rigorous difference between natural deformations—such as those wrought by aging or those that are naturally occurring—and nonnatural bodily deformations, such as might occur as a result of injury, abuse, or surgical intervention. Indeed—leaving aside the question of whether nonnatural deformations are accidentally or intentionally incurred. (is such a question ever decidable?)—it is important to note that *some* discretion between natural bodily deformation and nonnatural bodily deformation informs, at a profound level, all of our inherited modes of social recognition.

There are many reasons for this—belonging characteristically to our different ways of making social sense of bodily life, starting with medicine, health care, and other welfare activities. The line separating natural from nonnatural bodily deformation can be, and is, drawn differently in various contexts, and by diverse ethical discourses—hospitals, child welfare programs, prisons, and so forth. Without stopping to consider these in detail, I wish simply to suggest that it becomes *ethically impossible to distinguish the doing of harm from the provision of care in the absence of some assumed difference between natural and nonnatural bodily deformation.*[15]

The potential to tell—in our bodily perception of other embodied creatures—*whether or not bodily harm has been done* constitutes the very presumption on which inheritable forms of social rights and recognition rest. But because this potential rests on the distinction of natural from nonnatural modifications to bodily life, our socially inherited modes of recognizing bodily creatures—as human, animal, man, woman—can be troubled whenever nonnatural bodily deformation can be confused with natural bodily deformation.

"This is a strange thing as e'er I look'd on," declares Alonso on seeing Caliban for the first time (5.1.289–90). If inherited forms of social recognition are confounded by our perception of the embodied beings we see before us—routinely, but sometimes with astonishing visceral force—then how might we do other than acknowledge such embodiment as "natural facts" (or things of darkness) and come to recognize them as belonging to us in nonnatural ways as well?

How can we recognize one another anew while also acknowledging the "facts" of nature that we embody, and thereby perhaps better care for and about one another as natural creatures?

{8}

. . . all thy vexations
Were but trials of thy love, and thou
Hast strangely stood the test . . . (4.1.5–7)

The last scene of *The Tempest* compels us to reflect upon the possible recovery of a socially inheritable world, the renewal and rebirth of social ties, in the wake of exile, dispossession, and disinheritance.

It has appeared to many students of the play as though this recovery of the social world is the final aim of Prospero's "art" and the fullest accomplishment of his "project." Indeed, it is in light of this possible recovery that we are asked to understand the torments he has carried out.

Strikingly, Prospero challenges us to regard his torment of those who had trespassed against him as having created the conditions under which he might now pardon and forgive them—restoring to all not only their bodily life and psychic orientation, but also a collective future in the shared world of Milan and Naples, along with the return of his dukedom.

We are asked nothing less than to regard acts of torture as sharing the conditions—artificially produced by a unilateral sovereign power—under which forgiveness and reconciliation might occur.

How are we to understand this proximity between torment and forgiveness?

⁓

Because Prospero casts his final acts in the play as an alternative to revenge ("the rarer action is / In virtue than in vengeance" [5.1.27–28]), we might begin by approaching the play's final scene as a further reflection—already underway in *Hamlet* and *King Lear*—on possible ethical responses to transgressions other than the taking of revenge.

Chief among such responses are forgiveness and punishment. At a glance, therefore, we might assume that the "afflictions" (5.1.22) Prospero has performed on others are acts of punishment, undertaken in order to make possible forgiveness.

"Punishment," according to Hannah Arendt, is "the alternative to forgiveness." But, she continues, it is "by no means its opposite."[16] By indicating that punishment is not the "opposite" of forgiveness, Arendt means to suggest that punishment and forgiveness "have in common" the fact "that they attempt to put an end to something that without interference could go on endlessly."[17] Inasmuch as punishment is not collapsed into revenge, it shares with forgiveness the ability "to undo" what has been done by no longer identifying the doer with that past deed. If punishment is anything other than vengeance, we might say, then this is because punishment accomplishes the same end as forgiveness; namely, releasing doers from past deeds, such that "*what* was done is forgiven for the sake of *who* did it."[18]

But if punishment accomplishes the same end as forgiveness, how are we to distinguish acts of forgiveness from acts of punishment? If one cannot punish without also forgiving—lest the punishment collapse into revenge—can one forgive without punishing?

Arendt seems to suggest that, although punishment and forgiveness are not opposed to one another, they are nevertheless alternatives. And in the next sentence she explains: "Men are unable to forgive what they cannot punish."[19] Acts of forgiveness entail the capacity to punish but not necessarily the actual punishment. To forgive without punishing, we might now add to Arendt's thought, is to withhold a punishment that one could have inflicted, thereby accomplishing all at once what the punishment would accomplish only over the course of the penalty. Moreover, because punishment involves some further suffering or penance on the part of the transgressor, the transgressor is given a part to play in the detachment of his misdeed from himself.

By contrast, forgiveness is an act performed by the forgiver for the sake of the transgressor—on the latter's behalf, as it were—in order that the transgressor need do nothing more in order to release himself from his past deeds. In this way, forgiveness reveals itself as more "sovereign" than punishment in that its accomplishment depends on no one but the one doing the forgiving. Hence the historical-political connection between sovereignty and the power to pardon.

This does not mean that one must already have sovereign or divine power in order to pardon. But it does indicate, so to speak, the extent to which acts of forgiveness—insofar as they are nonpunishing—imply that the event of being forgiven is detached from any deed, activity, or agency proper to the one who is forgiven. And it therefore manifests the unilateral, quasi-divine power the forgiver holds.

To forgive another without punishing—without having to punish— implies the demonstration of a sovereign capacity to radically transform, undo, or remake another's social and ethical ties to others, independent of the wills, desires, actions, consent, or opposition of others. To forgive without punishing is to dissolve the worth and inheritability of all prior social bonds between the one forgiving and the one forgiven and to remake those bonds under conditions brought into being by the forgiver alone.[20]

In this way, the proximity of forgiveness to torment becomes clearer. Indeed, precisely where punishment (as nonavenging) would distinguish itself by returning to the one punished the chance to release *himself* from his misdeeds—forgiveness torments by divorcing the event of being forgiven from any activity proper to the one who is forgiven.

To forgive another, without punishing them, is to lay bare that person's helplessness to prevent, avenge, undo, or oppose what is being done to her.

Prospero's forgiveness of those who trespassed against him is thus the fullest realization of his torment of them. Forgiveness occurs not when the torment ceases; rather, forgiveness appears as the *accomplishment* of what Prospero has put them through. Forgiveness is in fact enacted precisely as Prospero's torment of others reaches its height, as if the pardon were its climatic moment. Thus, Prospero finally confronts his usurping brother, who stands "spell-stopp'd," unable to move or to speak, and in fact unable to distinguish what is being done to him from torment:

> Thou art pinch'd for 't now. . . . Flesh and blood,
> You, brother mine, that entertain'd ambition,
> Expell'd remorse and nature; whom, with Sebastian—
> Whose inward pinches therefor are most strong,—
> . . . I do forgive thee. (5.1.74–78)

{9}

. . . my ending is despair,
Unless I be reliev'd by prayer,
Which pierces so, that it assaults
Mercy itself . . . (epilogue, 15–18)

Can tormenting be forgiven, if forgiveness is itself a form of torment?

What "prayer" might assault mercy itself? By whom—what power, what god, what art—could Prospero himself be punished, or forgiven? To free ourselves from Prospero, would we not stand in need of a new Prospero? The viciousness of the ethical circle is not difficult to grasp.

So long as it is a "god" that stands before us—so long as we confront a supreme artist or demiurge, one who can force us to undergo formative experiences and events over which we have no control, and thereby turn "art" into historical fate—we ourselves cannot undergo self-induced transformations in our lives together nor recognize ourselves anew *in* a history in which necessity and freedom intertwine.

~

Several moments still seem to be required. First, the "god" must risk appearing otherwise than as a god. It is not (yet) a matter of the god's disappearance, pure and simple, but rather of a risk that the god would take—namely, to appear as otherwise than as a god. Certain trappings would have to be jettisoned.

> . . . I'll break my staff,
> Bury it certain fadoms in the earth,
> And deeper than did ever plummet sound
> I'll drown my book. (5.1.54–57)

This is not only a matter of trading one guise for another, nor is it merely that the "god" is undergoing a shift within himself. Rather, and this is the second requirement, it must be seen that the risk he has taken, in appearing otherwise than as a god, *also* means that the way things stand for others, too, changes. It would not be enough for the god to appear as otherwise than god if everyone persisted in their assumption or belief or stupor—if everyone were still held, as it were, by the enduring effects of the god's spell. The spell also must dissolve—so that we, too, might see how things between us really stand now.

> . . . The charm dissolves apace;
> And as the morning steals upon the night,
> Melting the darkness, so their rising senses
> Begin to chase the ignorant fumes that mantle
> Their clearer reason. . . . (5.1.64–68)

Third, to truly risk appearing to others as otherwise than a "god' "— if it is to be a risk and not merely a further demonstration of autonomous artistry—requires the recognition that letting go of art (if it is a real "letting go") cannot itself be artfully accomplished.

To appear as otherwise than a god therefore could not be accomplished by a god—lest that "appearance" be taken for another demonstration of godliness. Only a human being could appear as otherwise than as a god.

And so, finally, a human being stands forth—stepping away from the "art" he made and from what that art itself wrought.

> *Now my charms are all o'erthrown,*
> *And what strength I have's mine own*
> *Which is most faint . . .* (epilogue, 1–3)

But even at this point, another moment is still required. For the human being—claiming no strengths but his own—encounters the limits of autonomy and free invention. He cannot move further on his own. He remains confined by us, bound to us.

> *I must be here confin'd by you*
> *. . . Let me not*
>
> . . . . .
>
> *. . . dwell*
> *In this bare island by your spell;*
> *But release me from my bands*
> *With the help of your good hands[.]* (epilogue, 4–10)

But we ourselves are not yet released from the island. We may have believed that we left Prospero behind; however we find that he has followed us beyond the confines of the "play." Nothing is sacred in the play, it turns out; not even its (artistic) separation from us. We find ourselves implicated; evasion is not to be countenanced.

We are not yet "released" from what has transpired and cannot claim to be. At least, not until we undergo an as yet unscripted, self-induced transformation in our recognition of ourselves and one another.

Introduction: Disinheriting the Globe

1. All citations of Shakespeare come from the *Arden Shakespeare: As You Like It*, edited by Agnes Latham; *Hamlet*, edited by Harold Jenkins; *King Lear*, edited by Kenneth Muir; *The Tempest*, edited by Frank Kermode; *1 Henry IV*, edited by David Scott Kastan; *2 Henry IV*, edited by A. R. Humphreys.

2. Aristotle, *Poetics* 1453b.

3. Amélie Oksenberg Rorty articulates this point very nicely in her essay "The Psychology of Aristotelian Tragedy," in *Essays on Aristotle's "Poetics,"* ed. Amélie Oksenberg Rorty (Princeton: Princeton University Press, 1992): "Just whom do we pity and what do we fear? The tragic hero? Ourselves? Humanity? All three, and all three in one. . . . Since we are also essentially social and political beings, connected to others by civic *philia*, we treat the welfare of our friends and family as essential to our own welfare. Our *philoi* form a series of expanding circles starting from the closest family and friends, to partners in a common civic project (*koinonia*), and to those who—like members of the human species—share a common form of life" (13).

4. G. W. F. Hegel, *Phenomenology of Spirit*, trans. A. V. Miller (Oxford: Oxford University Press, 1977), 284, par. 470.

5. A. C. Bradley, *Shakespearean Tragedy* (New York: Penguin, 1991), 38.

6. For Aristotle, this refinement is, significantly, made manifest in the *katharsis* that tragic plot structures cannot fail to elicit: "The plot [of a tragedy] should be so structured that, even without seeing it performed, the person who hears the events that occur experiences horror and pity at what comes about" (Aristotle, *Poetics* 1453b1–4, trans. Stephen Halliwell, in *Aristotle: "Poetics"; Longinus: "On the Sublime"; Demetrius: "On Style"* [Cambridge, MA: Harvard University Press, 1995], 73).

7. Aristotle makes clear that the work of the tragic poet differs from that of the historian in precisely this way: "The difference between [the historian and the poet] is this: that the one relates actual events, the other the kinds of things that might occur." In this way, tragedy deals with the potentiality—and not just the actuality—of human actions and their consequences, and is therefore "nobler"

and more "philosophical" than historical writing (Aristotle, *Poetics* 1451b4–7, 59).

8. Hegel, *Phenomenology of Spirit*, 283, par. 468.

9. Aristotle, *Poetics* 1452a3–4, 63. For a very illuminating account of the abiding importance of Aristotelian *mythos*—or the "poetics of tragedy"—for the "dialectic" of the tragic that emerges in German philosophy, especially in the work of Hegel, see Peter Szondi's invaluable *An Essay on the Tragic*, trans. Paul Fleming (Stanford: Stanford University Press, 2002), 56 and passim.

10. Hegel, *Phenomenology of Spirit*, 282, par. 468.

11. This is obviously not to say that the terms proposed by Aristotle or Hegel for thinking about tragedy are of no use for thinking about Shakespeare; we clearly need all the analytical categories at our disposal to make sense of the experiences and actions portrayed in the plays. But I do want to suggest that our inherited categories for thinking about dramatic representation—plot, *katharsis*, experience, suffering, insight, reversal, recognition, and so forth—encounter a certain limit in Shakespeare's work (and, of course, in other works, too) and that therefore Shakespearean drama becomes an indispensable point of reference for thinking about our shared activities and forms of sociality beyond the philosophy and poetics of tragedy from Aristotle to Hegel and his school.

12. Hegel, *Phenomenology of Spirit*, 282, par. 468.

13. A concise history of the reception of the *Poetics* in neoclassical writings can be found in Stephen Halliwell, *Aristotle's "Poetics"* (Chicago: University of Chicago Press, 1998), 286–323.

14. Johann Gottfried Herder, "Shakespeare," in *German Aesthetic and Literary Criticism: Winckelmann, Lessing, Hamann, Herder, Schiller, Goethe*, ed. H. B. Nisbet (Cambridge: Cambridge University Press, 1985). For more on Herder and on philosophical interpretations of Shakespearean drama in general, see *Philosophers on Shakespeare*, ed. Paul A. Kottman (Stanford: Stanford University Press, 2009).

15. Herder, *Shakespeare*, 162. This is not to say that Herder managed to close the debate. Whether, or how, Shakespeare conformed to an Aristotelian unity of time and place continued to be an important point of contention well into the next century, among, for example, writers such as Stendhal and Alessandro Manzoni.

16. Herder, *Shakespeare*, 175.

17. This is not the place to expand on Shakespeare's place in baroque aesthetics. I simply wish to point out the extent to which non-neoclassical accounts of art—culminating with the writings of German idealist philosophy toward the end of the eighteenth century—took shape in large measure as a response to artistic practices and categories for which inherited philosophical or poetic concepts

could not account. Shakespeare's role in this is well worth considering; I have tried to offer my own discussion of this in my introduction to *Philosophers on Shakespeare*. An excellent bibliography on aesthetics in romantic German philosophy, including works that take up the relation of that philosophy to neoclassicism, can be found in *Classic and Romantic German Aesthetics*, ed. J. M. Bernstein (Cambridge: Cambridge University Press, 2003), xxxvi–xxxix. For the reader of Italian, an admirably clear overview of neoclassical debates and baroque aesthetics can be found in Jon R. Snyder, *L'estetica del Barocco* (Bologna: Il Mulino, 2005).

18. In stating my contention in this way, I realize that I run the many risks inherent in offering any blanket statement about Shakespeare's drama as a body of work. But, as I have just intimated, I do not even think that a "poetics" of Shakespeare's work is achievable. Likewise, in using the phrase "mature drama" I do not mean to attach excessive argumentative weight to the chronological development of Shakespeare's work, nor do I wish to stake my claims on a neat division of "early" from "mature" works; although I do regard the questions I raise as being posed with increasing intensity and insistence in Shakespeare's later works.

19. One could, I think, expand this list to include characters from plays I do not treat, such as Timon in *Timon of Athens*, Helena and Bertram from *All's Well That Ends Well*, Iago, or Macbeth.

20. By "ethical response" I mean to say some ulterior word or deed that reacts to the transgression. I am leaving out of consideration here other ways of understanding the psychic aftermath of an act of betrayal or transgression—such as, for example, the resentment that a victim might feel or the guilt that the criminal might suffer, regardless of whether or not any retribution for the criminal's deed comes to pass. Although I do not discuss these questions here, it is worth noting that Shakespeare represents such "guilt" in *Richard III*, for instance, when Richard is haunted in his dreams by the ghosts of those he has murdered. ("Soft, I did but dream / O coward conscience, how thou dost afflict me" [5.3.178–79].) Or, again, when Macbeth apprehends the ghost of Banquo—in a scene read by the young Hegel as follows: "The trespasser intended to have to do [away] with another's life, but he has only destroyed his own, for his life is not different from life. . . . In his arrogance he has destroyed indeed, but only the friendliness of life; he has perverted life into an enemy" ("The Spirit of Christianity and Its Fate," in G. W. F. Hegel, *On Christianity: Early Theological Writings*, trans. T. M. Knox [New York: Harper and Row, 1961], 229–30). This same predicament is explored in two films by Woody Allen—in *Crimes and Misdemeanors* and *Match Point*—in which the protagonist suffers a kind of "Shakespearean" guilt or destruction of the "friendliness of life" even as he gets away with murder.

21. Lukács's remarks—roughly contemporary with A. C. Bradley's more

elaborated lectures on the centrality of "character" in Shakespeare—can be fruitfully read alongside those lectures. See Georg Lukács, "Shakespeare and Modern Drama," trans. Arpad Adarky, in *The Lukács Reader*, ed. Arpad Adarky (Oxford, UK: Blackwell, 1995), 70–81. For more on Lukács's critique of the interpretation of Shakespearean tragedy as historical necessity, see my remarks about writings on Shakespeare by Walter Benjamin, Carl Schmitt, Georg Lukács, and Agnes Heller in my introduction to *Philosophers on Shakespeare*.

22. Of course, one of the great dramatic tensions in *1* and *2 Henry IV* concerns the force of Hal's own investment in the monarchy; for it is not clear in Shakespeare's drama, finally, whether Hal takes up the crown for what it might offer *him* (that is, out of personal ambition or desire) or for the sake of the monarchy's and his family's endurance as jointly a social organization capable of inheriting and bequeathing something of worldly value. However, inasmuch as this tension remains unresolved—precisely because Hal is, unlike Edmund or Richard of Gloucester, the sole clear and unquestionable heir to the throne—I am presuming that it is correct to see Hal's betrayal of Falstaff as performed for something more than sheer personal gain. For we know that Hal's ascension—his own "feelings" about it aside—will not only bring his own prosperity but his family's and his kingdom's as well. Henry V is, after all, a national hero, the victor of Agincourt.

23. To be sure, Falstaff's disregard for honorable duty hardly precludes him from desiring the prerogatives and privileges that fall on those invested with nobility. Falstaff, like many of us, would be perfectly happy to receive wealth without having to generate any. As a means to prosperity or gain, "honor" has as much instrumental value for the plebian Falstaff as for any practiced courtier.

24. "The pretensions of universal essentiality are uncovered in the self," writes Hegel. "It shows itself to be entangled in an actual existence, and drops the mask just because it wants to be something genuine" (*Phenomenology of Spirit*, 450, par. 744).

25. More generally, this truism appears in the notion that Shakespeare's drama both implies and instantiates a representational divide between art and life, play and reality. This truism continues to inform our general understanding of Shakespeare's work—both in academia and in the playhouse—inasmuch as it is routinely supposed, for example, that the plays have a quasi-universal significance that is not really limited by, and indeed makes possible, individual concrete interpretations and performances.

26. At the end of the day, how else is an actor's "worth" to be gauged? The self-defeating claims of an absolute mimesis are, after all, clear enough. For were an actor to really achieve a full disappearance of herself in each role that she played—appearing to us wholly as someone else, with every new role (were this

even possible)—then this "achievement" would come at a precise cost: namely, we would no longer be able to recognize *her* at all.

27. Hegel, *Phenomenology of Spirit*, 450, par. 742 and par. 744.

28. Cf. Harold Bloom, *Shakespeare: The Invention of the Human* (New York: Riverhead, 1998). That Hegel regards this movement as a moment of atheism is made clear when he writes that "the individual self is the negative power through which and in which the gods, as also their moments[,] . . . vanish" (*Phenomenology of Spirit*, 452, par. 747). For Bloom, too, Shakespeare's characters are such individual selves; but Bloom places Shakespeare as a "god" above the selves he invents for having "invented" them.

29. The other side of the coin, with respect to the deification of Shakespeare, is of course the unique and remarkable obsession with Shakespeare the *mere man*—and the concrete conditions of his existence—among biographers and historians. The proliferation of Shakespeare biographies and materialist studies of Shakespeare's life and times should not however be understood as the "opposite" of Bloom's deification of Shakespeare; on the contrary, materialist claims are symptomatic of—and imply—the same insistent separation of the concrete-material from the abstract, of actual self from universal value, albeit from the reverse side of the coin.

So far as I am aware, only one "biography" of Shakespeare manages to both address and collapse this separation. I am referring to Jorge Luis Borges's "Everything and Nothing," which concludes: "History adds that before or after his death [Shakespeare] found himself facing God and said: *I, who have been so many men in vain, want to be one man, myself alone.* From out of a whirlwind the voice of God replied: *I am not, either. I dreamed the world the way you dreamed your work, my Shakespeare: one of the forms of my dream was you, who, like me, are many and no one*" (in *Shakespeare's Other Lives: An Anthology of Fictional Depictions of the Bard,* ed. Maurice O'Sullivan [Jefferson, NC: McFarland, 1997], 203).

30. Harold Bloom, *Hamlet: Poem Unlimited* (New York: Riverhead, 2003), 2.

31. Hegel, *Phenomenology of Spirit*, 452, par. 747.

32. Is it because Shakespeare himself unfolds new forms of tragic expression, *Hamlet* and *King Lear,* in the wake of earlier comic structures? No, not only for that reason; indeed, the reification of "Shakespeare" into a body of work—a poetic corpus or new divinity—is symptomatic of the very gap between representational form and concrete individuals that was to have been closed by Aristophanes. Do we not resurrect the gods and masks and reinstate the separation of art from actualized lives by speaking of Shakespearean "tragedy" solely in poetic terms?

Chapter One: On As You Like It

1. This presumption informs even the most recent treatments of the play. In her book *Shakespeare's Drama of Exile* (London: Palgrave, 2004), for instance, Jane Kingsley Smith argues that both *As You Like It* and *King Lear* are shaped by "pastoral conventions" whose "classical consolations are invoked to assuage" the "anxiety of shared exile" depicted in the plays (106).

2. Jan Kott, *Shakespeare Our Contemporary,* trans. Boleslaw Taborski (New York: Anchor Books, 1964).

3. W. H. Auden, *The Dyer's Hand* (New York: Vintage, 1988), 520.

4. G. W. F. Hegel, *Aesthetics: Lectures on Fine Art,* 2 vols., trans. T. M. Knox (Oxford: Clarendon Press, 1998), 2:1161.

5. Similarly, Duke Senior and Jaques fail to agree on any meaningful response to—or any appropriate lamentation or grief for—the claims of nature on life in the forest or at court whether they take the form of the slaughter of forest animals or the spread of sexually transmitted disease. See 2.2.20–70; 2.7.58–70.

6. Hannah Arendt, *The Origins of Totalitarianism* (New York: Meridian, 1958), 277.

7. See Arendt's remarks on this principle in *The Origins of Totalitarianism,* 280.

8. "[I]t was . . . bequeathed me by will but poor a thousand crowns and, as thou sayst, charged my brother on his blessing to breed me well" (1.1.1–4).

9. We shall have occasion to reflect on this further when we turn to Caliban in the last chapter, on *The Tempest.*

10. In order for there to be "universal rights," the very conditions under which both those "rights" and that "universality" would make any sense would, themselves, have to become universal. "Nature" can, of course, appear a likely name for such "conditions"—insofar as human beings might be understood, say, to share certain anthropological features. Hence, our notion of "rights" as rooted in the fact of "all men being created equal" or naturally endowed with certain common characteristics. However, the problem remains: what nonnatural account of our shared nature is required in order for the bestowal of rights to seem inalienable? Particularly insofar as those worldly "rights" only acquire meaning through their being protected and bestowed.

11. I take it for granted that Orlando's father's "will" is not binding in a realm where brothers can banish brothers or usurp their positions.

12. As Oliver had envied Orlando's natural gifts, so, too, Duke Frederick suspects that Rosalind's innate attractiveness mars the fortunes of his own daughter. "[S]he robs thee of thy name," he tells Celia, "and thou wilt show more bright and seem more virtuous / When she is gone" (1.3.76–78).

13. I am reminded of Francisco de Quevedo's picaresque novel *El buscón*, in which the protagonist—like Orlando, denied from the outset any gentlemanly life—fails to find in criminal activity the necessary conditions for a "noble" or inheritable social life.

14. It should be noted that criminality here means more than sheer violence or the transgression of set laws; rather, it is a principle that, to use Arendt's words, was "devised to keep a community of people together who had lost their interest in the common world and felt themselves no longer related and separated by it" (*The Human Condition*, 2nd ed. [Chicago: University of Chicago Press, 1998], 53). Such is the bond between Orlando and Adam, who is now near death and who has followed Orlando "in pure love," in "service sweat for duty, not for meed" (2.7.131, 2.3.58). "[T]hou prun'st a rotten tree, / That cannot so much as a blossom yield, / In lieu of all thy pains and husbandry" (2.4.63–65), says Orlando to Adam at the moment of their exodus, as if to confirm that what binds them together is anything but the assumption of some material, worldly reward. This is why the criminality undertaken by Orlando is not mere violence or "force" but rather the natural outgrowth of the sheer charity Adam has already shown him, a sign of the bond they share.

15. Arendt nicely makes this point in her discussion of charity when she cites Augustine: "Even robbers have between them [inter se] what they call charity." *Caritas*, according to her, was simply Christianity's response to the need to "find a bond strong enough to replace the world" that had been lost with the fall of the Roman Empire (*The Human Condition*, 53).

16. *The Human Condition*, 53.

17. *The Human Condition*, 54.

18. Hence Arendt suggests that the post-Roman Christianity of Augustine offers a "politics" wherein the survival of the world is the last thing to be taken for granted.

19. Jaques's sentimental tears over the deers' "gor'd" haunches seem antiquated, and he is (for this reason, as it were) appropriately mocked

20. It is true that Rosalind ostensibly woos Orlando—or allows Orlando to woo her—while she is disguised as a young man. But there is ample evidence in the play to suggest that Orlando is never fooled. Anyway, there is certainly no plot suspense that hinges on Rosalind's disguise in the way that, say, Viola's disguise matters to the plot of *Twelfth Night*.

21. See, for example, René Girard, "Myth and Ritual in Shakespeare's *A Midsummer Night's Dream*," in *Textual Strategies: Perspectives in Post-Structuralist Criticism*, ed. Josué V. Harari (Ithaca, NY: Cornell University Press, 1979), 189–212; see also Anne Barton's discussion in *The Names of Comedy* (Toronto: Uni-

versity of Toronto Press, 1990), and Edward Barry, *Shakespeare's Comic Rites* (Cambridge: Cambridge University Press, 1984).

22. Such informal marriage ceremonies were not unknown in the period. See Silvana Seidel Menchi and Diego Quaglioni, eds., *Matrimoni in dubbio: Unioni controverse e nozze clandestine in Italia dal XIV al XVIII secolo* (Bologna: Il Mulino, 2001).

23. A good place to start is Jean Howard, "Crossdressing: The Theatre, and Gender Struggle in Early Modern England," *Shakespeare Quarterly* 39, no. 4 (1988): 418–40.

Chapter Two: On Hamlet

1. A. C. Bradley, *Shakespearean Tragedy* (New York: Penguin, 1991), 35; G. W. F. Hegel *Aesthetics: Lectures on Fine Art,* 2 vols., trans. T. M. Knox (Oxford: Clarendon Press, 1998), 2:1229.

2. Hannah Arendt suggests that we should read Hamlet's statement that "the time is out of joint" as his grasping at the stakes of this disinheritance. She does not develop the thought, or her reading of the play, however. See "The Crisis in Education," in *Between Past and Future* (New York: Penguin, 19993), 192–93.

3. For more on this point, allow me to refer the reader to my discussion in my introduction to *Philosophers on Shakespeare,* ed. Paul A. Kottman (Stanford University Press, 2009).

4. Hegel sees in *Hamlet* the tragedy of a new, modern subject that is irrevocably alienated from the world in a manner not at all unlike the Cartesian subject as he reads it. Stanley Cavell has expanded and developed this Hegelian connection into a theory of Shakespearean tragedy as staging the "advent of skepticism." See his *Disowning Knowledge in Seven Plays of Shakespeare* (Cambridge: Cambridge University Press, 2003), 17–18. Hegel's account is to be found in *Aesthetics: Lectures on Fine Art,* 2:1225–33. My friend and colleague Jay Bernstein has usefully suggested to me that it is as if the whole of Hamlet's subjectivity existed in the space between the end of Descartes' First Meditation, where the violence of the evil demon (Claudius, for Hamlet) requires the doubt of everything, and the commencement of the Second Meditation, where Descartes reclaims himself against doubt.

5. Gertrude, in turn, has Hamlet's bed on her mind in her last words at Ophelia's grave: "I hop'd thou shouldst have been my Hamlet's wife / I thought thy bride-bed to have deck'd, sweet maid, / And not have strew'd thy grave" (5.1.237–39).

6. Another way of understanding Gertrude's presence can be found in Janet Adelman's suggestive study of *Hamlet,* which develops and enriches arguments

introduced by Coppélia Kahn and other feminist and psychoanalytic readers of Shakespeare. Adelman argues that Gertrude's determining presence in *Hamlet* marks the "the point of origin of [Shakespeare's] great tragic period." Whereas Shakespeare's histories and romantic comedies had unfolded "without any serious confrontation with the power of female sexuality," *Hamlet* subjects "to maternal presence the relationships previously exempted from that presence" (*Suffocating Mothers: Fantasies of Maternal Origin in Shakespeare's Plays, "Hamlet" to "The Tempest"* [New York: Routledge, 1992], 11).

7. This connection is apparent in various places: in the dumbshow, in which the murderer woos the queen; in the ghost's lament that Claudius "won to his shameful lust / The will of the most seeming-virtuous queen" (1.5.45–46); and in Hamlet's lament that he is left with "a father kill'd, a mother stain'd" (4.4.57). Consider also Hamlet's last words to the dying Claudius as he raises the poisoned chalice to his lips, "Is thy union here? / Follow my mother" (5.2.331–32).

8. As Margreta de Grazia plausibly states the matter: "That a son's feelings for his mother should be sexual may have seemed less transgressive than prudent at a time when endogamous unions were used to keep dynastic power and property intact" (*"Hamlet" without Hamlet* [Cambridge: Cambridge University Press, 2007], 106–7). Likewise, as Lisa Jardine points out, it is not Hamlet's disgust with his mother's sexuality per se that is manifest here—for he already knew that his mother "would hang on [old Hamlet] / As if increase of appetite had grown / By what it fed on" (1.2.143–44). Rather, it is the remarriage that is the issue (*Reading Shakespeare Historically* [New York: Routledge, 1996], especially 46–47).

9. This would explain Hamlet's final, and most revealing, put-down of Claudius: "But come, for England. Farewell, dear mother," he says to Claudius. "Thy loving father, Hamlet," retorts Claudius, only to receive the appellation a second time—"My mother. Father and mother is man and wife, man and wife is one flesh; so my mother" (4.3.51–55).

10. In fact, it appears to be Gertrude's death by poison ("O my dear Hamlet! . . . I am poisoned" [5.2.315–16])—rather than old Hamlet's murder—that spurs Hamlet without delay to assassinate Claudius. ("Drink off this potion. Is thy union here? / Follow my mother" [5.2.331–32].)

11. The Q2 spelling is "sonne," which makes clear that "sun" puns on "son" here.

12. See G. W. F. Hegel, *Phenomenology of Spirit*, trans. A. V. Miller (Oxford: Oxford University Press, 1977), 269–70, par. 451.

13. Hegel, *Phenomenology of Spirit*, 271, par. 452, my emphasis.

14. Hegel, *Phenomenology of Spirit*, 270, par. 452.

15. Giambattista Vico, *The New Science*, trans David Marsh (New York: Penguin, 1999), 223, sec. 529.

16. Vico does not imagine such repulsion to be a "natural" instinct of the human species; rather it is a reaction that, where and when it occurs, serves to distinguish those primitive collectives that managed to make of themselves a society from those that did not.

17. Gertrude in fact speaks of Hamlet in terms of the twin young of the dove, hatched from the female; see 5.1.281–83. In Vico's idiosyncratic mythologeme, sheer brutish uterine bonds—in which "mothers merely nursed their infants and let them wallow naked in their own faeces, abandoning them forever once they were weaned"—predate and precondition all subsequent forms of social life (*The New Science*, 140, sec. 369).

18. Vico, *The New Science*, 224, sec. 529.

19. I am thinking, primarily, of Stephen Greenblatt's *Hamlet in Purgatory* (Princeton: Princeton University Press, 2001). I have tried to interpret the ghost scenes myself, in two essays: "Sharing Vision, Interrupting Speech: *Hamlet*'s Spectacular Community," *Shakespeare Studies* 36 (1998): 29–57, and "Speaking as One Witness to Another," in my *A Politics of the Scene* (Stanford University Press, 2008), 139–65.

20. Although, as I mentioned earlier, we might also consider Hamlet's assassination of Claudius as revenge for his mother's poisoning. Or, perhaps, we could consider the *addition* of the poisoning of Claudius—over and beyond killing him with his sword—to be Hamlet's signal that both parents are being avenged here.

21. Perhaps this explains Horatio's impression that "[o]nce methought / It lifted up it head and did address / Itself to motion like as it would speak" (1.2.215–17).

22. As Laertes makes clear toward the end of the play, it is the "natural" bond of blood that motivates revenge, 5.2.240–42.

23. Laertes' fate, again, parallels Hamlet's in this sense—enough to make the fate, to some extent, a shared social one.

24. This observation was already part of Goethe's reading in *Wilhelm Meister*. Hamlet, he writes, "is now . . . a stranger in the scene which from youth he had looked upon as his inheritance" (in *German Aesthetic and Literary Criticism: The Romantic Ironists and Goethe*, ed. Kathleen Wheeler [Cambridge: Cambridge University Press, 1984], 232). In *"Hamlet" without Hamlet*, de Grazia presents ways in which, by positing an elective monarchy, the plot of *Hamlet* "stages one contest over land after another." She moreover brings to light a number of interesting observations about the play's language, which "upholds the attachment of persons to land, human to humus" (2–3). The fruitfulness of her thorough scholarship in this regard makes her book useful and suggestive as a thematic study of *Hamlet*. At the same time, however, she frames her study of "land" and "property" in *Hamlet* by arguing, more broadly, that philosophical readings

of the play from Hegel to Freud and beyond have tended to extract Hamlet from the plot of *Hamlet,* making of the hero a paradigm of modern subjectivity and inwardness. The account that de Grazia offers of this philosophical tradition of grappling with *Hamlet* strikes me as an oversimplification, one that finally goes to the heart of her thesis about land and property. To pick two examples: de Grazia claims that for Hegel and Marx, "a radical and irreversible break with the past must occur before the advance into the modern can proceed, and in both cases it takes the form of a dissociation from the land." That for Hegel the modern subject is already figured in crucial ways by the Roman legal world, and in that world's emphasis on "legal personhood" through property rights and land ownership, as a way to overcome the sort of tragic conflict between family and polity that *Antigone* stages should remind us that things are not so simple for Hegel, any more than they are for Marx. Building on this questionable claim, de Grazia suggests that this "break" explains Hegel's limited reading of Hamlet: "Like Hegel's spirit of consciousness," she writes, "Hamlet is driven ahead and held back, not by outward circumstances but by the conflict within himself" (28). But Hegel's phenomenology of "spirit" unfolds as different configurations of sociality—not only as internal conflict. Indeed, Hegel's *critique* of Descartes and Kant compels his investigation into the dialectic of subjectivity and sociality, the "I" and "We" with which the *Phenomenology of Spirit* is so concerned: in Hegel's text "inwardness" is subjected to trenchant *critique,* not touted as such. Where de Grazia's own thesis finally goes awry, in my view, is in its suggestion that philosophers concerned with subjectivity in *Hamlet* have made "Hamlet's disengagement from the land-driven plot" the "very precondition" for their reading of Hamlet as "modern subject" (4). I would suggest that precisely the contrary is the case; it is only in dialectical relation to historical principles of social organization like property rights and landownership (as Hegel makes clear) that Hamlet's self-alienation/subjectivity—subjectivity in general—arises, and remains, a demanding problem.

25. As I noted earlier, this is given a perspicacious analysis in Hegel's *Phenomenology of Spirit,* 290–94, pars. 477–83.

26. That his sexual conquest of Gertrude remains essential to Claudius's legitimacy, as I have argued on the preceding pages, obviously makes of *Hamlet* more than the mere representation of the success of a new system of property rights. Rather, in ways I am trying sketch, *Hamlet* reveals this system's continuing tragic ties to a "natural" set of social bonds.

27. For more on the legitimacy of Claudius's ascent, see de Grazia, *"Hamlet" without Hamlet,* 87–89, especially her reference to the earlier work of William Blackstone.

28. The 2000 film version of *Hamlet,* directed by Michael Almereyda, rightly

updated "Denmark" in precisely this way—as a corporation, whose headquarters / palace is a high-rise in Manhattan.

29. In this, as in many other respects, Laertes both mirrors Hamlet and functions as his "foil." As Hamlet says of Laertes: "[B]y the image of my cause I see / The portraiture of his" (5.2.77–78)]. Laertes, indeed, does not waste time upon returning to Elsinore in stating his understanding of his predicament as being the insufficiency of his maternal ties for the maintenance of his own, now fragile, estate: "That drop of blood that's calm proclaims me bastard, / Cries cuckold to my father, brands the harlot / Even here between the chaste unsmirched brow / Of my true mother" (4.5.117–20).

30. Of course, this is not the whole picture; it is only how Hamlet and Horatio first see it. In point of fact, it is Hamlet who cannot distinguish the bones from mere nature; he must struggle to attribute to them the status of a unique individual. The gravedigger, it turns out, knows and remembers them. Or, at least, he claims to remember their names, when they died, where they lie now. "Here's a skull now hath lien you i'th' earth three and twenty years," he remarks—probably knowing that Hamlet will recognize the name once he hears it. "Whose was it?" wonders Hamlet. "Whose do *you* think it was?" replies the gravedigger, as if to show Hamlet who really cares for the dead in this scene. "Nay, I know not," admits Hamlet. "This same skull, sir," comes the answer, "was, sir, Yorick's skull, the King's jester" (5.1.166–75, my emphasis).

31. It is easy to read, or perform, these lines in an ironic mode—nothing, of course, prohibits such a reading. For my part, however, I read Hamlet as having failed to be ironic here, in the face of what he sees before him. For, he *starts* to wax ironical about the fact of decay; but he interrupts himself. "My Lady Worm's . . ." (5.1.87) he begins; but then he looks on the spectacle of the gravedigger at work. "Chopless, and knocked about the mazard with a sexton's spade" (5.1.87–88), he goes on, practically spitting the words, before arriving at a question that, to my ears, sounds dead serious: "Did these bones cost no more the breeding but to play at loggets with em? Mine ache to think on't" (5.1.90–91).

32. The precise ceremonial unfolding of Ophelia's burial is of the greatest concern to Laertes, whose own nobility is tied to Ophelia's fate. And Hamlet's own response concurs, saying of Ophelia's corpse, before he even knows it is her body: "Twas of some estate" (5.1.214). And the priest confirms: "[B]ut that great command o'ersways the order, / She should in ground unsanctified have been lodg'd" (5.1.221–22).

33. I am thinking, in particular, of Jacques Lacan's essay on Ophelia and Hamlet, "Desire and the Interpretation of Desire in *Hamlet*," *Yale French Studies* 55–56 (1977): 11–52.

34. I am aware that I am offering a counterintuititive definition of "honor"

with respect to our typical understanding of the period. I am not suggesting a "historical" definition of honor but rather what I take to be Shakespeare's critique of the concept. For a detailed history of the concept of honor from Plato through Shakespeare, see Curtis Brown Watson, *Shakespeare and the Renaissance Concept of Honor* (Princeton: Princeton University Press, 1960).

35. His dismissal of his "friends" is quite astonishing in this regard: " [T]o be demanded of a sponge—what replication should be made by the son of a king?" (4.2.11–12). And, later to Horatio: "Why, man, they did make love to this employment. / They are not near my conscience . . . / 'Tis dangerous when the baser nature comes / Between the pass and fell incensed points / Of mighty opposites" (5.2.57–62).

36. Harold Bloom, *"Hamlet": Poem Unlimited* (New York: Riverhead, 2003).

37. Bloom, *"Hamlet,"* 129–30.

38. J. G. Herder, "Shakespeare," in *German Aesthetic and Literary Criticism: Winckelmann, Lessing, Hamann, Herder, Schiller, Goethe,* ed. H. B. Nisbet (Cambridge: Cambridge University Press, 1985), 172.

39. See Paul A. Kottman, "The Limits of *Mimesis*: Risking Confession in Shakespeare's *Hamlet,*" *Shakespeare Studies* 42 (2005): 42–70.

40. Plato, *Ion,* trans. W. R. M. Lamb (Cambridge, MA: Harvard University Press, 1962), 425, translation modified.

41. Plato, *Ion,* trans. W. R. M. Lamb, 427.

42. I have in mind something not unlike what Socrates refers to, in the *Ion,* as the hermeneutic chain that binds actors and audience in a common state of affective ecstasy.

43. For a different elaboration of the relationship between affect and dramatic representation in tragedy that diverges from the Aristotelian inheritance, see my discussion of Phyrnichus's *Fall of Miletus* in *A Politics of the Scene,* chap. 6.

Chapter Three: On King Lear

1. Jan Kott, *Shakespeare Our Contemporary,* trans. Boleslaw Taborski (New York: Anchor Books, 1964), 152. Peter Brook's production of *King Lear* with Paul Scofield in the role of Lear—one of the most influential performances of Shakespeare of the past half century—was inspired, according to Brook himself, by Kott's essay.

2. Burgundy, for example, appears to have agreed on a precise dowry before the scene even began. "Most royal majesty, / I crave no more than your Highness offer'd, / Nor will you tender less" (1.1.193–95).

3. Harry Jaffa has offered what seems to me a plausible account of the open-

ing scene as the prevention of future strife. See his "The Limits of Politics: *King Lear*, Act 1, Scene 1," in Allan Bloom with Harry Jaffa, *Shakespeare's Politics* (Chicago: University of Chicago Press, 1996), 113–45.

4. As I shall make clear, I understand Lear's retaining of the hundred knights, title, and "all th' addition to a king" (1.1.136) to run contrary to his initial intentions to give "all" away and as an error made, without premeditation, only subsequent to the disastrous exchange with Cordelia.

5. As is well known, thanks to Ernst Kantorowicz's celebrated book on the subject, the history of European monarchical rule is particularly preoccupied with the development of a theory of the king's two bodies. As the Middle Ages waned, this doctrine connected the immortality of the body politic to the mortal body of the king. See Ernst H. Kantorowicz, *The King's Two Bodies: A Study in Medieaval Political Theology* (Princeton: Princeton University Press, 1957).

6. To be clear, what is at issue here is not the unavoidable reality of individual, bodily mortality—as invoked, for example, in Hamlet's observations about the "base uses to which we return" (5.1.196). By the same token—to address a question I have been asked more than once on this point—the necessity of individual deaths for generational devolution should not be confused with Heidegger's notion that the apprehension of one's own death is the existential condition for self-individuation. In *Lear*, Shakespeare addresses the community of the living and the dead, the inheritance of a worldly form of life—everything implied by Lear's trilogy ("rule, interests of territory, cares of state")—rather than *Dasein*. (For a reading of Shakespearean tragedy that builds on Heidegger's notions of being-toward-death, the interested reader could consult Northrop Frye, *Fools of Time: Studies in Shakespearean Tragedy* [Toronto: University of Toronto, 1967], 3–4.) The world would be neither inheritable, inhabitable nor desirable were it not for the knowledge that nature tends to allow the young to survive the old, that children tend to live to bury their parents and thereby take their place in the world as members of an intergenerational community of the living and the dead. Lear's continuing survival thus amounts to the deferral of that bequeathal, as Regan and Goneril understand full well. ("[I]f our father carry authority with such disposition as he bears, this last surrender of his will but offend us" [1.1.304–6].) Hence, they are themselves amazed by "how full of changes his age is" (1.1.288) and by what has befallen them in the opening scene of the play.

7. After all, Lear does not—as might reasonably be expected—merely name those on whom he *intends* or *wishes* to bestow the various effects of his kingdom subsequent to his death; nor, as Stephen Greenblatt has rightly observed, is Lear effecting a contractual "maintenance agreement" with his children. Lear does not establish or institute his *will*. Lear seeks instead to *enact* the inheritance in open

defiance, as it were, of the first natural precondition of this deed—namely, his own disappearance and return to nature. He refuses to recognize that he is the one person who cannot, who must not, *live* to see this deed done.

8. Northrop Frye, *Fools of Time: Studies in Shakespearean Tragedy*, 4.

9. Stephen Greenblatt's fascinating reading of the play—which begins with the history of an early nineteenth-century father's attempt to coerce his toddler into showing him love and obedience—aims to shed light on *King Lear*'s opening scene by contrasting Lear with medieval fathers who entered into "maintenance agreements" with their children ("The Cultivation of Anxiety: King Lear and His Heirs," in *Learning to Curse: Essays in Early Modern Culture* [New York: Routledge, 1990], 95). He argues that Lear's "demand for unbounded love . . . then takes the place of the older contractual bond between parent and child" (97). I agree with Greenblatt's general claim that Lear is here endeavoring to suspend and supersede this "medieval device, linked to feudal contractualism" (95). And, as I shall try to make clear, I likewise share Greenblatt's sense that the "transformation" of power presaged by the play (from early to late modernity) concerns the increasing confusion or substitution of contractual obligation for "tributes of the heart," and "public deference" for less ritualized acts of love from subjects or children (97). However, I shall try to get at the sources, and consequences, of this tragic confusion through a different path of argument.

10. At this juncture it is worth mentioning a point to which we shall return—namely, that this notion of sovereignty is in many respects consistent with the theory of sovereign power offered, a generation later, in Thomas Hobbes's *Leviathan*. Like Hobbes, Shakespeare is implying that a form of sovereign power that aims to do without traditional modes of generational devolution—a power, therefore, that claims duration by denying the necessity of binding the living to the dead—can only claim that power *by contesting nature's role in the inheritance of the world*. It is this contest that is staged in *King Lear*. However, Shakespeare's drama, unlike Hobbes's mythologeme, does not allow us to avert our eyes from the interpersonal consequences of the struggle; he gives it a dramatic retrospective.

11. In the discussion of patrimonial sociality that follows, I am taking for granted what many critics have painstakingly endeavored to demonstrate regarding the thematic predominance of patriarchal ideology in Shakespeare, namely, Shakespeare's repeated representation of the overcoming of matrilineal descent as the determinant principle of social organization and generational devolution. Some demonstrations that come to mind are Louis Montrose's essay "*A Midsummer Night's Dream* and the Shaping Fantasies of Elizabethan Culture: Gender, Power, Form," 65–87, and Coppélia Kahn's "The Absent Mother in *King Lear*," 33–49, in *Rewriting the Renaissance: The Discourse of Sexual Difference*

in Early Modern Europe, ed. Margaret Ferguson, Maureen Quilligan, and Nancy J. Vickers (Chicago: University of Chicago Press, 1986). Kathleen McLuskie's suggestion that our affective response to tragic representation is conditioned by our conscious or unconscious submission to its patriarchal ideology is not one that I find convincing (although I confess that I also do not fully understand McLuskie's claim here); however, it is instructive that she sees *King Lear* as a paradigm of this "misogynistic aesthetics." See her essay "The Patriarchal Bard: Feminist Criticism and Shakespeare: *King Lear* and *Measure for Measure,*" in *Political Shakespeare: New Essays in Cultural Materialism,* ed. Jonathan Dollimore and Alan Sinfield (Manchester: Manchester University Press, 1985), 88–108.

12. Incidentally, this same absence of maternal figure characterizes the patrimonial world that Shakespeare represents in earlier plays, too—notably in *1* and *2 Henry IV,* for example, where the relationship between father (or father figure) and son (or surrogate son) structures the drama. What distinguishes *King Lear* from these earlier plays in this regard, first and foremost, is that in this later play Shakespeare appears to want to track the breakdown of patrimonial bequeathal —its tragic impasse rather than its successful transmission. For a different take on this impasse, one that sees Lear as subservient to the same maternal power he would overcome, see Janet Adelman's chapter on *King Lear* in her *Suffocating Mothers: Fantasies of Maternal Origin in Shakespeare's Plays, "Hamlet" to "The Tempest"* (New York: Routledge, 1992).

13. On this point, I am unconvinced by Stanley Cavell's argument that Gloucester "still feels shame about his son" and that his shame "is the cause of his withholding of recognition [from Edmund]." Cavell uses a certain account of shame—namely, "the failure to recognize others" as "a failure to let others recognize you"—to interesting effect in his reading of the play. However, I fail to see what Gloucester is hiding in this scene—nor do I see, as Cavell does, that Gloucester is hiding himself. This may merely be a difference in sensibility to the words here. But I confess that I wonder more generally about the "motive" of shame as Cavell articulates it: namely, as a version of what Lear (and Hegel) call hard-heartedness—the "withdrawal of recognition" from others and "the attempt to avoid recognition." In giving priority to shame ("shame comes first, and brings rage and folly in its train"), Cavell seems to me to be attributing the tragedy's consequences to what I take, instead, to be merely one of its manifestations or symptoms ("The Avoidance of Love," in *Disowning Knowledge in Seven Plays of Shakespeare* [Cambridge: Cambridge University Press, 2003], especially 55–59). Even if Shakespeare is tracking in *King Lear* different forms or moods of shame (or hard-heartedness), it still does not necessarily follow that these need to be given originary, causal, or motivational status.

14. In the context of his reflection on paternity and patrimonial inheritance in

Shakespearean drama, James Joyce's Stephen Dedalus memorably describes paternity in light of the naked emptiness of such "obedience." "Paternity may be a legal fiction," he says. "Who is the father of any son that any son should love him or he any son?" (*Ulysses* [New York: Random House, 1961], 207).

15. In fact, this is precisely how Edmund later (falsely) demonstrates his supposed defense of Gloucester against Edgar's alleged murderous intentions, namely, by refusing to "murther" Gloucester. Edmund's totally disingenuous reasoning is of course meant to convince the old man that Edmund still believes in some deep ethical bond between father and son: "Sir, when by no means he could . . . // persuade me to the murther of your lordship; / But that I told him, the revenging Gods / 'Gainst parricides did all the thunder bend; / Spoke with how manifold and strong a bond / The child was bound to th' father" (2.1.42–48).

16. Of course, it is perhaps *because* Kent embodies, as Hegel says of him, the "liege-service of chivalry" that he responds to Edmund in this way ("Dramatic Motivation and Language," in *Hegel on Tragedy,* ed. Anne and Henry Paolucci [New York: Anchor, 1962], 204). But my point is that Edmund's being a bastard hardly denies him social standing and formal recognition.

17. In my opinion, the numerous readings of *King Lear* that see the play's characters as representatives of moral goodness (Kent, Cordelia) or badness (Edmund, Regan, Cornwall) are attributing to Shakespeare's drama a set of moral universals that must be imported from outside the play's context. In perhaps no other play is it clearer that Shakespeare, as Samuel Johnson famously put it, "writes without any moral purpose." Even W. H. Auden (one of my very favorite interpreters of Shakespeare) identifies Edmund as a "villain"—as opposed to a mere "criminal," like Macbeth or Claudius—because he understands Edmund's "primary satisfaction [as] the infliction of suffering on others." I am suggesting, by contrast, that whatever pleasure Edmund takes in sadistic violence, his primary motive is what he says it is: his own prosperity and growth. Auden rightly observes that "Edmund does not need to betray his father to Cornwall and Regan in order to inherit," because he has already persuaded Gloucester of Edgar's unworthiness (Auden, "The Joker in the Pack," in *The Dyer's Hand* [New York: Vintage, 1988], 248). But whereas Auden takes this as a sign of Edmund's gratuitous malevolence, I take it to be an indication that Edmund is closer to a Hobbesian individual who is inclined to remove with all possible expediency any obstacle to his felicity. That is, I see Edmund as no more "wicked" than the "individual" that Hobbes places at the center of his political philosophy. Iago—who is Auden's primary focus in the essay I am citing here—strikes me as the figure who, more than any other in Shakespeare, compels us to think about motiveless wickedness, precisely because Iago seems rather unconcerned with his own "felicity," prosperity, or growth.

18. We might pause here to consider the evidence of Edmund's dying attempt to save Cordelia from execution in light of what I am saying here. Edmund does not undertake his final (attempted) good deed because his impending death changes or converts him or, as Cavell suggests, because "all who have loved him, or claimed to love him, are dead" (*Disowning Knowledge*, 70; I find Cavell's take on this implausible, not only because Gloucester's loving recognition of Edmund was always far from clear but also because I cannot read Edmund's hilariously egocentric remark on seeing Goneril's and Regan's dead bodies—"Yet Edmund was belov'd / The one the other poison'd for my sake, / And after slew herself" [5.3.239–41]—as anything more than a hyperbolic display of individual self-interest, not, as Cavell has it, as showing us that Edmund can finally "acknowledge" being loved.) Instead, I see Edmund's remark—"*I* pant for life; some good *I* mean to do / Despite of *my* own nature" (5.3.243–44, my emphasis)—as telling us that "doing good" is now nothing more the only type of felicity available to Edmund in his current mortally wounded state. That he is not "wicked through and through" does not mean than he has, in the end, undergone a moral conversion.

19. Allow me to refer to my longer discussion of Hobbes's political philosophy as the foreclosure of dramatic action and representation, which can be found in "Hobbes; or, Politics Without a Scene," chap. 3 of my *A Politics of the Scene* (Stanford: Stanford University Press, 2008).

20. Hobbes, *De cive* (New York: Appleton-Century-Crofts, 1949), 100.

21. In the paragraphs that follow, I will suggest just the opposite of what Greenblatt (who is far from alone in this regard) supposes when he writes that Lear wished "to avoid at all costs the drastic loss of status that inevitably attended retirement in the early modern period" and that Lear's later rage "is a response not only to his daughters' vicious ingratitude but to the horror of being reduced" to begging for what had been his (*Learning to Curse*, 95–96).

22. Cavell's invocation of shame in his essay as meant to serve as a counterweight to this traditional reading. As I indicated in note 13 above, I am not convinced that shame has motivational status in the play. But I share with Cavell the view that Lear's "madness" is not pursuant to the pain and humiliation he suffers subsequent to the opening scene—being made to supplicate, for example, or being abandoned in the storm. Rather, his behavior manifests the failures and misdeeds of the opening scene; later scenes merely reflect and refract these mistakes under different light.

23. This is the logic with which Lear defends his retinue of knights to the end. When Regan and Goneril later question his "need" for this company, Lear replies by making clear his refusal to debase himself in their presence. "O! reason not the

need; our basest beggars / Are in the poorest thing superfluous: / Allow not nature more than nature needs, / Man's life is cheap as beast's" (2.4. 266–69). I understand his reluctance to shed tears in front of Regan and Goneril in the same vein; that is, as a sign of his trepidation of what it would mean for them to see him as a mere man, exposed to their provision of care or harm.

24. Although Lear does not seek the love of lover, as Cavell points out, the love he wants from Cordelia is nevertheless incompatible with her loving anyone else.

25. That Lear winds up accomplishing the inverse of his aim—turning, as the fool says, his daughters into his mothers ("thou mad'st thy daughters thy mothers; for . . . thou gav'st them the rod and putt'st down thine own breeches" [1.4.179–81])—does not diminish the power and significance of the *desire* for this dreamed-of sociality, this longed-for love.

26. I am, of course, not claiming that Regan and Goneril *are* hollow or empty beings—mere mechanisms for flattering discourse. (As I have already intimated, I see Regan and Goneril, like Edmund, as consummately desirous individuals, whose drive for "felicity" does not shy away from murderousness.) Rather, I am suggesting that in telling Lear how much they love him—indeed, already in being bidden to speak in this way—they show themselves to be capable of performing a kind of self-evacuation; they demonstrate that, by flattering, they can actively vacate themselves from their own words.

27. It is probably worth admitting that Cordelia may simply be expressing, at this moment, nothing more than the worry that she won't be able to hold her tongue; she knows it would be better for her not to speak—not because of some ineffable love but because she knows what she will not be able to help herself from saying, and she knows full well how her words will be received.

28. Cavell, *Disowning Knowledge*, 62.

29. Another possibility is that Cordelia is simply naive, that she does not understand this demand for what it is. For her dilemma is not, as she might want to believe, whether to speak flatteringly or to speak in some other way. Perhaps she simply does not realize that, in this context, she can only speak flatteringly or not at all.

30. Sources on which Shakespeare likely drew, as well as those he probably did not know directly, do not qualify Cordelia's "bond" or "love" as merely following on her blood relation to Lear. The emphasis on begetting and breeding—that is, on natural propagation—is a Shakespearean innovation. In earlier versions where Cordelia's "love" is explained, it is generally given a patrimonial valence, as for instance in Geoffrey of Monmouth's *Historia* where Cordelia responds "Quantum habes, tantum vales, tantum que te diligo." Enigmatically, other folktale versions

have Cordelia remark that she loves her father as "fresh meat loves salt." See Jay Halio, ed., *The Tragedy of King Lear* (Cambridge: Cambridge University Press, 1992), 10.

31. Cavell, *Disowning Knowledge,* 63.

32. Cordelia makes her understanding of love clear again when she rebukes Burgundy for equating "love" with patrimonial inheritance. "Peace be with Burgundy! / Since that respect and fortunes are his love, / I shall not be his wife" (1.1.247–49).

33. G. W. F. Hegel, "Tragedy as a Dramatic Act," in *Hegel on Tragedy,* 86.

34. I am citing from the opening paragraph of an insightful essay by Richard Eldridge, "How Can Tragedy Matter for Us?" *Journal of Aesthetics and Art Criticism* 52, no. 3 (1994): 287.

35. These failures of recognition might be interestingly compared to, and perhaps contrasted with, Hegel's reelaboration of tragic ignorance. Hegel writes: "The son does not recognize his father in the man who has wronged him and whom he slays, nor his mother in the queen whom he makes his wife. In this way, a power which shuns the light of day ensnares the ethical self-consciousness, a power which breaks forth only after the deed is done, and seizes the doer in the act" (*Phenomenology of Spirit* trans. A. V. Miller [Oxford: Oxford University Press, 1977], 283, par. 469). In contrast to the situation Hegel sees in *Oedipus,* the consequences of Lear's and Cordelia's failure to recognize one another is, so to speak, simultaneous with that very failure. From this simultaneity there arises a "tragic" predicament in which the stakes of the failure to recognize do not "break forth only after the deed is done"; rather, it is that failure to itself that itself determines the ethical character of their doings. I try to suggest in the following pages that Shakespeare offers a tragic blindness of a murkier kind.

36. It is France who utters these last words, discovering newly "inflam'd respect" for Cordelia's principled stance. "Love's not love / When it is mingled with regards that stand / Aloof from th' entire point," he says with a perfectionist's self-certainty (1.1.238–40). He is indeed the near-perfect match for Cordelia in that he, too, is ready to tell others what loving recognition *ought* to be. I fancy that France comes pretty close to embodying the "pride" that Lear scornfully intoned with the words, "Let pride, which she calls plainness, marry her" (1.1.129).

37. Says Albany, later, in a telling aside to the audience: "This judgment of the heavens, that makes us tremble / Touches us not with pity" (5.3.231–32).

38. In this sense, *King Lear* eludes and confounds the "ever-spreading morality of pity" to which Nietzsche refers in *The Genealogy of Morals.*

39. I have often been struck by how many theater critics refer to the role of King Lear as one of the most "exhausting" or "demanding" that an actor might play. It is, of course, a physically demanding role; but, except for the fact that the

actor playing Lear perhaps ought to be of advanced age, playing Lear is no more demanding physically for an actor than playing many of Shakespeare's other tragic protagonists. I have therefore come to think of this truism as an expression of the audience's *own* exhaustion at the end. We are exhausted from watching Lear, not because we are bored or unattentive but because our dramatic investment in the play's worldly stakes has itself been depleted by the sequence of events the play represents. This sense of exhaustion, of having nothing left, must, I think, be part of our collective, affective response. Rather than undergoing *katharsis* or purgation, we are left drained.

40. See Aristotle, *Poetics* 1453b29–36.

41. Aristotle, *Poetics* 1452a3–4, trans. Stephen Halliwell, in *Aristotle: "Poetics"; Longinus: "On the Sublime"; Demetrius: "On Style"* (Cambridge, MA: Harvard University Press, 1995), 63.

The understanding that tragedy is a form of ethical reflection on the unexpected consequentiality of our actions—and therefore constitutes an implicit critique of such moral and literary categories as "intentionality," "desire," "will," and so forth—continues, for instance, to inform most of the essays in even the most recent collection of critical essays on tragedy, *Rethinking Tragedy*, ed. Rita Felski (Baltimore, Md.: Johns Hopkins University Press, 2008); in this regard, see especially the essays by Elizabeth Bronfen, Simon Goldhill, and Kathleen Sands. For another example of the continuing influence of the Hegelian account of the tragic—which also contains a good account of *why* the Hegelian account continues to determine literary and philosophical reflection on the tragic—see Dennis J. Schmidt's recent contribution, *On Germans and Other Greeks: Tragedy and Ethical Life* (Bloomington: Indiana University Press, 2001). Not coincidentally, perhaps, none of these writings includes more than a passing, glancing reference to Shakespeare's drama.

42. I am again citing Hegel's elaboration of tragic blindness (*Phenomenology of Spirit*, 282, par. 468).

43. "Negativity" is of course Hegel's word, too. Tellingly, it is to Regan—at the height of her ego's indifference to her father's life—that Shakespeare gives lines that express this thought: "O! Sir, to wilful men, / The injuries that they themselves procure / Must be their schoolmasters" (2.4.304–6).

44. I am, of course, again referring to Cavell's powerful reading, *Disowning Knowledge*. My understanding of the "grotesque walk" taken by Edgar and Gloucester is akin but not identical to that of Cavell, with whom I agree when he writes: "There are no lengths to which we may not go in order to avoid being revealed . . . especially to those we love and are loved by" (56). Like Cavell, I am not compelled by readings of this scene that would make their walk into a version of the Christian ordeal, or purgatory. I wish, however, to push Cavell's thought in

a different direction by suggesting that the avoidance of love is not a "literal . . . consequence of avoiding the facts" (55) but rather an indication that such avoidance is only "consequential" inasmuch as it forecloses all future consequences. That is, I understand Cavell's reading to still be bound to the understanding of Shakespeare's tragedy as plot driven, whereas I take the grotesqueness of these moments as further proof that historical meaning and consequences founder on the walk to Dover.

45. Cavell, *Disowning Knowledge,* 56.

46. These are questions I tried to address in *A Politics of the Scene,* inasmuch as I was concerned there with understanding the anticipatory dimension of human actions and scenes as essential for politics, defined as beginning anew. My reading of *King Lear* is, for me at least, thus an attempt to test again my own hypotheses.

47. O you mighty Gods!
This world I do renounce, and in your sights
Shake patiently my great affliction off;
If I could bear it longer, and not fall
To quarrel with your great opposeless wills,
My snuff and loathed part of nature should
Burn itself out. . . . (4.6.34–40)

48. I see this wish repeated, as if for emphasis, in two subsequent moments: First, in Oswald's attempted murder of Gloucester. Of course, there is nothing for which Gloucester more devoutly wishes than a way out—as he says to Oswald, "Now let thy friendly hand, / Put strength enough to 't" (4.6.231–32). But here again, Edgar interposes, killing Oswald and saving Gloucester's life, suggesting he simply will not let his father leave him. And, yet again, when Edgar perceives Lear's defeat in battle, Gloucester responds to the news of approaching enemy troops by reiterating his wish: "No further, sir; a man may rot even here" (5.3.8) But still Edgar will not abandon him: "Men must endure / Their going hence, even as their coming hither" (5.2.9–10).

49 Kent, being in somewhat better health and inclined to service and duty, sees in Lear's final acknowledgment of him a glimmer of hope that there might be something new for them to say to one another. "Who are you? / Mine eyes are not o' th' best" (5.3.278–79)—remarks Lear who, having just borne his dead daughter in his arms, is far from enthusiastic about responding to the demand Kent now places on him. Still, he does not deny that he knows Kent: "Are you not Kent? // . . . You are welcome hither" (5.3.282, 289). Having "follow'd" Lear throughout in dutiful service, Kent nevertheless finds no loving recognition; indeed—his declaration of untiring fidelity (5.3.287–88) is interrupted by barely more than a

word acknowledging the mere fact that he, too, has borne with some measure of dignity his coming "hither."

50. Cavell, *Disowning Knowledge*, 95.

51. Cordelia, it should be noted again, does not answer Lear's explicit request for forgiveness here.

52. For a nonfictional account of the destruction of ethical orientation, see Jean Améry's writings and his discussion of the way in which torture destroyed his worldly bonds to others.

53. Hannah Arendt, *The Human Condition*, 2nd ed. (Chicago: University of Chicago Press, 1998), 209.

54. Gloucester naively believed that Edmund loved him; he believed this merely because he knew himself to be Edmund's father, as if that gave him the "right" to this love, and because Edmund had duplicitously encouraged the false belief that Gloucester was owed love *as a father.* But no one will avenge Gloucester, because he has outlived the significance of his own paternity. "Such children" (3.7.65) now pluck him by the beard. Gloucester cannot, as old Hamlet's Ghost was still able, command his sons to "mark" (1.5.2) him and "list" (1.5.22). He henceforth depends on the support of others for every single step he takes. Because he sees not the ones to whom he speaks, Gloucester is now unable to, in contrast to the dead king's ghost, "fix his eyes . . . most constantly" (1.2.33, 34) on anyone. Gloucester cannot even appear to us as the terrifying return of a dead paternal authority, a "winged vengeance" that will "overtake such children" (3.7.65). Hereafter, Gloucester appears instead as the living reminder that paternal authority as such can die along with the ethical obligations, the calls to vengeful duty, such authority might have once commanded. His sons owe him no duty, no love, no remembrance. If they prosper, they do so in spite of him. If he is afflicted, he suffers alone.

55. That Cornwall is himself killed by his servant as he performs the torture on Gloucester serves to further foreclose the possibility of retribution, punishment, or revenge.

56. Arendt, *The Human Condition*, 209. See also her discussion of forgiveness on 216.

57. Philosophers have long considered certain human acts to be neither forgivable nor punishable. For Hegel, murder is such an action; Arendt's reflections on human wickedness turn on the thought that we "are unable to punish what has turned out to be unforgivable" (*The Human Condition*, 209). Adorno's writings on Auschwitz similarly challenge the "speculative philosophy of history" to which principles of revenge and forgiveness remain bound by disputing our sense of "history as a narratable if horrific learning process." See J. M. Bernstein,

Adorno: Disenchantment and Ethics (Cambridge: Cambridge University Press, 2001), 379.

58. This emphasis on the violation as such is heightened by Gloucester's age and fragility.

59. Hobbes, *Leviathan*, ed. C. B. Macpherson (Baltimore, Md.: Penguin, 1968), 183. For even "the weakest has strength enough to kill the strongest." Moreover, Hobbes locates an originary, natural form of sovereign power, or absolute "dominion," in the "power of the mother" to "nourish" or "destroy" the infant, who is not only "vulnerable" but a wholly defenseless "subject." See *Leviathan*, 254.

60. Adriana Cavarero, *Horrorism: Naming Contemporary Violence*, trans. William McCuaig (New York: Columbia University Press, 2008), 30.

61. "Defenseless and in the power of the other, the helpless person finds himself substantially in a condition of passivity, undergoing violence he can neither flee from nor defend against. The scene is tilted entirely toward a unilateral violence. There is no symmetry, no parity, no reciprocity" (Cavarero, *Horrorism*, 30).

62. This is obviously not to claim that one can torture a dead body; rather, it is to point out that torture shows that the infliction of suffering need not be measured against the given fact of human mortality. In *King Lear*, for example, Cornwall does not set out to kill Gloucester or even to test Gloucester's "mortal" threshold for pain. Torture is not concerned with "discovering" natural givens but in creating its own conditions.

63. This, again, expresses part of Hegel's reading of *Antigone*. As J. M. Bernstein puts it in a commentary on Hegel's *Phenomenology*, "Antigone cannot be without Creon and the community he represents and misrepresents" ("Confession and Forgiveness: Hegel's Poetics of Action" in *Beyond Representation: Philosophy and Poetic Imagination*, ed. Richard Eldridge [New York: Cambridge University Press], 45). An analogous claim could be made about Arendt's discussion of natality and action in *The Human Condition*. According to her, we can begin something new because we are ourselves newcomers. Hence, the very newness of our actions already corresponds to, and affirms, the given "plurality" of newcomers among whom we intervene by acting. For more on this point, see my discussion of Arendt in *A Politics of the Scene*.

64. Cavarero, *Horrorism*, 32.

65. To be precise, it is Cornwall's first servant who acts as civil disobedient in this scene—by acting in defense of Gloucester in spite of the fact that has "serv'd [Cornwall] ever since [he] was a child" (3.7.72). The first servant mortally wounds Cornwall before himself succumbing to Regan's sword. His "transgres-

sion" therefore serves not to prevent or forestall the torturous act; he merely ensures that the torturer himself does not survive.

66. Most editions give this line to Kent, but Q gives it to Lear. Because Lear has ostensibly died by this point, most editors presume Q is wrong or corrupt. But the textual ambiguity reflects the ambiguity of the line: *who is addressing whom here?*

Chapter Four: On The Tempest

1. Jan Kott, *Shakespeare Our Contemporary,* trans. Boleslaw Taborski (New York: Anchor Books, 1964), 244.

2. It is perhaps worth noting that the folio version of this passage of the play is punctuated so that Ferdinand, leaping from the ship, is described as being himself "afire." Most editors amend this punctuation to interpret the passage as meaning that it is the "vessel" that is on fire, not Ferdinand himself. "However," writes Frank Kermode in an astonishing bit of commentary on this passage as he edits it, "the idea of Ferdinand leaping overboard with flaming hair and fingertips is very attractive" (23, note to l. 212).

3. In this respect, as some commentators have recognized, Prospero appears as a quasi-divine demiurge who produces, as it were, the events of human history without having to suffer their consequences himself. In this sense, Prospero can be placed in a long tradition whereby human beings have understood human history and suffering as a "spectacle" produced for and by divinities—whose "divinity" is defined precisely by the capacity to "make" history without having to suffer its fallout. Symptomatically, early humanist writers from Erasmus to Pico della Mirandola increasingly define the "dignity of man" as lying in the human capacity for such divine fabrication. For more on the figure of the demiurge and *poietes* as it is expropriated from the philosophical writings of Plato and Plotinus into the Renaissance, see my *A Politics of the Scene* (Stanford: Stanford University Press, 2008), 193–201.

4. The significance of the distinction between "making" and "suffering" (and the correspondent activities of *poiesis* and *praxis*) for historical understanding is interestingly developed in the work of Hannah Arendt, especially in *The Human Condition,* 2nd ed. (Chicago: University of Chicago Press, 1998), and in her essay "The Concept of History," in *Between Past and Future: Eight Exercises in Political Thought* (New York: Penguin, 1977), 41–90. I have tried to reelaborate this distinction as well in my *A Politics of the Scene.*

5. G. W. F. Hegel, *Elements of the Philosophy of Right,* trans. H. B. Nisbet (Cambridge: Cambridge University Press, 1991), 130.

6. I am not insinuating that revenge and punishment are identical. They dif-

fer, again, in that punishment seeks to return the criminal to society whereas revenge wishes simply to harm the criminal. In this sense, the possibility of punishment coincides with the possibility of forgiveness, as we saw in the previous chapter. (This is nicely teased out, in a reading of Arendt and Hegel, in J. M. Bernstein, "Confession and Forgiveness: Hegel's Poetics of Action," in *Beyond Representation: Philosophy and Poetic Imagination,* ed. Richard Eldridge [New York: Cambridge University Press], 57–59.)

7. G. W. F. Hegel, *Aesthetics: Lectures on Fine Art,* 2 vols., trans. T. M. Knox (Oxford: Clarendon Press, 1998), 2:1161.

8. "My son is lost"; "he's gone" (2.1.105, 118). Likewise, Prospero must know the unsettling "thoughts" that will not let Alonso sleep (2.1.186–88)—"O thou mine heir / Of Naples and of Milan, what strange fish / Hath made his meal on thee?" (2.1.107–9); or, again, "he is drown'd / Whom thus we stray to find; and the sea mocks / Our frustrate search on land" (3.3.8–10); or, yet again, "I wish / Myself were muddled in that oozy bed, / Where my son lies" (5.1.150–52).

9. Prospero will know, too, that Alonso has already worried about being "responsible" for the loss of his daughter as well. Indeed, the sea voyage was the return trip from Africa, where Alonso has married her off. "Would I have never / Married my daughter there! for, coming thence, / My son is lost, and in my rate, she too, / Who is so far from Italy removed / I ne'er again shall see her" (2.1.103–7).

10. Actually, it is not at all clear that Miranda recognizes *herself* bodily as a woman, independent of Ferdinand's external affirmation. She claims to have only the faintest recollection of "[f]our or five women once that tended me" (1.2.47). It is Ferdinand who seeks to assure her that she embodies a "maiden"—referring to his prior apprehension of other women. "Full many a lady / I have ey'd with best regard, and many a time // . . . for several virtues / Have I lik'd several women; never any / With so full soul . . . / but you, O you / So perfect and so peerless, are created / Of every creature's best!" (3.1.39–48).

11. "Canst thou remember," inquires Prospero of Miranda, "a time before we came unto this cell? // . . . by any house or person? / Of any thing the image tell me, that / Hath kept with thy remembrance?" (1.2.38–44). Miranda's "remembrance"—"rather like a dream than an assurance" (1.2.46, 45)—recalls the image of "four of five women that tended" her. But, as she later makes clear, she remembers, "no woman's face . . . / Save, from my glass, mine own" (3.1.49–50). From this, again, we can surmise that Miranda's apprehension of those she encounters on the island is not conditioned by her prior recognition of other embodied beings; she encounters each creature as a newcomer—"O brave new world, / that has such people in it!" (5.1.183–84).

12. This starts, in fact, with Prospero's own assertion of paternity of Miranda. See 1.2.56–58.

13. Prospero can further deform Caliban's body, through physical abuse or acts of degradation, but he cannot shape or mold it entirely.

14. I realize that it may seem exaggerated to call these rights "social" or anachronistic to call them "rights"—given the fact that we are on a fictional island, populated by only three embodied beings, in a play composed in or around 1611. By using these terms, however, I hope to draw attention to the relationship—thematized in the play, although obviously not in the language of "rights"—between the perception of embodied beings as "human" and the form of social life that might follow or correspond to such perception and recognition.

15. This is not to suggest that the distinction between the provision of care and the doing of harm is reducible to the distinction between natural and nonnatural bodily deformation. Rather, it is to suggest that the former presupposes the latter in crucial ways.

16. Arendt, *The Human Condition*, 241.

17. Arendt, *The Human Condition*, 241.

18. Arendt, *The Human Condition*, 241.

19. Arendt, *The Human Condition*, 241.

20. Hence, Prospero's "forgiveness" is what allows him to take back his dukedom; there is nothing the others can do to stop him. "I do forgive / Thy rankest fault,—all of them; and require / My dukedom of thee, which perforce, I know, / Thou must restore" (5.1.131–34).